bezonomics

HOW AMAZON IS CHANGING OUR LIVES
AND WHAT THE WORLD'S BEST COMPANIES
ARE LEARNING FROM IT

BRIAN DUMAINE

SCRIBNER

New York   London   Toronto   Sydney   New Delhi

Scribner
An Imprint of Simon & Schuster, Inc.
1230 Avenue of the Americas
New York, NY 10020

Certain names have been changed.

First Scribner hardcover edition May 2020

For information about special discounts for bulk purchases,
please contact Simon & Schuster Special Sales at 1-866-506-1949
or business@simonandschuster.com.

The Simon & Schuster Speakers Bureau can bring authors to your live event.
For more information or to book an event, contact the Simon & Schuster Speakers
Bureau at 1-866-248-3049 or visit our website at www.simonspeakers.com.

Manufactured in the United States of America

1   3   5   7   9   10   8   6   4   2

Library of Congress Cataloging-in-Publication Data has been applied for.

ISBN 978-1-9821-1363-6
ISBN 978-1-9821-1365-0 (ebook)

For Caroline

CONTENTS

bezonomics

Introduction

In the early days of Amazon, Jeff Bezos held biannual all-hands meetings for his employees at a small movie theater across the street from the company's old downtown Seattle headquarters. Since then Amazon has grown, and the all-hands meeting that Bezos called in the spring of 2017 was held at the city's KeyArena, a sports center on the site of the 1962 World's Fair, which holds 17,459 people. On that day, the place was packed. The last question Bezos took from the audience was: "What does Day 2 look like?" The question got a laugh from the crowd, because Amazonians are programmed to think in terms of Day 1 from the first minute they start working at the company. In Bezos's lexicon, Day 1 means that Amazon will always act as a start-up—every day has to be as intense and fevered as the first day of running a new business. Even the downtown Seattle high-rise where Bezos has his office is named Day 1.

Dressed in a white-collared shirt and gray jeans, Amazon's founder, letting out one of his explosive signature guffaws, said: "I know how to answer this. Day 2 is (and then he took a long pause) stasis." After another long pause, he continued: "Followed by irrelevance (pause), followed by excruciating, painful decline (pause), followed by death." Bezos smiled, and the crowd broke into laughter and applause as he walked off the stage. Their leader had articulated what these employees knew in their gut:

that Amazon may be a gigantic tech company, but it's a very different kind of company, a place where intensity and drive are expected and where complacency is strictly taboo.

Despite his massive success so far, Bezos really does run his corporation, which was worth $1 trillion as of 2018 (at the time more than any other company in the world), as if it were a small business whose very existence is threatened daily. At another all-hands meeting in November of 2018, in response to an employee question about big companies like Sears going bankrupt, Bezos rattled the crowd by saying: "Amazon is not too big to fail. In fact, I predict one day Amazon will fail. Amazon will go bankrupt. If you look at large companies, their life spans tend to be thirty-plus years, not a hundred-plus years." At the time he made that comment, Amazon was twenty-four years old.

Why would Bezos talk to his troops about the demise of Amazon? Perhaps he didn't want to jinx all the good luck the company had experienced by sounding smug and invincible. Perhaps he worried that some huge competitor such as Walmart or Alibaba would figure out Amazon's magic and take the company by surprise. There's some truth in both of those things, but at heart Bezos fears most that Amazon will succumb to what is known as big-company disease, where employees focus on each other instead of on their customers, and where navigating a bureaucracy becomes more important than solving problems.

At his all-hands meetings, Bezos was making a heartfelt plea to his employees not to bask in Amazon's success but to work even harder to invent new products and services that please customers, thereby delaying that day of reckoning for as long as possible. The best way to make customers happy, in Bezos's playbook, is to make living their lives cheaper and easier. As Bezos put it: "It's impossible to imagine a future ten years from now where a customer comes up and says, 'Jeff, I love Amazon; I just wish the prices were a little higher.' Or, 'I love Amazon; I just wish you'd deliver a little slower.' Impossible."

This is textbook Bezos. He's a hard-driving leader and unconventional thinker—imagine the CEO of GM or IBM talking about bankruptcy without panicking the troops or triggering a run on its stock. In many ways, Amazon is Amazon because Bezos built a culture in which everything is questioned, and nothing is taken for granted—not even the very existence of the company—and everyone must focus on the customer because all else flows from that. As Bezos put it in Brad Stone's 2013 book, *The Everything Store*, which adeptly tells the origin story of the company: "If you want to get to the truth about what makes us different, it's this: We are genuinely customer-centric, we are genuinely long-term oriented, and we genuinely like to invent. Most companies are not those things. They are focused on the competitor, rather than the customer. They want to work on things that will pay dividends in two or three years, and if they don't work in two or three years, they will move on to something else. And they prefer to be close followers rather than inventors because it's safer. So if you want to capture the truth about Amazon, that is why we are different. Very few companies have all of those three elements."

All this might sound like trite management-speak, but Bezos is one in a billion—a leader who stands apart from other business titans because he figured out how to use his high IQ, combative style, and boundless energy to build a culture at Amazon that really does care about the customer. He chastises executives who worry more about the competition than the customer. When he sees an email from an unhappy customer, he forwards it to the appropriate executive with a simple "?" This sets off an alarm bell in the mind of the poor soul receiving the message, a Pavlovian response that makes that person drop everything and solve that problem for the customer—now. Of the scores of Amazon employees, both current and former, whom I interviewed for this book, all at some point mentioned the line "Everything starts with the customer," as if their brains had been hardwired by one of the company's ace computer scientists.

Yet, as I dug deeper while researching this book, I became dissatisfied with the "Everything flows from the customer" mantra. Yes, it helped explain Amazon's success, but it was far from the whole story. I wanted to find the answer to the question: What does Amazon *really* want? After spending two years on research and interviewing more than a hundred sources, including many of the company's top executives, I came to this conclusion: Amazon wants to be the smartest company the world has ever seen.

A lot of businesses do smart things all the time, but Bezos has built a company that runs largely on big data and artificial intelligence. A lot of hype surrounds AI, but in essence, this entrepreneur has created the first and most sophisticated AI-driven business model in history, one that gets smarter and bigger on its own. Increasingly, the algorithms are running the company. The algorithms are *becoming* the company.

Bezos has designed Amazon to spin like a flywheel—a term Amazonians use religiously. Less a formula and more a high-tech perpetual-motion machine for growth, the "flywheel" paradigm is deeply embedded in Amazon's culture. Picture a three-ton stone wheel resting on a suspended axle. Getting it moving is tough. The trick is to apply enough energy day in and day out to get the flywheel spinning faster and faster until it keeps moving on its own. When Amazon offers perks to its Prime members, such as free one- or two-day shipping, free Amazon TV shows, or a discount at Whole Foods, it brings more customers to its site. More customers attract more third-party sellers to Amazon.com because they want to reach this large pool of potential customers. (Today, independent, third-party sellers account for more than half of all the products sold on Amazon. The company sells the rest directly to consumers.) Attracting more sellers increases Amazon's revenues and creates more economies of scale that allow it to lower prices on its site and offer more benefits. That attracts more customers to Amazon.com, and that brings more sellers, and the flywheel keeps turning faster and faster and faster.

Other successful companies have built flywheels before. Jim Collins in his 2001 seminal book, *Good to Great: Why Some Companies Make the Leap . . . and Others Don't*, coined the term and cited examples such as Kroger and Nucor Steel, whose executives spent years patiently building successful businesses by driving their own versions of the flywheel. Nucor, as Collins points out, was facing bankruptcy in 1965 when CEO Ken Iverson discovered that the company was good at making cheap steel through a new technological process called mini-mills. Nucor started with one mill, which attracted more customers, which boosted revenues and allowed it to build another, more cost-effective mini-mill, which in turn attracted more customers, and so on. For two decades, Iverson and his team focused on pushing this mini-mill flywheel faster and faster, and by the mid-1980s Nucor had become the most profitable U.S. steel company. As of 2019, Nucor remained the largest American steel company.

But Amazon's flywheel is very different. It has evolved into an even more formidable machine. What Bezos has done is taken the flywheel concept to a new level, a move that is revolutionizing the way we do business and one that has given the company an almost insurmountable competitive advantage over its rivals. He has created the next-generation corporation, the twenty-first-century model for how the world will do business. Bezos is now accelerating his flywheel through the shrewd use of AI, machine learning, and big data. The company has gotten so good at applying computer technology that it has started to learn and get smarter on its own. No corporation has ever done this as successfully as Amazon. A lot of CEOs pay lip service to AI and hire a handful of data scientists in an effort to tack this technology onto their business model. At Amazon, technology is the key driver to everything it does. Consider that for the development and upgrading of its magic genie, Alexa, which runs on AI voice software, the company as of 2019 had deployed some ten thousand workers, the lion's share of which were data scientists, engineers, and programmers.

From day one, Amazon has been a technology company that just happens to sell books. Since those early days, Bezos has made big data and AI the heart of the company. The original Amazon website, which went live in July of 1995, promised the convenience of a million-book library in which you could search by "author, subject, title, keyword, and more." If customers scrolled down to the bottom of that original site, they'd find the first example of Amazon's use of computer intelligence, a technology it would use to turn the retail industry upside down in the decades to come. That paragraph boasted of something called "Eyes, our tireless, automated search agent." When a book by a favorite author was published or came out in paperback, Eyes would email readers to let them know.

Since then, Amazon has used its technological prowess to improve the way its site makes suggestions to its customers and to make sure it always has the right products in stock in the right warehouse for speedy delivery. It has collected massive amounts of data on its customers to build the algorithms that help provide them with the best service, low prices, and a mind-boggling selection of goods. More recently, its system has even reached the point where many of the retailing decisions that used to be made by executives are now being made by machines that get smarter and smarter each time they act. Every time these machines make a decision—ship ten thousand coolers to the Pasadena warehouse the week of the Rose Bowl or a thousand knit mittens to the Ann Arbor warehouse when winter is coming—it activates a subsequent check to see whether that decision turned out to be the correct move. The goal is to make sure the company gets it right the next time. And the flywheel keeps turning faster and faster.

Bezos's relentless spinning flywheel has helped make Amazon the world's most formidable and feared company. The research firm CB Insights tracked the content of investor calls in 2018 and found that American executives brought up Amazon more often than they mentioned any other company, more than they mentioned President Trump—and almost as often as they talked about taxes.

And notwithstanding Bezos's warning his troops of a corporate apocalypse, this unconventional founder seems unstoppable. In early 2019, he was the richest man in the world with a net worth of $160 billion, and he remained in that top spot even after giving his ex-wife, MacKenzie, a quarter of their jointly owned Amazon stock (worth at the time $38 billion) in a divorce settlement. The company he founded controlled, as of 2019, nearly 40 percent of all online retailing in the U.S. and is one of the largest e-tailers in Europe. Amazon has expanded its Prime membership program to seventeen countries, and the number of people who have signed up for the service globally has hit more than 150 million. Bezos built Amazon Web Services (AWS) into the world's largest cloud computing company, and Prime Video into a streaming media giant nipping at the heels of Netflix, and he's the driving force behind the Echo, a smart speaker with Alexa inside that sold nearly 50 million units in its first few years of existence. Throughout the 2010s, this profitable company grew at an average rate of 25 percent a year—an astounding performance for such a large corporation (as of 2018, it had $233 billion in annual revenues). Next, Bezos has set his sights on becoming a major player in brick-and-mortar retail, advertising, consumer finance, shipping, and health care—all driven by his AI flywheel.

I call this new corporate model Bezonomics. It's shattering the way we think about business, and its widespread adoption in the coming decades will have a profound impact on society. The business world is quickly dividing into those companies pursuing the status quo and those pursuing their own brand of Bezonomics by building up their AI technological skills so they, too, can have massive amounts of detailed knowledge about what their customers want and do. Established tech giants Alphabet, Alibaba, Apple, Facebook, JD.com, and Tencent fall into this camp. So do some traditional companies such as Goldman Sachs. Harit Talwar, the head of Goldman's consumer bank division Marcus, talked about the Amazonization of banking at a 2019 conference: "Our purpose is to disrupt the distribution and consumption of financial services—pretty much what Amazon has done, and is doing, to retail." Of course, Amazon itself is already trying to disrupt the banking industry, too.

Echoing Talwar's refrain, Uber CEO Dara Khosrowshahi says that he wants his ride-sharing platform to be the Amazon of transportation—using big data to conquer all aspects of transportation, from food delivery to scooter-sharing services to pay systems. "Cars are to us what books were to Amazon. Just like Amazon was able to build this extraordinary infrastructure on the back of books and go into additional categories, you are going to see the same from Uber." As of late 2019, the company had a stock market value of $52 billion, suggesting that Khosrowshahi's adoption of Bezonomics is working—so far.

Walmart, the largest company in the world by revenue, is working hard to join the club by investing heavily in AI and big data. It's trying to prove that an old-school retailer can transform itself into a twenty-first-century tech platform and it's spending billions as it girds for battle. Other businesses have responded to the Amazon threat by trying to protect their niche, offering their customers a highly curated experience and the kind of human touch that the Amazon machine can't match. Best Buy, Williams-Sonoma, British fashion e-tailer ASOS, Swiss luxury retailer Richemont—owner of Cartier—and Crate & Barrel, owned by the German e-commerce giant Otto, fall into this category. So do feisty small outfits such as Stitch Fix, Warby Parker, and Lulus. Those left untouched by Amazon are either lucky enough to be in sectors of the economy where this AI giant doesn't play—heavy industry, law, restaurants, and real estate— or are just dallying cluelessly until the Amazon steamroller crushes them.

The repercussions of Bezonomics on how we work and live are also profound. Amazon is a master of robotics, and although the company has created more than 650,000 jobs from its inception to 2019, it's about to unleash a wave of automation that— when copied by others—will roil our labor markets to the point where governments will need to take seriously the idea of a universal basic income. At the same time, as more companies pursue their own Bezonomics business model, life will become even more digitized, ushering in a world where, instead of visiting malls or small neighborhood stores where we can interact with friends and neighbors, we'll sit in isolation in the glow of a screen and do our shopping with a click of the buy button.

During the writing of this book, many thoughtful friends and colleagues have asked me whether Amazon is good or bad. That's a fair question but a complex one, and in the case of most complicated things no simple answer exists. My hope is that readers of this book will grow to understand this complexity and recognize the ways Amazon both helps or harms business and society so that they'll be better equipped to survive in an age of Bezonomics and check the power of such big-tech platforms when warranted.

How one thinks about Amazon depends to a large degree on where one stands. For Amazon's Prime members around the globe, it's hard to argue that Amazon is evil. It offers a vast selection of goods—Amazon will not confirm how many, but one source puts it at nearly 600 million. It offers these goods at low prices and can deliver millions of them within two days or fewer for free. And it does this with very few mistakes and great customer service. For movie and music lovers, Amazon streams 2 million songs for free and has produced award-winning films such as *Manchester by the Sea* and popular TV series such as *Transparent* and *The Man in the High Castle*. In the U.S., Amazon consistently ranks as the most trusted and beloved brand. Globally, in a 2019 survey, it ranked first in brand reputation among the Fortune Global 500 corporations.

Amazon has been accused by politicians of crushing mom-and-pop businesses, and there's some truth to that. Small retailers who don't carry exclusive goods or provide outstanding service, low prices, or fast delivery have been crushed by Amazon and will continue to be. At the same time the company has been a spawning ground for start-ups. As of 2019, millions of independent businesses—1 million in the U.S. alone—from 130 countries sold 58 percent of all items on the company's Marketplace platform. Worldwide, Amazon says that the small businesses selling on its site have added, as of 2018, 1.6 million jobs. Amazon also helps small businesses in other ways. Its cloud computing service, AWS, has brought the power of big-corporate computer systems to entrepreneurs at a reasonable price. Its Alexa AI voice software has created a huge opportunity for app developers and smart-appliance makers.

Yet all this comes at a cost. Amazon employs hundreds of thousands in their vast global warehouse network, and these jobs are hard, demeaning, and non-union. As bad as that situation is, those workers have to worry that they'll be replaced by robots who can do their tasks more quickly and cheaply. And that day is coming sooner than most think.

The company's culture is fast-paced, aggressive, and largely unforgiving for both white- and blue-collar workers alike. On the environmental front, the company's billions of deliveries and its energy-sucking server farms aren't helping the world's greenhouse gas emissions. Its dominance in online retailing has politicians calling for its breakup. On top of all that, in 2017 and 2018, the *Wall Street Journal* estimated that Amazon legally paid little or no U.S. federal income taxes—a fact that's hard to swallow given that the company posted $10 billion in annual profits in 2018 alone. One of many reasons is that Amazon can deduct historical losses against today's profits, which helps keep the tax man at bay, much in the same way Donald Trump and his money-losing businesses have allowed him at times to pay little or no taxes.

These are certainly serious issues, but they're also ones that arise from the very nature of capitalism itself. As one of the largest and most successful of the new tech platforms, Amazon has come under intense scrutiny for some of its behavior, and in some cases it deserves blame. Its failure to address the concerns of community groups during its failed effort to place its second headquarters in New York City is a case in point. The amount of greenhouse gas emissions the e-tailer creates from shipping billions of packages and running its server farms doesn't help Mother Earth. But in the main, the solutions lie not in publicly attacking a single company but discerning the problems it and its ilk are creating (and will create) and then taking the appropriate steps to reform tax law, institute sensible carbon emission regulations, and enact government support and training for workers displaced by automation.

In the meantime, the best one can do is to take a close look at Amazon and learn how it's shaping the future. The point is that whether we like it or not, Bezonomics will keep engulfing a larger and larger share of the global economy. My modest hope is that by reading about Amazon, those working to reform capitalism will better understand where business is headed in the twenty-first century, how Bezonomics has put us at a critical pivot point, and how it will roil society. For business leaders this book will explore in more depth how Bezos built his AI flywheel, why it works so well, and what one can do to compete against this behemoth. For the rest of us, I hope this journey through the world of Jeff Bezos will help us understand what's really happening to our life every time a smiling brown box arrives at our doorstep.

The first step is to grasp just how massive and powerful Amazon has become—and how it's more pervasive in our lives and intertwined in the global economy than most of us imagine.

CHAPTER 1

Bezonomics

As she wakes in the morning, Ella asks Alexa to brew her coffee, check the weather, and order groceries from Whole Foods to be delivered to her apartment that evening. Ella is twenty-six years old and has hardly known a world without Amazon. She bought all her college textbooks used from the website, then sold them back. Although she's had an Amazon Prime subscription since she was eighteen years old, she still feels an endorphin surge when she comes home to find a package on her doorstep sealed with Amazon-branded packing tape.

After breakfast, Ella takes the subway to her office. For her work, she searches for Bluetooth keyboards; no surprise, Amazon has the best selection. She clicks twice and knows they'll be at her desk the next or maybe even the same day if she really needs them fast. She backs up important company files on the cloud built by Amazon Web Services, researches small-business loans offered by Amazon Lending, then gathers her team to discuss her start-up's next major milestone: launching a new product on the Amazon site. That evening, on her way home, she stops at a cashier-less Amazon Go store to pick up a snack, and when she leaves, sensors and cameras automatically charge her Amazon account for what she carries out. She returns home, where she asks Alexa to read her a recipe for dinner. After eating, she relaxes by asking Alexa to play the Amazon Prime Video hit *The Marvelous Mrs. Maisel* on her TV, and then falls to sleep reading her Kindle.

Ella is a fictional character, but the world she lives in is very real. We all know that many others like her exist in the Amazon ecosystem—Amazon Prime members in America pay $119 a year for the privilege of being fully enmeshed in it. Millions of Amazon's products can be shipped to them in seventeen countries in two days or less for free. Not all Amazon shoppers, however, are Prime members. Around the globe, an estimated 200 million additional online shoppers have, whether they realize it or not, signed on for Bezos's operating system for life. And Bezos has only started to penetrate world markets. The company is extending its tentacles through Europe, India, Africa, South America, and Japan. Only in China, with its formidable homegrown digital giants Alibaba and Tencent, has Amazon been thwarted.

To the person on the street, Amazon is a business that delivers lots of stuff in little brown boxes. Walk down an avenue on any given afternoon in L.A., London, or Mumbai and you'll see Amazon's smile boxes piled up in lobbies or dropped at doorsteps. A former Amazon executive who served for a decade in high-profile positions at the company told me that what Amazon is really doing is creating a new operating system that will be broader and more pervasive than Apple's iOS or Google's Android. "Everything we did at Amazon," he said, "was about becoming a tightly woven part of the fabric of [people's] lives. We did that on Amazon.com and now here comes the Amazon Echo with Alexa, who tells us the weather, plays music for us, controls the lights and cooling in our houses and, yes, helps us buy things on Amazon.com. We're getting to the point where there is going to be a massive integration. Amazon is becoming an operating system for your life."

It's hard to fathom just how popular and addictive and all-encompassing Amazon has become. During the 2017 holiday season, three-quarters of Americans who shop online said they would make most of their purchases on Amazon. The next closest destination was Walmart.com, with 8 percent saying they'd do most of their shopping there. U.S. Post Office trucks in suburban areas made extra runs to deliver the stream of Amazon packages. In some areas, mailmen started their routes at 4:00 a.m. to keep up with the volume. On New York's Fire Island, the local ferry each morning was taking so long to unload Amazon deliveries that some ferry riders had to take an earlier boat to avoid missing their commuter train to New York City.

In an age where people are losing trust in our institutions, Amazon has earned deep respect. In 2018, the Baker Center at Georgetown University asked Americans which institutions they believed in the most. Democrats picked Amazon above all others—quite surprising, given the mounting attacks from the Left targeting the company's tough warehouse working conditions and its ability to squeeze large tax breaks from local governments and the fact that it paid little or no federal income tax in 2017 and 2018. The Republicans polled picked Amazon third after—no shocker—the military and the local police. Whether Democrat or Republican, those surveyed respected Amazon more than the FBI, universities, Congress, the press, the courts, and religion. That perhaps helps explain that while 51 percent of American households attend church, 52 percent have Amazon Prime memberships.

The reverence for Amazon runs particularly deep among the millennials and Gen Zers. The Max Borges Agency polled 1,108 people from the ages of eighteen to thirty-four who'd bought tech products on Amazon in the last year. An astounding 44 percent said they'd rather give up sex than quit Amazon for a year, and 77 percent would choose Amazon over alcohol for a year. This, however, might reveal as much about the lifestyles and sex drives of millennials and Gen Zers as about Amazon's allure.

That kind of stellar reputation among consumers translates into dollar signs. A ranking of the world's most valuable brands, released in mid-2019 by the data firm Kantar, a division of the advertising giant WPP, put Amazon for the first time at the top of the list. Its brand, Kantar estimates, is worth $315 billion—up by an impressive $108 billion from the previous year. Amazon beat out Apple and Google for the top spot. The company outpaced both Alibaba and Tencent by more than a two-to-one margin.

Amazon has become so addictive that it's now taking a significant share of Americans' income. The company siphons off 2.1 percent of all household spending—or some $1,320 for a U.S. family that earns $63,000 a year. The main reason consumers open their wallets for Amazon is that it saves shoppers the time, hassle, and expense of driving or taking public transport to a store to purchase mundane items such as diapers or batteries. A case in point: when Charlotte Mayerson, a retired book editor living on Manhattan's Upper West Side, needed new batteries for her old landline phone, she hopped a bus to the nearest Best Buy for a replacement. The helpful clerk said: "Best Buy does not carry that battery, but I'd be happy to help you out." He walked to his computer screen and ordered the woman her replacement batteries—on Amazon.

Even some shoppers who despise Amazon can't live without it. Nona Willis Aronowitz, in an op-ed for the *New York Times*, said that on principle she hated Amazon because of the reports she'd read about the way it treated its warehouse workers. Yet, after her eighty-five-year-old father, who'd been a labor activist at one point in his career, had suffered a debilitating stroke, Aronowitz came to depend on Amazon for making sure her house-ridden dad had everything he needed—from physical therapy balls to cheap tubs of protein powder. Aronowitz saw using Amazon as a "deal with the devil," yet wrote of her father: "He can't shop on his own, and his caretaker can't spend her life going to specialty pharmacies and medical supply stores. So Amazon Prime has been his lifeline."

No one has any hard statistics on the topic, but there's plenty of anecdotal evidence that some shoppers develop a psychological addiction to Amazon. At one point, a forty-year-old man in Saco, Maine, had his account suspended for returning too many smartphones—Amazon's algorithms secretly decide who is worthy and who is not. The man spent months trying to get himself back in good standing. After much pleading to an Amazon customer service employee, his account was finally restored. As he told the *Wall Street Journal*: "It was dizzying and disorienting. You don't realize how intertwined a company is with your daily routine, until it's shut off."

For some time now, scientists have known that using social media platforms such as Facebook, Twitter, and Instagram can be addictive. Every time someone's phone pings with a notification announcing the latest number of likes or an enthusiastic comment, the brain releases dopamine, a neurotransmitter that among other things can trigger a sense of pleasure. Users get used to these little highs and compulsively check the site to see if someone has commented on their latest post. Sean Parker, the founding president of Facebook who resigned from the social media company in 2005, once explained that to hook its users, the company exploited a "vulnerability in human psychology. Whenever someone likes or comments on a post or photograph, we . . . give you a little dopamine hit."

Both adults and children are susceptible to Internet addiction although the phenomenon is particularly evident in children who become glued to their screens at a time when they should be developing social and reading skills. It has reached the point where some Silicon Valley titans won't let their kids use phones or at least strictly reduce their access to these devices. Chris Anderson, the former editor of *Wired* and now the chief executive of a robotics and drone company—hardly a Luddite—expounded upon children and screen use in a *New York Times* interview: "On the scale between candy and crack cocaine, it's closer to crack cocaine. Technologists building these products and writers observing the tech revolution were naïve. We thought we could control it, and this is beyond our power to control. This is going straight to the pleasure centers of the developing brain."

While social media sites such as Facebook, Instagram, and Twitter can cause social and psychological problems, Amazon is responsible for aggravating an equally serious phenomenon—shopping addiction. So powerful is its allure that some people get caught in a kind of compulsion feedback loop with dire financial consequences. The 1-Click buy button is the equivalent of getting a ping of affirmation on Facebook or Instagram. But instead of a "like" from a friend, a person with a single click knows they'll get a reward—a package arriving at their home in a day or two with some item they desire—the equivalent of receiving holiday or birthday gifts throughout the year. So, they get a double hit of dopamine—one when they click and the other when the doorbell rings with a delivery.

Some have become financial victims of Amazon's compulsion feedback loop. April Benson is a New York City psychologist who specializes in shopping addiction. In the course of her research she discovered some serious cases of addicted online shoppers, including a middle-aged woman named Constance from Long Island who recently filed for bankruptcy after accumulating $150,000 in debt. As Constance told Benson: "I don't know what it's like to be a crack head, but shopping is my crack. . . . I work 7 days a week to support my habit. . . . Something's got to give."

Shopaholics are not new, but the Internet has made it easier to become one because of the convenience of shopping online. The Max Borges Agency poll of millennial and Gen Z shoppers found that 47 percent have shopped online while using the bathroom, 57 percent while working, 23 percent while sitting in traffic, and 19 percent while drunk (although one might have thought that the number of besotted shoppers would be higher). One high school teacher in the Northeast said she'd occasionally sit in bed drunk, buy stuff on Amazon, and not remember the next morning what she ordered.

The addictive ease of shopping by the press of a button or with an Alexa voice command means that some shoppers might simply end up buying more junk than they need. The other day I found myself ordering on Amazon a stainless-steel coffee canister that had a carbon dioxide vent to keep the grounds fresh. Who even knew that CO_2 was a threat to coffee, and why did I care? I bought it anyway. The more we know we can buy, the more we buy. Online shopping is also a great way to procrastinate at work. Tired of designing that spreadsheet or writing that memo? Somehow your brain reminds you that you really do need a new pair of flip-flops for your upcoming weekend excursion to the beach, and off one's fingers go to Amazon.

One reason shoppers get hooked on Amazon is that they can find pretty much anything they want. In fact, as of 2018, Amazon and the millions of third-party retailers who sell on its site listed an estimated 600 million products worldwide. That's more than eight times the number of products offered by Walmart, the largest brick-and-mortar retailer in the world, which offers 120,000 items in its Super Stores and roughly 70 million online.

A deep dive into the Mariana Trench of Amazon's website dredges up some curiosities. Shoppers can buy a sixteen-color, motion-activated toilet bowl night-light ($9.63); a men's black silicon wedding band ($12.99 for a four pack), for the budget-minded and apparently pessimistic groom; Honest Amish Beard Balm Leave-in Conditioner ($11.43); a live, sexed pair of Madagascar hissing cockroaches (*Gromphadorhina portentosa*) for $13.50, but alas no longer available; and my favorite: a pillowcase imprinted with a photo of a bare-chested Nicolas Cage ($5.89). The item earned 239 reviews and a four-star rating. As one happy reviewer named Kara said of her purchase: "I feel so protected knowing that Nicolas is in bed with me."

And it's not all tchotchkes. Shoppers can order a three-and-a-half-ton power lathe for $35,279, which weighs more than a Ford Expedition and gets free delivery—but one has to be home to receive it. Also eligible for free delivery: a 674-pound GM engine—no assembly required—a set of 300-pound barbells, and a quarter-ton gun safe. One customer warned that free delivery does not include lugging this heavy safe up a flight of stairs.

Because Amazon has access to prodigious amounts of data regarding which categories of products are selling well, it's extremely well positioned to sell its own products, and it's doing just that. When the company sees that a category like blue cashmere sweaters or smart microwaves is popular, it finds a manufacturer to produce it under its own brand. The classic example is AmazonBasics batteries, which compete directly with Eveready and Duracell and often underprice those premium brands. In 2016, the company had about twenty private label brands, including AmazonBasics and its women's contemporary line,

Lark & Ro, and the kids' clothing label, Scout + Ro. By 2018, that number had grown to more than 140 private label brands, including Rivet for midcentury furniture and Happy Belly for food and beverages. House brands have the potential to become a big business for Amazon. Amazon's private label sales hit $7.5 billion in 2018, according to analysts at SunTrust Robinson Humphrey. By 2022, they are expected to hit $25 billion.

Though the surveys suggest that most shoppers love Amazon, there's mounting anecdotal evidence—especially among some millennials I interviewed—that the Amazon search results are getting too crowded with sponsored items and Amazon "picks." The clutter, they say, turns them off. Then there's the feeling of being overwhelmed by the sheer volume of products offered. It's hard to get one's brain around the vast wasteland of online shopping. Type in "running shoes" and a shopper gets more than seventy thousand results. Which one to choose? I have no idea. With the emergence of fake reviews as well as reviewers who are offered free products in exchange for their opinion, it's hard to know which product is superior.

Ironically, research suggests that shoppers who have fewer choices make better choices and are more likely to buy. Sheena Iyengar, a professor of business at Columbia University and the author of *The Art of Choosing*, conducted in 1995 what she called "the jam test." She set up a table in a California market with samples of Wilkin & Sons jams. Every few hours she switched between a selection of twenty-four jams and a group of six jams. She found that about a third of the people who sampled the smaller assortment ended up buying the jam compared to only 3 percent who had to select from among twenty-four jars. Too much choice can be debilitating.

As much as Amazon's customers like being able to order almost anything on the site—including Nicolas Cage pillowcases—it's the fast and accurate delivery of those items to their doorsteps that keeps them coming back for more. Recently, a pile of Amazon boxes I deposited next to my trash bin was so big that I received a $120 charge from my garbage company for an oversized pickup. Fortunately, most cardboard box material does get recycled into new boxes and other paper products both in the U.S. and abroad. However, the amount of greenhouse gas emitted in making and delivering all those smile boxes has become a real concern.

Since Amazon's inception, Bezos has been driving down the delivery time of what the company sells. When Prime was introduced in 2005, members got free two-day delivery on certain items, and the company has been expanding the number of items eligible for Prime ever since. In early 2019, it announced that it was working on converting its Prime free two-day shipping program to a free one-day shipping program. For those who need things even quicker, Amazon offers Prime Now, in which members get free *same-day* delivery on more than 3 million items on orders over $35. Besides the U.S., same-day has been rolled out in Australia, England, Germany, and Japan, among other countries. (The most popular item for Prime Now deliveries is bananas. Who would guess?) In 2018, Amazon delivered 2 billion items in one day or less, and the delivery times are getting shorter and shorter. A Nintendo NES Classic was delivered to a customer in Kirkland, Washington, and a High Sierra Loop backpack to a shopper in Charlotte, North Carolina—both in nine minutes.

Nor is Amazon content to fully depend on the local post office or delivery companies such as UPS to move their packages over that crucial last mile from the warehouse to the customer. In 2018, Amazon said it would buy twenty thousand Mercedes vans to launch a program whereby entrepreneurs could, with Amazon's help, start their own local delivery companies. The company also has a program called Amazon Flex that makes it possible for Uber and Lyft drivers to deliver packages. It's also experimenting with drone deliveries. It made its first such test delivery in England in 2016 when a drone carried an Amazon Fire TV and a bag of popcorn to a customer near Cambridge. From the time the customer clicked the buy button to the time the drone landed at his home was only thirteen minutes.

As big as they are, UPS and the U.S. Post Office aren't big enough to handle the surging flood of deliveries. Amazon is amassing a fleet of container ships, jumbo cargo jets, and tractor-trailer trucks to create what it hopes to be one of the world's most robust shipping companies. In an initiative called Dragon Boat, Amazon has leased its own fleet of container ships to import items from Chinese factories. It's building an air-delivery service called Amazon Air that will have seventy cargo jets deployed by 2021. In late 2018, the company announced that it was building an air hub shipping center at the Fort Worth Alliance Airport. This is no idle threat. As the company was beefing up its shipping business, Morgan Stanley lowered its outlook for the stocks of FedEx and UPS because Amazon would likely eat into the growth of those two giants.

One key to fast delivery is to build warehouses near where Amazon's customers are, whether that's Hertfordshire, England; São Paulo, Brazil; Osaka, Japan; New Delhi, India; or Tianjin, China. As of 2019, Amazon operated 175 warehouses around the globe and it keeps expanding, even buying up abandoned malls and turning them into fulfillment centers. In early 2019, it bought two malls in the Cleveland area that were near the city center, already had electric, water, and parking, and were adjacent to a bus stop for warehouse workers who couldn't afford cars.

The scale of Amazon's distribution network is hard to grasp. From its massive complex of warehouses, Amazon shipped an estimated 3.3 billion packages in 2017, the equivalent to sending a parcel to nearly half the world's population. In 2018, that number is expected to rise to 4.4 billion packages, which adds up to 12 million packages a day.

Today's shoppers want not only fast delivery but also the option to either buy online or browse in a real store. With its $13.7 billion acquisition of Whole Foods in 2017, Amazon is in a position to become a leader in a new hybrid form of retailing that promises to disrupt traditional brick-and-mortar retail. Whole Foods' five-hundred-plus stores give Amazon's customers the choice of ordering groceries online and having them delivered to the home, or putting them in their trunk on the way home from work.

A year after the acquisition of Whole Foods, press reports suggested that Amazon would build a national chain of lower-cost grocery stores to compete more directly with Walmart and Kroger. One expert suggested that Amazon convert abandoned Sears locations into their new grocery stores. The company is striving to operate on a smaller scale, too. As of 2019, Amazon operated forty-two of its own physical retail stores, including Amazon Go, Amazon 4-star, and Amazon Books. So far Amazon has opened only fifteen Go stores, where shoppers can buy sandwiches, salads, and drinks without checking out. Ceiling cameras scan purchases and charge them directly to the shoppers' Amazon account. Weights in the shelves determine whether the person has returned the item. The stores have proved popular, and the company says it will keep rolling them out. Wall Street analysts predict that the Go Stores will be a multibillion-dollar business by the middle of this decade.

While Bezos has built the most expansive and powerful online retail operation in the world and now threatens brick-and-mortar stores, that's only part of the story. A new pattern is emerging that is threatening businesses in other industries. As Amazon invents something to please its customers, as it pushes the AI flywheel a little harder, it often ends up creating a product or a service that becomes a business of its own. This is what has enabled Bezos to enter one new industry after another, from cloud computing to media to consumer electronics. It's what has many in the business world worried—and they should be— that the Amazon AI flywheel could come crashing through their industry.

Over its two decades of existence, Amazon invested billions in making its site the most intuitive and dependable online shopping destination. The company then took some of the programming talent and computer expertise that it used to build up its online business and created its cloud service, AWS. Cloud computing lets businesses and individuals use the Internet to store, manage, and process data on large server farms instead of on a local server or a personal computer, and it's one of the fastest-growing sectors of the tech industry. Amazon was one of the first to market with its cloud service in 2006. As of 2018, AWS remains the largest cloud company in the world with revenues of $35 billion, making it the most profitable in Amazon's suite of businesses.

In the mid-2000s, Bezos came to the conclusion that offering Prime members a free streaming video service would be a great way to attract and retain customers. He launched Prime Video, and since then the service has created scores of original television programs, including Tom Clancy's thriller *Jack Ryan*, *Homecoming* with Julia Roberts, and *The Marvelous Mrs. Maisel*, which won multiple Emmys, including Outstanding Comedy Series. In 2019, Amazon spent approximately $7 billion on original programming and music, making it a major force in Hollywood. That number still trails Netflix, which spent an estimated

$15 billion on original content that year (more than any Holly-wood studio), but it means Amazon is playing to win. Amazon offers its streaming services in more than two hundred countries. Netflix, with 104 million members, has more subscribers, but industry watchers say that Amazon, with 27 million of its Prime members watching its video service regularly, is starting to close the gap. That's thanks to deals like the one Amazon struck with the NFL in 2018 to stream ten Thursday Night Football games.

Maybe Amazon's Prime members would like free music. In 2007, Bezos launched the streaming service Amazon Music—free for Prime members. A decade later, the company spawned Amazon Music Unlimited, a paid service with 50 million songs and curated playlists. It's now a direct competitor with Spotify, Pandora, and Apple Music. As Steve Boom, the vice president of Amazon Music, told *The Verge*: "I see us as one of the top global streaming services. I expect us to grow faster than everybody else."

And wouldn't it be nice, thought Bezos, if his company could make ordering products, listening to Amazon Music, and watching Amazon Video easier for its customers. That led to the introduction in 2014 of the Amazon Echo with its AI voice assistant, Alexa. The Echo has sparked nothing less than the biggest shift in personal computing and communications since Steve Jobs unveiled the iPhone. The Echo uses artificial intel-ligence to listen to human queries, scan millions of words in an Internet-connected database, and provide answers from the pro-found to the mundane. Alexa, named for the ancient Egyptian library in Alexandria, can take musical requests, supply weather reports and sports scores, and remotely adjust a home thermo-stat. By 2019, Amazon had sold a total of nearly 50 million Echo devices globally. Other companies are selling tens of millions of Alexa-capable products. Amazon had long made Kindles, Fire TVs, and other consumer electronic devices, but it's now moving into manufacturing Alexa-controlled security cameras, microwaves, and lightbulbs. Amazon has become a major consumer electronics company.

And that's just the beginning of the disruption Bezonomics is causing. The threat that Amazon poses doesn't stop at retailing, cloud computing, media, and consumer electronics. The company is moving into finance, health care, and advertising. When Bezos applies his AI flywheel to these industries, many competitors are likely to be ground into dust or at best lose significant market share. Take as just one example, health care.

In 2018, Amazon partnered with Warren Buffett's Berkshire Hathaway and JPMorgan Chase to form a nonprofit dedicated to reinventing health care for the 1.2 million employees who work at the three companies. The head of this new initiative is the renowned Boston surgeon and *New Yorker* writer Atul Gawande. Amazon aims to use this laboratory to find new ways to disrupt the sector. What the health-care industry needs is lower prices and better customer care, and that's exactly what Amazon does best. In 2018, the company acquired PillPack, an online pharmacy. Amazon could also build pharmacies in its Whole Foods stores, not only offering low prices but also employing its predictive analytics and customer data capabilities to track and influence patient behavior.

In the near future, Amazon's Echo and Alexa could give the company a leg up in telemedicine. It could create a vast platform for new voice-activated services, such as helping patients book physician visits. The video capability of its new Echo Show device with its ten-inch screen could make virtual house calls a reality. Amazon's deep AI capabilities could help doctors more accurately diagnose their patients. Alexa already delivers first-aid information and offers tips for keeping yourself healthy. Adding tasks such as auto-refills for prescriptions and medication reminders would not be a stretch. CVS Health, Humana, UnitedHealth, and other health providers should be worried.

As Bezos applies his AI flywheel to new domains, he will change the rules of business dramatically. Big data, AI, and an extreme focus on the customer will become mere table stakes. Anyone competing with Amazon must realize that business as usual won't hack it. They must learn to embrace the fundamentals of Bezonomics or find safe harbors where they can operate outside of its impact.

It's not possible to fully grasp the implications of Bezonomics without understanding the man behind it. Jeff Bezos left a lucrative job at a Wall Street hedge fund in 1994 to start an online bookstore. A little more than twenty years later, he'd built one of the most valuable companies in history and become the world's richest man.

A desire to make money, however, wasn't what drove him to those heights.

CHAPTER 2

The Richest Man
in the World

Jeff Bezos is a man of contradictions.

He has created more than half a million new jobs, but his company is also a threat to the livelihood of millions as it perfects robotics and AI and spreads that knowledge to businesses around the globe.

He runs Amazon as if every penny counts—even going so far as to use old doors as desktops. Yet, as he has amassed more wealth than anyone on the planet, he has spent lavishly. His possessions include a Gulfstream G650ER private jet that lists for $66 million; estates in Los Angeles, San Francisco, Seattle, Washington, D.C., and New York City; plus 400,000 acres of land, most of it in West Texas. His most recent purchase, in mid-2019, involved combining three apartments (including the penthouse) on four floors at 212 Fifth Avenue in the tony Madison Square Park neighborhood of Manhattan. The combined apartments give Bezos 17,300 square feet of living space, twelve bedrooms, sixteen bathrooms, a ballroom, library, private elevator, and 5,730 square feet of terraces with park and city views. The price tag: $80 million.

He portrays himself online as a family man who likes to putter around the house in the morning, reading the newspaper and having breakfast with his four kids, occasionally whipping up blueberry–chocolate chip pancakes. Sometimes he even gets dish duty. Yet, in 2019, he divorced MacKenzie Bezos, his wife of twenty-five years, to pursue a sexy former Fox News anchor who flies helicopters for a living and was the wife of one of Hollywood's most powerful talent agents. The headline pasted on the cover of the *New York Post*: "Amazon Slime."

He has pledged $2 billion for early childhood education and to combat homelessness. Yet many in the public perceive him as a ruthless capitalist who won tax breaks for his planned second headquarters in New York City that would starve local schools and services. (Never mind that Amazon would have generated tens of billions more in taxes than the breaks were worth, plus brought jobs to the community.)

These contradictions suggest that on one level Bezos is indeed human, prone to both greatness and folly. But on another, they also indicate that he's a force of nature, moving at warp speed through a vast canvas and with such unparalleled resources that contradictions become inevitable. When a person creates one of the most valuable companies in the world and has more money than every other human on earth, their life doesn't lend itself to a tidy story line. Bezos himself believes in the narrative fallacy, a term popularized by Nassim Nicholas Taleb in his 2007 book, *The Black Swan*, a work that Bezos requires his top executives to read. Taleb argues that humans are biologically wired to turn complex situations into oversimplified stories. By that line of thinking, Bezos likely is not bothered by the contradictions in his life.

The narrative fallacy of Bezos's life is that he is a hard-driving, brilliant executive who cares about pleasing his customers more than anything else. He will drive his engineers to near madness until they come up with popular new innovations such as Kindle, Fire TV, or Echo with Alexa to make his Prime members happy. He will take as long and spend as much money as it takes to keep Amazon growing and moving into new industries like media, advertising, cloud computing, and health care. There is much truth to that characterization, but like all false narratives it doesn't tell the whole story. Look beyond this script, and a different, more complex picture emerges.

Bezos embodies three characteristics that separate him from all other mere mortal entrepreneurs. He believes that resourcefulness is the greatest virtue. He faces the truth no matter where it leads him. He is a visionary who thinks in terms of not years but decades and centuries. Those qualities help explain the contradictions in his life and they're what makes Bezos . . . well . . . Bezos.

"Jeff Bezos" wasn't always his name. The founder of Amazon was born Jeffrey Preston Jorgensen on January 12, 1964, in Albuquerque, New Mexico. When his mother, Jacklyn (née Gise, which rhymes with "dice"), gave birth, she was seventeen and still in high school. His father, Ted, had just graduated from high school and worked as a trick unicyclist with a local group that toured county fairs, sporting events, and circuses. The two high school sweethearts married before Jeff was born.

Ted and Jackie suffered many of the challenges of young newlyweds. Ted's unicycling job didn't pay much and he had to pick up part-time work at a local department store. Money was tight and put a strain on the marriage. Jackie's father, Lawrence Preston Gise (from whom Jeff got his middle name), tried to help the struggling couple. He paid for his son-in-law's tuition at the University of New Mexico, but Ted dropped out. He tried to pull strings for a position for Ted at the New Mexico State

Police, but Jorgensen wasn't interested. When Bezos was three, his father left the family and disappeared.

Bezos never saw his biological father again. It was not until 2012 that journalist Brad Stone found Jorgensen and wrote about him in his book *The Everything Store*. Jorgensen, as Stone discovered, owned a small bike store north of Phoenix called the Road Runner Bike Center. He had no idea that his son had founded Amazon and was one of the richest people in the world. When Stone first mentioned his son, Jeff, to him, Jorgensen's reply was: "Is he still alive?"

After Stone unearthed Jorgensen, the ex-unicyclist reached out to Bezos, saying he just wanted to meet with him, stressing that he had no interest in his son's vast fortune. He simply wanted to see him and acknowledge that they were father and son. But Jorgensen's efforts were to no avail. As he told the *Daily Mail* after trying to reach out to Bezos: "I don't think he will come to me now. I haven't heard a word from him or had any sign that he wants to connect with me. I hoped with the publicity it might happen, but I can't blame him. I guess I wasn't a very good father." There is no evidence that Bezos ever made contact with his biological father. Jorgensen died on March 16, 2015, at the age of seventy. His obituary only mentions that he was survived "by his son, Jeff," and nowhere does the Bezos family name appear.

After Jackie got divorced from Jorgensen, she started dating and eventually met a Cuban refugee named Miguel Bezos, whose family owned a lumberyard on the island. Miguel's parents, not wishing their son to fall into trouble with the Castro regime, had sent him to Miami in 1962. He and Jackie met in New Mexico and soon fell in love, and in April of 1968, they got married and then moved to Houston, where Miguel (who Americanized his name to Mike) had landed a job as a petroleum engineer at Exxon. When Jeff was four, Mike officially adopted him, and the parents gave their toddler the Bezos name. Throughout his life Jeff considered his real father to be Mike Bezos, and saw him as a warm, supportive father.

So how does the son of a struggling unicyclist and a teenaged mother become the richest man in the world? Bezos likes to tell how lucky he has been en route to becoming one of the most influential figures in business history. And he's correct in saying so. He has been in the right place at the right time, launching a book business just as the Internet was taking off, surviving the dot-com meltdown, riding the wave of streaming media, and the massive shift in shopping from brick-and-mortar stores to online. He even had a near brush with death, as we'll learn later. That, however, is not the whole story.

It seems that Jeff Bezos inherited a love for technology, a knack for running large organizations, and his resourceful nature from his maternal grandfather, Lawrence Preston "Pop" Gise, whose role, says Bezos, "was super important for me." Bezos spent every summer from the age of four to the age of sixteen at the Lazy G, his grandfather's ranch in south Texas. Pop took in Jeff, his stepsister Christina, and his stepbrother Mark to give Jackie and Mike Bezos a break from parenting. Those summers spent with Pop Gise helped shape Bezos. He recalls his grandfather being patient and willing to involve Jeff and his stepsiblings in the work on the ranch. As Bezos later recalled his first summer on the ranch when he was four years old: "He created the illusion for me that I was helping him on the ranch, which of course could not have been true, but I believed it."

Bezos has always portrayed his grandfather as a kind old man who liked to putter around the Lazy G, and he was indeed that. But what he doesn't talk about is what Gise did before he retired, a career that helps explain—at least in part—why Bezos ended up with the aptitude, energy, and the pedigree necessary to run an organization of roughly 650,000 employees.

When hearing Bezos's claims that he was plain lucky, keep in mind that Pop Gise was no aw-shucks Texas rancher. He was a man who had a tremendous influence on Bezos and his career. Bezos's grandfather was a well-respected and highly placed government official, whom Congress, in 1964, appointed to run the Atomic Energy Commission's Albuquerque operations office, which included the Sandia, Los Alamos, and Lawrence Livermore laboratories, sites that drove the development of the atomic and hydrogen bombs. He was in charge of some 26,000 employees and oversaw some of the most sophisticated and secretive technology of his time. Gise was also a top manager at what became known as the Defense Advanced Research Projects Agency (DARPA)—the R&D arm of the Pentagon—that was created in 1958 as a response to the Soviet launching of the Sputnik 1 satellite in 1957. Among other things, DARPA created a communications system that was designed to keep working after a nuclear attack had knocked out conventional communications channels. That technology helped lead to the formation of what we know today as the Internet. Gise had deep experience in the way the government worked and was privy to some of the most advanced and secretive technology of his day.

During those summers on the ranch, Bezos says that his grandfather would tell him stories about the missile defense systems he worked on during the Cold War with the Soviet Union. That made a deep impression on the young Bezos. Today, among the Silicon Valley titans, he is one of the most pro-government CEOs. Amazon's cloud computing business has won multibillion-dollar contracts from the Pentagon and the CIA. The significance of that business to Amazon is one reason why, in 2018, Bezos put his new second headquarters in northern Virginia, near Washington, D.C., and why he paid $23 million for an old textile museum in D.C.'s swish Kalorama area—his neighbors are the Obamas and Jared Kushner and Ivanka Trump—and is converting it into the city's largest single-family home at 27,000 square feet. The *Washingtonian* obtained blueprints of the $12 million renovation, which includes twenty-five bathrooms, eleven bedrooms, five living rooms, three kitchens, and a massive ballroom.

Amazon's tight relationships with governments has led to controversy. The company's Rekognition facial recognition software is one of the most sophisticated systems of its kind. In the U.S., Amazon sells the technology to both federal and local law officials, who use it to track down suspected criminals and terrorists. In late 2018, a group of 450 Amazon employees, worried that the technology has the potential to violate one's civil liberties, sent Bezos a letter protesting the company's decision to sell its facial recognition software to police. Bezos didn't respond publicly to the letter, but at a conference on the same day the letter was released, he made it clear where his priorities lay when it came to selling technology to the government: "If big tech companies are going to turn their back on the U.S. Department of Defense, this country is going to be in trouble."

Bezos's positive attitude toward the military industrial complex stood in stark contrast to Google, which announced in late 2018 that it wouldn't sell general-purpose facial recognition software to governments before working through important technology and policy questions. There's nothing wrong in helping one's country, but the field of facial recognition is so new and so fraught with privacy issues, that it would behoove Amazon to follow Google here and make sure that proper safeguards are in place before letting loose this technology. In a 2018 experiment using Amazon's Rekognition program, the American Civil Liberties Union found that the software confused twenty-eight members of Congress with publicly available mug shots and that a disproportionate number of them tagged as criminals were people of color. Amazon responded by saying the ACLU did not apply the software properly.

A love for his country wasn't the only thing Bezos learned from Pop Gise during those sweltering days on the Lazy G ranch. He says he took to heart a crucially important lesson about human relations that to this day he tries to bring to both his professional and family life. In 1974, when he was ten years old, he took a long road trip with his grandparents, who hitched an Airstream trailer to the back of their car and joined a caravan of three hundred other fellow travelers on a trek throughout the West. His grandmother Mattie was a chain-smoker, and at that time the networks were running a major TV ad campaign to get people to stop smoking—Bezos saw these ads while watching the *Days of Our Lives* soap opera during afternoons at the ranch. One of the advertisements had a statistic that said every puff of a cigarette takes two minutes off your life. One day during the trip, while sitting in the backseat of his grandparents' car, he calculated how much time Mattie had taken off her life. When he was finished with his arithmetic, he proudly announced to her how many years she'd lost, but got a reaction he didn't expect. She burst into tears. His grandfather stopped the car and took Bezos out of the backseat. He had no idea what was about to happen because Pop Gise had never before said a cross word to him. Recalls Bezos: "I thought he might actually be angry with me, but he wasn't. He said these incredible words, 'You're going to find out one day that it's harder to be kind than clever.' That's very powerful wisdom."

Later in his career, Bezos, whose occasional flashes of hot

temper have been widely documented, wouldn't always heed Pop Gise's advice about being kind to others, but his grandfather's lessons about the importance of being resourceful made a huge impression on the young man. On the ranch, Pop Gise liked to do almost everything himself, and to teach self-reliance, each summer he had his grandson take on more and more responsibility. They built fences, water pipelines, and assembled a prefab house. They fixed windmills and barns and spent a summer overhauling an old Caterpillar bulldozer. Bezos even helped his grandfather do veterinary work. Pop Gise used to make his own suture needles for his cattle. He'd take a piece of wire, use a torch to sharpen the tip, flatten the end, and put in an eye. Bezos later joked that they were on "a farm in the middle of nowhere and you could not just order from Amazon."

Part of being a resourceful person is being able to laser-focus on a task until it's finished—and done right. When Bezos was in Montessori school, he'd get so wrapped up in what he was doing that the teacher couldn't get him to switch tasks when it was time, so she'd literally have to pick up his chair with him in it and move him to the next task station. Bezos today says that he has the focus to not check his emails every few minutes. He jokes that he "multitasks serially. If something really important is happening, someone will find me."

When he was in sixth grade, Bezos became obsessed with a device called an Infinity Cube, whose motorized mirrors allow one to stare into "infinity." The mirrors bounce the light that is caught between them, creating the illusion that the images go on infinitely. His mother, Jackie, thought that $20 was too much for such a bauble and refused to buy it for him. Bezos figured out that the pieces of the cube could be bought cheaply, so he did—and built it himself. According to a book written about the gifted children at his school, Bezos the sixth-grader said: "You have to be able to think . . . for yourself." The author describes him as "friendly but serious," even "courtly," and possessed of "general intellectual excellence," though, according to teachers, "not particularly gifted in leadership."

After graduating from high school at the top of his class, Bezos headed for Princeton, where he wanted to be a quantum physicist. He found that others in the major had more of a knack for the esoteric principles of that field, so he switched to electrical engineering and computer science where he felt more at home. He graduated with a rare 4.2 grade point average (4.3 is an A+) and headed for New York City, where he worked on Wall Street.

Not long after arriving in New York, Bezos decided he wanted to marry, and he was pretty sure he knew what criterion counted the most. "You don't want to go through life with teammates who aren't resourceful," he recalled. His ideal woman, he said, would possess the ability to get him out of a third-world prison.

He found that woman in MacKenzie Tuttle, a fellow Princeton alum whom he met at work. Although she was working on Wall Street, she wanted to be a novelist. At Princeton she'd been an assistant to the bestselling novelist Toni Morrison. MacKenzie would go on to publish two well-regarded works of fiction. During the early days of Amazon, MacKenzie displayed plenty of resourcefulness, acting as the start-up's accountant, helping with hiring, and even packing books, and driving to UPS or the post office.

Bezos applied the same philosophy of resourcefulness to the raising of his four kids (he has three sons and an adopted daughter from China). He let them play with knives when they were four years old and power tools when they were eight or nine. MacKenzie had a saying: "We'd much rather have a kid with nine fingers than a resourceful-less kid with ten fingers." Even the woman Bezos left MacKenzie for, Lauren Sanchez, showed a sense of resourcefulness Bezos must have admired. This former cohost of Fox's *Good Day LA* and of the dancing competition series *So You Think You Can Dance* became a helicopter pilot and started her own aerial photography company—a skill that might come in handy if she ever has to free Bezos from a third-world prison.

In those early days in New York City, Bezos eventually landed a job at the secretive hedge fund D. E. Shaw, which, among other things, engaged in high-speed arbitrage—a kind of mathematical black box trading approach that searches for price discrepancies in markets around the globe. One day Bezos figured out that the Internet was growing at 2,300 percent a year. He'd never seen anything like it and knew he had to be a part of it. He decided that selling books would be a good place to start because they didn't spoil, came in relatively uniform sizes for easy packing and shipping, and shoppers knew pretty much what they were getting thanks to reviews.

When he decided to start Amazon in 1994, he was thirty years old, had a promising job—he was one of the youngest senior vice presidents in D. E. Shaw's history—an apartment on the Upper West Side, and had been married to MacKenzie for a year. He did a lot of soul-searching because he enjoyed his job, had a bright future, and could make serious money if he stayed. He approached his boss and told him he wanted to start an Internet bookstore. His boss said it sounded like a good idea, but not for Bezos, who already had a good career.

Bezos wrestled with the decision for a couple of days, and the data-driven computer whiz uncharacteristically looked to his heart to make the decision. He looked ahead to his life at age eighty and then looked back at his life and realized: "I don't want to be eighty and having to look back at a string of regrets. And our biggest regrets—you can murder someone, you'd regret that—but our biggest regrets are those of omission. It's the paths not taken that haunt us." He then knew that at eighty he'd never regret trying something big, even if he failed.

Bezos and MacKenzie packed their belongings and headed across the country to Seattle. He picked that city because of its reputation as a tech hub—Microsoft was headquartered there. More important, he selected it because of its small population. If he settled in California or New York he'd have to pay huge amounts of sales tax on the books purchased in those highly populated states. Under the laws back then, Amazon only had to collect tax on the books purchased in Washington State. Bezos started Amazon in the proverbial tech-start-up garage with a $100,000 stake provided by his parents. Bezos chose to sell books, but from the start had much larger ambitions. Yes, he cared about books, but what he really cared about was building a machine that would eventually become his AI flywheel, one that could deliver massive amounts of goods quickly and cheaply. He invented Amazon.

The company's rise to the top has been well documented. Bezos hired the most brilliant programmers he could, drove home his mantra of extreme customer service, and drove his employees to the limit in a culture that valued data, the truth, and high performance. He hired a talented team of editors who reviewed books and interviewed authors in an effort to make Amazon a destination for book lovers. His algorithms could help make reader recommendations based on what else was being read by other purchasers of the same book. He offered low prices, a broad selection, and fast delivery.

Not everything in those early days was data-driven, however. One of the ways that Bezos built traffic on his site involved old-fashioned marketing. In 1997, the two-year-old company was growing, but not fast enough for Bezos. To attract eye-balls to the site, the marketing department came up with a concept called "The Greatest Tale Ever Told," where Amazon's customers could collaborate with a famous writer. According to the memoir *Amazonia* by James Marcus, who was Amazon employee number 55 and one of the site's book editors, novelist John Updike agreed to write the first paragraph of a mystery titled "Murder Makes the Magazine," set in an office not unlike that of *The New Yorker*. His opening sentence ran: "Miss Tasso Pok at ten-ten alighted from the elevator onto the olive tiles of the nineteenth floor only lightly nagged by a sense of something wrong." Amazon invited its customers to write a new paragraph each day for the next forty-four days, and the company's editorial staff would pick a winner each day. The winners would get $1,000 each, and Updike would write the final paragraph of the mystery and collect $5,000. The contest became a magnet for book lovers—Amazon attracted 380,000 submissions—and a public relations home run: the Updike literary challenge got a mention in three hundred different news outlets. By that fall, Amazon had grown to become one of the twenty-five most visited sites on the web.

The company would go to any length to get its customers the best prices and the fastest deliveries. No free lunchroom for employees, and to this day lavish expense accounts are out of the question. During a holiday season early in Amazon's history, for example, Bezos ordered his executive team to work a series of night shifts in its Seattle warehouse to help catch up on the swell of orders arriving. Bezos held a contest to see who could pick items off the shelf the fastest. He always encouraged his employees not to focus on the competition, but when a competitor got in its way, Amazon could be brutal. When, in the late 2000s, it was battling with the start-up Diapers.com, Bezos, according to the book *The Everything Store*, said that if the start-up didn't agree to be taken over, Amazon would keep cutting the price on its diapers to zero if it had to until a deal could be made. Amazon swallowed the business.

The lessons about self-reliance that Bezos learned from his days on Pop Gise's ranch served him well at Amazon. In the late 1990s, Bezos was looking for a way to expand the number of products sold on Amazon.com, so he decided to allow independent or "third-party" merchants to sell on his site. His first idea was to launch an Amazon auction where customers bid for products—a lot like eBay—but nobody came. (Although his stepbrother, Mark, says he bought a coffee cup.) So Bezos folded that operation and opened Z shops, where prices were fixed by the third-party retailers, and no one came to those, either. These experiments had been going on for about a year and a half until the idea arose inside the company to sell those third-party products on the same page as Amazon's products. Bezos jumped on the strategy, called it Marketplace, and it started working right away. Today, Marketplace accounts for more than half of all products sold on Amazon, and it has better profit margins than its core online business.

"The whole point of moving things forward," says Bezos, "is that you run into problems, into failures, and you have to back up and do things again. You use resourcefulness and you try to invent yourself out of a box."

But being resourceful isn't all that makes Bezos tick.

CHAPTER 3

In God We Trust,
All Others Must Bring Data

When taking stock of someone's character, Bezos, as we've seen, puts resourcefulness at the top of his list, and he expects everyone who works for him to show the same level of smarts, initiative, and ingenuity. The company's web page in the early 2000s explained what kind of person Bezos liked to hire. "There is no Amazon.com 'type.' There are Amazon.com employees who have three master's degrees and speak five languages . . . people who have worked at Procter and Gamble and Microsoft . . . a professional figure skater . . . a Rhodes scholar." Joy Covey, the CFO in the company's early days, finished second in a field of 27,000 the year she took her CPA exam, and one early Amazonian was a National Spelling Bee champion. As Bezos told the *Washington Post*: "You can shout out 'onomatopoeia' in the hallway, and you'll get an answer."

Recruiting resourceful superstars is not enough, however, to explain Amazon's phenomenal success. One of Bezos's most striking personality traits is his ability to face the unvarnished truth no matter how inconvenient, to make decisions based on cold, hard facts. At the company, some managers had signs outside their offices that said "In God we trust. All others must bring data," a philosophy that Bezos lives and breathes. Unlike many CEOs, he doesn't surround himself with sycophants who tell their leader what they want to hear; instead, he reaches out to those willing to confront him with stark reality. He deeply believes that the facts should trump hierarchy every time.

The clearest manifestation of his propensity for the truth is his famous—or some would say infamous—six-pager, which to this day can instill fear and loathing in the hearts of Amazon's managers. Any Amazonian who wants to pitch an idea for a product or a service must, before writing a single line of code, compose a document no longer than six pages in length. His mantra of "always starting with the customer" comes into play here. The memos, in the form of a hypothetical PR release, typically start by laying out the long-term impact of the new project and why it's meaningful to customers. Then an FAQ section helps determine the nuts and bolts of the proposed service or product, and how the development team should build it. In the early days of Amazon, Andy Jassy, who now runs AWS, says that before the six-pagers, employees sometimes had "great high-level ideas, but they'd get deep into a project only to find the result wasn't going to be that important." It was the discipline of the six-pager exercise that helped avoid going off on the wrong track. Teams within Amazon work tirelessly on these reports, crafting them sometimes for weeks until they make sure they get the concept right and that the document includes all the crucial facts.

One former Amazon manager who spent three years at the company in the mid-2010s says the six-page memo process works like an internally funded venture capital firm. "Amazon has all these smart young people with great ideas. It encourages people—if they have a good idea—to pitch it. Bezos is hiring the best brains from Silicon Valley and has created a system to fund the best ideas that those people have. Yes, they will have failures, but they are willing to kill things fast and are good at limiting their downside."

When a team brings a six-pager to a meeting, Bezos insists that everyone spend the first twenty minutes or so carefully absorbing the memo so no one can fake having read it. Once the reading period ends, the group engages in an animated, confrontational discussion, challenging the premise, the underlying facts, and the viability of the project from the customer's point of view. Every big innovation at Amazon, such as Prime, the creation of Alexa, or of Amazon's cloud service, has had to survive the crucible of the six-page memo. Not all proposals, however, are complicated or data-driven enough to require all six pages. Shorter memos are better for simpler problems. As a new project progresses, the memo gets revised and revised until the project is ready for prime time. In some instances, an edited version of the six-pager becomes the actual press release for the product.

The goal of every meeting at Amazon—whether triggered by a six-pager or not—is to get as close to the truth of the matter as possible. James Marcus recalls a meeting in the late 1990s in which Bezos and a handful of executives were discussing book sales. The young CEO, who'd declared that he was building "a culture of metrics," proudly cited a new readout from the company's database showing that book sales on the site's home page were booming. A manager named Marilyn, who happened to check actual sales with the warehouse on a daily basis, noticed that the numbers were too high by a factor of two or three. According to Marcus, she said to Bezos:

"Jeff, these are wrong."

"We pulled them straight from the database," he replied.

"But they are wrong," she insisted.

Bezos wouldn't budge. Then, one day he appeared at a meeting and announced: "My suspicion is that we're getting a count of shopping bag adds rather than actual sales." In other words, the computer was counting any book put in the shopping cart as a sale, while the truth was that not all shoppers hit the buy button, a subtlety that the database jockeys had missed. That an underling such as Marilyn was willing to stand up and bluntly contradict Bezos says a lot about the Amazon culture. But what perhaps says even more is that Bezos took the time and effort to get to the bottom of what was going on—it would've been easy for the CEO to simply believe his state-of-the-art database and the brilliant techies who built it. Truth prevailed.

A manager who worked at Amazon Prime Video and then left the company in 2017 to start his own firm says—speaking on background—that it was Amazon's egalitarian atmosphere that allowed underlings to challenge higher-ups with no negative repercussions. He recalls being at meetings at one of his previous jobs at a major national broadcaster where no one got to sit at the table unless they were a vice president or higher. "At Amazon it was completely different," he recalls. "Amazon encourages everyone to engage in healthy conflict. I've never been in such a flat organization with the ability to connect with super influential people. It was really about building, about being your own CEO and your own brand and working quickly and collaboratively with everyone else. And it was quite refreshing to work first and foremost for the customer. It was all about how we connect with customers and thinking of them first—and it was not bullshit."

Of course, that doesn't mean that these meetings were all kumbaya sessions. Another Amazon executive who spent nearly a decade at the company describes what some of these truth-telling sessions were like. "It's a fucked-up place to work, and I know because I've worked at investment banks," he says. "We'd have weekly meetings, and it would be like a game show. You were put to the test. Did you hit your numbers? You needed the answer, or it was 'get the fuck out of here.'" Behind all that intensity was the relentless drive to do away with friction in the lives of Amazon's customers. The company took responsibility for lazy customers who wouldn't read the manual—the product had to work intuitively. Readers could order a book on Kindle without leaving their living rooms. Alexa was designed to make shopping and listening to music easier. "We kept banging on getting friction out of our customers' lives," says the executive. "Customers always came first and we'd work backwards from there. At Amazon, the employees are not customers. We were never going to get brunch or sushi, and no one had an assistant."

One present-day fan of the six-pager is Greg Hart, who runs Prime Video, Amazon's movie and TV streaming service. He says that Bezos favors six-pagers over PowerPoints and whiteboards because he believes that when someone uses these common corporate tools most of the information about a project stays stuck in the head of the person presenting. A presenter has to be phenomenally communicative to share a lot of detailed information in a coherent fashion—in a way where the key points come through clearly. At the same time, the PowerPoint cowboy has to get everybody else to pay attention as one dense data-filled slide flips to the next and the next in a dark room.

By contrast, the six-pager forces employees to think carefully about what they want to say. The author of the memo must figure out how to craft a narrative about the project that clearly describes the potential of the product or service and includes only the most necessary and relevant details. Others might have questions after they read the document, but hopefully, the majority of those questions have been addressed in it. Crucially, it is a live document that tracks the project's life span, with the manager constantly refining and updating until launch.

The creation of Alexa best shows the six-pager at work. Before Hart ran Prime Video, he was in charge of the team that created Alexa. As early as 2011, Bezos was leading internal discussions about whether speech would become a key way that humans would interact with machines and how that would work. Out of those discussions, Bezos came up with a simple goal for Alexa: a device that would have no screen, with a person interacting with it entirely by voice. No keypads; no touch screens. Bezos asked Hart to lead the initiative, whose code name was Doppler, and to write a six-pager. "The amount Bezos thinks about the future," says Hart, "is amazing. His ability to look ahead and connect unrelated pieces of information and patterns and to find a thread that's of value between them is different than normal humans can do."

At first Hart was daunted. An English major from Williams, he had no experience with consumer electronics—never mind cutting-edge voice recognition software. The very first thing Hart did was to start learning as much as he could about speech and hardware. He spent a lot of time with the engineers at Amazon's secretive R&D center Lab126 (the lab's name is a reference to the alphabet, with *1* representing the letter *A* and *26* representing *Z*), trying to figure out how to make a device that works.

As they learned more about the technology, Hart and his team would edit and re-edit the six-pager before the official presentation to the top brass. Hart composed his six-pager as if it were a press release. It included the specs, price, launch date, and even ways in which Amazon would communicate with the press about the new device. It also addressed a slew of internal questions others at Amazon might have. How could it hear over background noise? How could it distinguish regional accents or colloquialisms? What would people use it for? Why would someone use it for shopping if they couldn't see what they were buying?

Over the months that followed, Hart kept revising the memo as the product and its capabilities changed, and as he received feedback from Bezos and other executives who made sure the six-pager was sticking to the CEO's original vision. As the original memo outlined, Alexa was supposed to be able to have a "normal conversation." Bezos regularly pushed Hart and his team to reduce what's called latency—the time it would take Alexa to answer questions. Bezos knew well how fickle retail customers are, so years earlier, in building Amazon.com, he pushed his programmers to make the site respond to a customer's click as fast as possible. Alexa had to be fast or it would be painful for customers to use her.

Just before the launch of the Alexa device—now called the Echo—in 2014, Hart updated the six-pager once more to reflect the product they were actually launching and then compared it to the original memo. "We asked ourselves," recalls Hart, "do we still feel good? Did we make compromises on things that were far too valuable to actually compromise on? Or are those compromises okay? Did we have feature creep that's caused us to change this or that?" The six-pager forced him to confront the truth about what he and his team had done. If the final product had fallen short of Bezos's original vision, Hart would be back to the drawing board. Bezos, satisfied with what he saw, gave the go-ahead, and the Echo became a major hit.

Even after the launch, Amazon didn't stop improving the product. At one point, Bezos and his executive team debated whether the Echo's hearing was good enough on its own or needed a small, handheld microphone for users who were trying to speak to it from across a noisy room. (Alexa, can you hear me now?) To learn the answer, Amazon once again turned to the customer. The first Echos were shipped with a voice-activated remote allowing people to use the device from across the room. The company immediately started monitoring how the Echo was used and soon the data told them that people almost never picked up the remote. In later shipments, it was quietly removed from the box—and therefore Amazon was able to lower the cost of the device, saving money for the consumer. Amazon removed some friction in their customers' lives. And the AI flywheel kept spinning.

The Alexa project is a microcosm for how Bezos innovates, motivates, and handles an enormous number of interconnected details. The six-pager works on many different levels. First, it helps the company deal with complexity. If the six-pager is written correctly, everyone on the team should get the critical information they need to get on top of a new complex project like Alexa. It helps level the playing field in terms of information— after a close reading of a memo, everyone at least gets the basics of the project.

Bezos sets the tone here. He reads with a high level of concentration. One executive who has been in many six-pager meetings says that Bezos reads at an Olympic level, meaning that when he is reading, he looks like an Olympic skier right before a run who is closing his eyes and visualizing and moving his body with the turns he knows he'll face on the run. Bezos, in other words, is absorbing all the information in the memo and anticipating the bumps and icy patches he will hit once the meeting begins. Once prepared, he will be able to give both strategic and tactical feedback on the memo in minute detail.

In a corporation as large and complex as Amazon, Bezos doesn't have the time to meet with all his leaders regularly, so he uses the six-pager sessions to make sure his top lieutenants are aligned with the goals of any particular project. In turn, these lieutenants spread the word down to the next level of teams, and those teams to the level beneath them. This works in part because he has surrounded himself with a cadre of longtime loyal leaders he calls the S-team, his eighteen top executives who know how he thinks, understand his values, and have a fierce desire to ferret out the truth. Many have worked with Bezos for years (some for more than a decade), rarely leave the company, and are fiercely loyal to him. "I'm very happy that we don't have a lot of turnover on the S-team," Bezos said at a 2017 all-hands meeting. "I don't intend to change that—I like you guys a lot."

Building an S-team takes a lot of hard work, but Bezos has a secret weapon. A number of his key S-team members were at one point in their career one of Bezos's technical advisors— more informally known as a "shadow." Up-and-coming executives lucky enough to become one of Bezos's shadows can follow him around for as long as two years, attend meetings with him, and get special assignments. Other companies besides Amazon have used shadows. In the 1990s, a young executive named Paul Otellini shadowed Intel CEO Andy Grove and eventually became the chipmaker's top executive. What makes Amazon's shadow program particularly effective is that these aren't run-of-the-mill mentorships but full-time positions.

Early in Amazon's history, Bezos would mentor a few select executives, but the effort wasn't paying off as well as he had hoped—some of those mentees ended up leaving the company. The CEO's first full-time shadow was Andy Jassy, a Harvard MBA with no technical background. Jassy's only job was to trail Bezos, attend meetings, learn how he thinks, how he ferrets out the nub of a problem, and where he thinks the world is headed. Jassy, who shadowed Bezos from 2003 to 2004, eventually, as we've seen, helped build and now runs AWS, the largest cloud service business in the world—an amazing feat for anyone, never mind someone with a non-tech background. Bezos wouldn't have been likely to assign such a key role to a non-techie if Jassy hadn't gained the CEO's trust during his stint as a shadow.

From that point on, the technical advisor program became an integral part of Amazon's culture, and over the years Bezos has put a string of successful executives through the program. Shadowing Bezos today is Wei Gao, originally from China, a female software developer with a fourteen-year career at Amazon. And the shadow program is spreading. Jeff Wilke, who runs e-commerce globally for Amazon and is by many accounts the second most powerful person at the company, has his own shadow, Yunyan Wang, also of Chinese descent, who previously was a director of Amazon's Marketplace, where independent retailers sell their wares. That two women currently hold these coveted shadow roles sends a strong signal that Amazon is trying to shake up its heavily male tech culture.

Greg Hart, the head of Prime Video, remembers vividly the day Bezos asked him to be a shadow.

Hart says he was surprised when he was asked to be his boss's shadow—he was happy at his current job—but a lunch with Bezos quickly persuaded him. Hart recalls that Bezos was very gracious about it. The CEO said: "Look, if you don't want to do it, if you love your current job, that's fine. Nobody outside will know." Says Hart, who accepted the offer immediately after the lunch: "It was a tremendous opportunity. That night I went home and said to my wife that I felt it was like Henry Ford asking somebody to be there, shadowing him at the dawn of the industrial revolution."

The S-team and the farm-club shadow system play another, equally important role inside the company—they make sure Amazon has a strong roster of executives who could one day take Bezos's place as CEO. Amazon is one of those corporations like Apple, Microsoft, Tesla, Google, and Facebook that is identified with its founder. Bezos, as of the writing of this book, is only fifty-five, but investors—not to mention employees—worry what would happen to Amazon should Bezos leave or something happen to him. With his S-team, the signal that Bezos seems to be sending to the world is that if something were to happen to him or if he retired (although no one believes *that* will happen anytime soon), Amazon has a deep bench of all-pro players who could step in and drive the company. Of course, it is unclear whether any of these talented executives have the vision, intuition, and genius of a Jeff Bezos. His leaving would doubtless be a negative for the company in the same way that Apple is still struggling to find its creative way after the death of Steve Jobs. That said, the message being sent to Wall Street—and bought into by some stock analysts—is that Amazon and its AI flywheel will keep rolling ahead even without Bezos.

The amount of trust Bezos has in his S-team allows him to delegate tremendous amounts of autonomy to these executives and helps explain why Bezos has been able to manage a multi-industry business as large and complex as Amazon. There's nothing really new or startling in having a loyal, experienced management team. What distinguishes Bezos is that every time a new product gets proposed he makes sure his lieutenants don't leave the room until they have a firm grasp on the project. Often this process isn't pretty. Bezos will keep challenging everyone in the meeting on the facts, allowing little room for wishful thinking or guesses. If someone isn't prepared or tries to fake it, Bezos might erupt into one of his well-documented "nutters," as some employees have come to call these outbursts. At meetings he has snapped at unprepared team members: "I'm sorry, did I take my stupid pills today?" "Are you lazy or just incompetent?" or "If

I hear that idea again, I'm gonna have to kill myself." In these situations, he is certainly being more clever than kind, although some who've worked closely with him say that his nutters are justified because he's almost always right.

Hart has seen plenty of nutters and has been a victim of them, but he's never taken them personally. "It's really important," says Hart, "for any leader to be able to have moments where they apply heat. When Jeff gets frustrated at people or teams, he's very good about saying that he's not frustrated with the person, he's frustrated with the *performance* of the team or the person, that they're not bringing their best thinking." Sometimes, Hart concedes, Bezos is right—the employee really hasn't done his best work.

To get at the truth, Hart says that Bezos and his reports often go back and forth on the issue—sometimes the frustration arises from someone simply not doing a good job of explaining themselves. Once Bezos understands their point of view—or they accept his—they can move on and have a good constructive dialogue.

Marc Lore, who worked at Amazon in the early 2010s, has a different take on the company's confrontational culture. In 2010, Lore, who had cofounded Quidsi, an online retailer that owned Diapers.com, agreed to sell his company to Amazon for roughly $500 million and then stayed on to work with Bezos. A few years later he left Amazon to start Jet.com, which he sold to Walmart in 2016 for $3.3 billion in a deal that made him the giant retailer's U.S. e-commerce chief.

One reason Lore left Amazon is that he didn't like the culture Bezos had created in which executives used sharp elbows and raised voices to get to the truth. Sitting in his modern Hoboken, New Jersey, office overlooking the Hudson River, Lore, dressed in a very un-Walmart-like black T-shirt and jeans, reflected on his years at Amazon. "Jeff said he didn't believe in social cohesion because you can get to the wrong answer that way," explains Lore. "There are some benefits to that approach. If you tell people exactly what you're thinking—even if you hurt their feelings—you get to the right answers." The downside, Lore believes, is that if you hurt coworkers' feelings, maybe they don't have as much trust in the leadership or they won't speak up the next time or they'll be risk averse or leave the company. "There are pros and cons to both approaches, but I personally love the Walmart culture of social cohesion where feelings matter. How you interact with people is very important and how you make them feel is very important. It's not always about just getting to the right answer."

Lore makes a good point, but the search for truth at all costs is a formula that has created some of the world's great companies. Apple's Steve Jobs was famous for driving his coworkers to the edge until he arrived at what he thought was the right solution. He could sometimes convince them to do the impossible, often by being very brusque and rude. Jobs liked to say that "my brutal honesty is the price of admission for being in the room with me." He'd tell his employees that they were full of it. Sometimes they told him *he* was full of it, but in the end they accomplished great things. Ray Dalio, the billionaire founder of Bridgewater, the world's largest hedge fund with $160 billion under management, has a philosophy of business called "radical truth and radical transparency," which he believes is the best way to cultivate independent thinkers in an organization. Workers get rated in real time during meetings to gauge how truthful, transparent, and right they are. It's an extreme culture, but also a productive one. Not everyone can survive such pressure and scrutiny—as with the Navy SEALs, it's "up or out"—but in the long run both Jobs and Bezos ended up with a very loyal group of top-notch players whom they could trust to take on bigger and bigger responsibilities.

It's not only those confrontational meetings that make working at Amazon tough. In 2015, the *New York Times* ran a long piece describing a corporate culture in which workers are "encouraged to tear apart one another's ideas in meetings, toil long and late (emails arrive past midnight, followed by text messages asking why they were not answered), and held to standards that the company boasts are 'unreasonably high.'" The piece went on to describe how the internal phone directory instructed colleagues on how to send secret feedback to one another's bosses, and how it wasn't uncommon to see workers weeping at their desks. One former Amazon employee in the piece summed up the culture as "purposeful Darwinism."

After the piece was published, Bezos said he didn't recognize the company described by the *Times*'s journalists. Of the dozens of current and former Amazon employees I spoke with, no one could recall such horror stories or were too intimidated by Amazon's tough nondisclosure agreements to mention them. That said, all described the culture as extremely exacting and not for the faint of heart.

Amazon doesn't hide the fact that it demands excellence, and any manager or engineer talented enough to get hired there would certainly be able to easily move on to a new job if they didn't like how the place was run. When Bezos started the company, the contracts that new hires had to sign included a paragraph stating that the employee acknowledged that working at the company "may involve a high degree of job-related stress" and that the employee wouldn't bring any action against the company arising from that stress. Hart believes that the culture is less about being confrontational and mean and more about being manically focused and persistent. Pursuing the truth and believing there is a right answer can lead to heated debates, but people, he says, don't start out being confrontational. The bottom line, according to many in the company, is that Bezos's relentless search for the truth has more often than not helped improve their thinking.

A deep addiction to data does have its downside. The kind of fact-driven, relentlessly focused mind that Bezos possesses can be an Achilles' heel, making him appear in the public eye as less than empathic, as sometimes blind to the grayer areas of life. His critics view him as a plutocrat who, in the name of enriching his shareholders, is so obsessed with his customers that he neglects his employees and his community. They point, for example, to the tough working conditions at Amazon, which seem driven by a devotion to the customer, and to Bezos's unwillingness to soothe the fears of local politicians and residents when Amazon announced its Long Island City second headquarters, presumably because working out those problems would have taken valuable time and resources away from serving customers.

Ironically, what made Bezos so successful in the short run might ultimately work against him. In all likelihood, Bezos thinks of himself as a good guy, creating jobs and donating billions to charity. That's little solace, however, to those who have been crushed by Amazon's wheel as well as to the politicians who represent them. A rising tide of political antipathy toward Amazon could someday dramatically alter its trajectory.

Bezos is not alone in displaying big tech hubris. Other Internet titans, such as Facebook's Mark Zuckerberg, Uber's cofounder and ex-CEO Travis Kalanick, and Google's cofounder and CEO Larry Page at times have displayed the same Silicon Valley social blindness. All are brilliant technologists who feel more comfortable with things they can quantify rather than with things they can't, such as human emotions. While at Uber's helm, Kalanick had a "Don't ask for permission but beg for forgiveness" attitude, sometimes flouting local regulations to expand his car-hailing service and leaving a trail of upset community members behind him. Zuckerberg's growth-at-all-costs philosophy—he was described by former Twitter CEO Dick Costolo in a *New Yorker* article as "a ruthless execution machine"—rankles many. His seeming aloofness during the Russian manipulation of Facebook during the 2016 presidential elections and throughout the Cambridge Analytica scandal, in which personal Facebook data was hijacked to help sway voters toward Trump, certainly didn't help his reputation. Similarly, Google CEO Page waited for a public insurrection from a group of his employees before agreeing to stop selling face recognition software to law enforcement agencies until certain safeguards were met. As Bill Gates told *The New Yorker*: "Somebody who is smart, and rich, and ends up not acknowledging problems as quickly as they should will be attacked as arrogant. That comes with the territory."

Bezos, of course, is hyper-smart and he might soon become more adept at communicating with the public and displaying a more human touch. Perhaps he'll hire his own version of Zuckerberg's Sheryl Sandberg, who, as the CEO's deputy and a regular on the conference circuit, is more skillful than her boss at trying to explain Facebook to the public. In a sign that he may be adapting to this new reality, Bezos has given Amazon's head of Global Corporate Affairs, Jay Carney, the go-ahead to build up Amazon's public relations team, which has grown from a handful of spinmeisters to, as of 2019, an army of 250. If they do their job right, this team will help better explain Amazon to the world and perhaps limit the number of future anti-Amazon eruptions.

While he might lack empathy in the eye of the public, Bezos, as we have seen, does possess positive qualities: his turbocharged resourcefulness and his uncanny ability to confront the truth have helped him build his empire. Also essential to his success has been his long-termism. While most business leaders think in terms of the next quarter or perhaps the next two or three years, Bezos thinks in terms of centuries.

CHAPTER 4

The 10,000-Year Man

A two-hour drive east from the Cavern City Air Terminal in Carlsbad, New Mexico, brings you to the dusty town of Van Horn, Texas. This sleepy outpost in far-west Texas—population 1,919—has a typical commercial strip with a Budget Inn, a Shell gas station, and Chuy's Mexican restaurant. But Van Horn is different from small-town America in one extraordinary way. Just to the north lies a 300,000-plus-acre ranch owned by Bezos—a stretch of land only slightly smaller than Los Angeles. The ranch isn't just a place for him to get away from it all. It is the launching site for his rocket company, Blue Origin, whose ultimate aim is to colonize space. The project is symbolic of Bezos's long-term frame of mind. It helps explain why Bezos is of a different ilk than most people, why he was able to build Amazon into arguably the most formidable capitalist machine in history. While the rest of humanity is focused on the short term—a few months or a few years out—Bezos, as this book has pointed out, thinks in terms of decades and centuries.

In Bezos's first letter to his public shareholders, released in early 1998, he laid out the importance of the long view, a philosophy that to this day Amazon follows. He wrote about taking bold steps, making investments in new technology and businesses that might or might not pay off, and a willingness to wait years to find out. In the first section of the letter, under the subhead "It's All About the Long Term," he wrote that Amazon "will continue to make investment decisions in light of long-term market leadership considerations rather than short-term profitability considerations or short-term Wall Street reactions." That meant that boosting cash flow and market share always trumped short-term profitability. This approach allowed him in many ways to run Amazon as if it were a private company. Its soaring growth rate and the promise of future profits—even while the business kept piling up losses—granted him the ability to raise capital in the face of scathing criticism and skepticism from some on Wall Street. (Of course it doesn't hurt that Bezos controls 16 percent of Amazon's stock, which gave him the kind of leeway to run the company that most CEOs can only dream of.) In 2014, Bezos told Henry Blodget of *Business Insider* that he spends only six hours a year talking to investors and then only to the ones who are long-term holders of Amazon stock. He basically doesn't care what people think who trade in and out of the stock on a regular basis.

Bezos is the ultimate long-term thinker. He believes that thinking in terms of decades and centuries is the lever that enables people to accomplish things that they couldn't even conceive of doing if they only thought about the short term. Ask someone to alleviate world hunger or solve peace in the Middle East, and most will throw up their arms in dismay. Ask them to solve those issues in one hundred years, and suddenly the problem becomes more addressable. This is the kind of long-term thinking that helped make Amazon a success. While most CEOs worry about the next quarter or two, Bezos expects to get his results in five, six, or seven years. That gives his employees the time to be creative and solve problems. "If everything has to work in two to three years," says Bezos, "then that limits what you can do. If you give yourself the breathing room to say okay, I'm okay to take seven years, all of a sudden you have way more opportunities."

Getting his employees to think long term changes how they spend their time, how they plan, and where they put their energy. Their ability to look around corners improves. It's not an easy kind of corporate culture to create. As Bezos puts it: "By the way, it's not natural for humans. It's a discipline you have to build. The get-rich-slowly schemes are not big sellers on infomercials."

Bezos's long-term strategy has yielded big dividends at Amazon. Over the last two decades, he has taken a large portion of the e-tailer's cash flow and, rather than give it back to shareholders, used it to expand the business, invest in R&D, and hire the best people. While Wall Street cried for quarterly profits and Amazon's stock rode a roller coaster, Bezos ignored all the static to focus on his crusade to build the world's smartest company.

Perhaps the best example of Bezos's long-term vision was his uncanny decision in 2003 to gamble on what eventually became the world's largest cloud computing business: AWS. At an off-site meeting in 2003 at Bezos's home on Lake Washington, the discussion turned to the difficulty Amazon's software engineers were having when they designed new features for Amazon.com. Every time they wrote the code for a new feature, they had to wait for the IT department to figure out how to make it work on Amazon's sprawling computer infrastructure. As Andy Jassy, who was Bezos's shadow at the time, recalled to the *Financial Times*: "They were all reinventing the wheel . . . nothing they were building scaled beyond their own projects." Jassy's idea was to build on-demand computing power in the cloud to make it easier and faster for Amazon's engineers to design new features. This, however, required Amazon to build a major computer service within the company. At the time, the fallout from the dot-com crash was still being felt—how could a struggling online retailer justify starting a computer services company?

Despite the risks, Bezos gave the go-ahead to build a cloud service. It worked so well that eventually Amazon started to offer these same software tools to other businesses. Today, AWS is Amazon's most profitable business line—a service that counts among its thousands of customers Netflix, Airbnb, and the CIA. It was a huge long-term gamble that has paid off handsomely. In mid-2019, the investment research firm Cowen estimated that AWS alone was worth north of $500 billion, more than half the total stock market capitalization of Amazon itself.

The bold, long-term bets that Bezos made over the years didn't always pay off. In 2019, the company closed its Amazon Restaurants food delivery business, finding it difficult to compete in a highly crowded field that included players such as Door-Dash and Uber Eats. That same year it discontinued its Dash buttons, which allowed consumers to reorder laundry detergent and other everyday items with a push of a button—customers didn't find them very useful. During the dot-com bubble, Amazon invested in the delivery service Kosmo.com and Pets.com, two online businesses that flopped spectacularly.

Perhaps the company's most public failure was the Amazon Fire Phone. Apple's iPhone, launched in 2007, had become a huge success, and Google had its fast-growing Android operating system. Why not, thought Bezos, develop a phone that would appeal to Amazon's Prime members? In 2014, Amazon launched the Fire Phone, a smart device that sold for $650, making it competitive with the iPhone and Samsung's Android phones. The phone, however, didn't support many popular apps, including Google Maps and Starbucks, and some users complained how awkward it was to import programs such as the Apple iTunes library. The phone never caught the public's imagination, and soon after the product's launch Amazon took a massive write-down on its unsold inventory.

As painful as that litany of losses was to the company, Bezos, who has called Amazon "the best place in the world to fail," wouldn't have it any other way. He believes that if the size of a company's failures doesn't keep growing, it can't be inventing at a scale that can achieve major breakthroughs. Bezos encourages his people to be bold, to make large long-term wagers, including winners such as AWS, Prime, and Kindle. But that risky approach also generated many big flops like the Fire Phone and Pets.com. He has survived this string of flops because while these failures were all big bets, none were "bet the company" bets. If a company is constantly innovating, a few of those winning bets are bound to more than make up for the losses. If a company doesn't innovate, it might one day find itself in a position where it will have to make a Hail Mary bet to save the company. "I've made billions of dollars of failures at Amazon.com. Literally billions of dollars of failures," Bezos told *Business Insider*'s Blodget. "You might remember Pets.com or Kosmo.com. It was like getting a root canal with no anesthesia. None of those things are fun. But they also don't matter." Losses like that do matter to Wall Street, but Bezos throughout his career has been tenacious, persuasive, and successful enough to weather the sharp criticism from those in the investment community looking for quick payoffs. All the while, he is building a loyal following of investors with patient money.

Successful CEOs like Bezos don't go long for the sake of going long. It's what a company gets from acting long-term that matters. Long-term companies can leapfrog competitors and position themselves for a bright future five, ten, or even fifteen years out. Amazon, for example, wants to penetrate the market in India with its 1.3 billion consumers. The company soon learned that it needed a way to overcome a tangle of local Indian regulations. With his trademark shrewdness, Bezos positioned Amazon as a good guy by playing to Prime Minister Narendra Modi's goal of boosting India's exports. Amazon now offers a significant suite of services to help Indian retailers reach U.S. consumers on their site. As of 2019, more than fifty thousand Indian businesses sell through Amazon into the American market. While it's too early to tell whether Amazon's foray into India will succeed—India's regulators are taking a tough stance on foreign e-commerce companies such as Amazon, Walmart, and Alibaba—it is hard to imagine any other company doing something that forward thinking as part of its international expansion plans.

Bezos's obsession with the long run even extends to his corporate board. Over the years he has picked directors who have expertise in markets where the company is seeking growth. For example, Amazon has been making a big push into Hollywood, investing billions each year in original programming. Thus, it was no coincidence that Bezos picked Judith McGrath to join the board in 2014. She had served as the CEO of MTV Networks Entertainment Group, which oversaw Comedy Central and Nickelodeon. Another example: a crucial part of AWS's business is providing cloud services to the U.S. government, including the Pentagon and the CIA. It doesn't hurt, therefore, that Jamie Gorelick sits on Amazon's board. She is a member in good standing of the military industrial complex, having served as deputy attorney general of the United States and general counsel of the Department of Defense.

The linkage between corporate priorities and board member backgrounds doesn't stop there. Amazon, a major consumer electronics manufacturer, builds Kindles, Fire TVs, and Alexa-driven Echos. So the expertise of Jonathan Rubinstein, a board member since 2010, has surely come in handy. He was CEO of the smartphone manufacturer Palm and before that oversaw the iPod division at Apple. Similarly, the acquisition of Whole Foods was a clear signal that Bezos is serious about cracking the $700 billion U.S. grocery business. It's no surprise, then, that the company in February of 2019 appointed two new board members with deep food experience. One was Indra Nooyi, the recently retired CEO of the food and beverage giant PepsiCo. The other was Rosalind Brewer, the COO of Starbucks. Starbucks not only has deep experience running brick-and-mortar stores but also has a large presence in multiple grocery chains. It's also worth noting that Brewer at one point in her career ran the warehouse chain Sam's Club, a division of Amazon's archrival Walmart.

Bezos doesn't apply his long-term perspective only to business matters. It informs, in a certain sense, his social consciousness. An examination of some of his moves outside of Amazon suggests that Bezos has an ambition to be seen as more than a businessman—as, rather, a cultural force, an idea merchant. Politically, Bezos has libertarian leanings, although a company spokesperson says he doesn't label himself a libertarian. He has given money to candidates from *both* the Democratic and Republican parties, in effect hedging his bets over the long run. In 2012, sensing which way the social winds would blow in years to come, he donated $2.5 million to a campaign to defend gay marriage in the state of Washington. In 2018, he donated $10 million to a nonpartisan super PAC that aims to elect military veterans to Congress. When he acquired the struggling *Washington Post* in 2013 for $250 million, he did it because he thought it was a pillar of democracy worth saving. As he told Charlie Rose in a 2016 interview: "I bought it because it's important. I would never buy a financially upside down salty snack food company. You know, that doesn't make any sense to me."

When his friend and former *Washington Post* owner Don Graham approached him about buying the struggling newspaper, he laid out all the *Post*'s positives as well as its problems, including a shrinking subscriber base and falling advertising revenues—a list of woes that would deter even the most stalwart buyers. Bezos, however, trusted Graham so much that he bought the paper without doing any financial due diligence. Years later, Bezos said that "every single thing he told me on both sides of that ledger turned out to be true."

Since the acquisition, the *Washington Post* has seen an increase in subscriptions, bolstered its news staff, and, most important, become profitable. The dramatic turnaround certainly has a lot to do with the renewed thirst for political news in the wake of Donald Trump becoming president. But journalists who work at the *Post* say Bezos has brought some of Amazon's tech magic to the paper, investing for the long term—whatever it takes in infrastructure and good journalists to ensure a strong future for the publication. To the relief of the *Post*'s staff, he has also stayed out of day-to-day editorial decisions.

Bezos takes the long view when it comes to Amazon, Wall Street, and even journalism, but the "looking toward the distant future" aspect of his thinking is also showcased with respect to his efforts to colonize outer space. In 2003, Amazon had survived the collapse of the dot-com bubble and its stock was on the rise again. With the company in the clear, the young entrepreneur thought it a good time to start a private rocket firm. He opened an office in Seattle and named the start-up Blue Origin.

For Bezos, it was more than a rich man's hobby. "In a kind of long time frame, the most important work I'm doing is to build Blue Origin and pushing forward to get humanity established in the solar system," he said in 2017. Yes, Bezos still spends four days out of five focusing on Amazon, but this Tony Stark of

Seattle won't feel that he's a true success unless Blue Origin succeeds. It can sound strange to some, but one of the reasons he built Amazon is so he'd have the wherewithal to fund his rocket company. He has pledged that each year he'll sell $1 billion of his Amazon stock to fund the project.

Why space? Bezos believes it is the only way to save the planet. As the earth's population grows, he argues that it will not be able to provide the resources for humans to survive. So he thinks we have to travel to other planets to get the minerals we need and to make the machinery we need to allow the population of the earth to grow. He calls his idea "the great inversion." In a nutshell, he wants to make earth a residential and light industrial zone and move all the mining and heavy industry to space. Humans could live not only on earth but also on giant space stations spread throughout the universe. "In space," says Bezos, "we have unlimited resources. We could have a trillion humans in the solar system and it still wouldn't be crowded. If you had a trillion people, you could have a thousand Einsteins and a thousand Mozarts and da Vincis, and how cool is that. We have to go to space to save earth and we have to do it in a hurry."

After a few mishaps and setbacks during Blue Origin's early history, including a rocket exploding into an orange ball in the skies over its operations center in Van Horn, Texas, Bezos's dream to make space flight affordable started to gain lift. By 2018, the company had secured a contract from the air force to carry payloads to space. The company has also said it will offer rides to the public, taking passengers high enough into space to see the curvature of the earth—for as much as $300,000 per passenger. (Bezos has said that he and his family will be on the first voyage.) In the spring of 2019, he held an event in a Washington, D.C., ballroom that resembled an iPhone launch. There,

Bezos unveiled the *Blue Moon*, a manned vehicle—affordable by NASA standards—that he said could land humans on the moon by the mid-2020s. It was another significant step in his building a road to space.

Bezos realizes that the grand vision of a trillion people traveling and working throughout the solar system and beyond is hundreds of years away, but given the way he thinks, that's just around the corner. The most conspicuous example of his long-term perspective may be his funding of the so-called 10,000-year clock, a device to keep time for the next ten millennia. Bezos has pledged $42 million to build it. The clock rests at an altitude of 1,500 feet on the shrubby side of a Bezos-owned limestone mountain—about a day's hike from Van Horn, Texas, and the Blue Origin facility. The entrance to the clock is hidden and protected by a jade door rimmed in stainless steel, and then a second steel door beyond it—to keep out dust and intruders. The entry brings you to the base of a five-hundred-foot-tall tunnel, about twelve feet in diameter, carved into the heart of the mountain.

As this book went to press, workers were still building the 10,000-year clock, much of it made of titanium, marine-grade stainless steel, and high-tech ceramics. Near the top of the five-hundred-foot-tall tunnel will rest the clock's face, a disk about eight feet in diameter that displays the natural cycles of astronomical time, the pace of the stars and the planets, the galactic time of the Earth's procession, and, well, the time of day. The clock will tick once a year, its century hand will advance once every one hundred years, and a cuckoo will come out on the millennium. A mechanical computer will calculate more than 3.5 million different melodies that the clock's chimes will play over the centuries.

The clock project, which the foundation says has no public completion date, is the brainchild of Bezos's friend Danny Hillis, a pioneer in parallel supercomputers and the creative force at Disney's Imagineering division—he once designed a full-sized dinosaur to saunter around Disney's theme parks. In 1996, he and Stewart Brand, a biologist, cultural pioneer, and the editor of the 1960s bible *Whole Earth Catalog*, launched a nonprofit to build the clock. The rock musician Brian Eno helped name the organization the Long Now Foundation, to indicate, as the foundation's website puts it, "the expanded sense of time the clock provokes—not the short now of next quarter, next week, or the next five minutes, but the 'long now' of centuries."

When the 10,000-year clock opens to the public, Bezos hopes it will encourage long-term thinking, that it will help put things in perspective and assist humans in solving big challenges. It was this kind of long perspective that helped him create one of the most potent engines in the history of capitalism: the AI flywheel.

CHAPTER 5

Cranking the AI Flywheel

Amazon's Seattle headquarters is a sprawling campus with forty-seven office buildings, including the Day 1 tower, where Bezos has his office. Between the Day 1 and the Day 2 towers sit the Spheres, two giant glass and steel igloo-shaped structures that Bezos built for his employees to hold a meeting in, relax, or concentrate. The steel-framed buildings, fashioned in a pattern of pentagonal hexecontahedrons, hold 2,634 panes of glass and resemble what a science fiction writer might imagine to be a biosphere on Mars. The Spheres, which are connected, act as a giant terrarium, containing some forty thousand different species of plants from more than thirty countries. The flora include a fifty-five-foot-tall, thirty-foot-wide, forty-thousand-pound *Ficus rubiginosa* tree, nicknamed Rubi, that was lowered by crane through the top of one of the spheres.

Inside, the atmosphere is hushed as employees, tucked away at tables and comfy chairs partially hidden by the flora and fauna, glance down at their laptops or talk quietly in small groups. A stroll through the suspended plank walkways that wend up to the top of the Spheres feels like traipsing through a rain forest as mist sprayers keep the atmosphere humid and the exotic plants happy. It's no coincidence that Bezos created a rain forest at his new headquarters. At the launch of his company in the mid-1990s, he first wanted to name it Relentless.com. Then he came up with Amazon.com, named for the mighty river coursing through the rain forests of Brazil. Even in those early days, he saw his start-up growing into a huge river of goods flowing to the far corners of the globe.

Signing in to the Day 1 building one late-August day—an unusually crystal-clear day for Seattle—I noticed a bowl of treats next to the receptionist and started to reach for one when I realized they weren't for human consumption—they were actually multicolored dog biscuits. Amazon has more than seven thousand dogs registered on its urban campus, although the number of pooches present on any given day is much smaller. Just outside the reception area there's an outdoor fenced-off area where about a half dozen dogs were joyfully chasing Frisbees and one another. Bezos's fondness for dogs started early in the company's history when he and his employees were working inhuman hours. According to *The Everything Store*, Bezos, to make life a little easier, told two of his employees, Eric and Susan Benson, that they could bring their Welsh corgi, Rufus, to the office every day. He became a combination of a mascot and talisman. Every time Amazon launched a new feature on its site, Rufus had to put his paw on the keyboard for good luck. Today a building on campus is named after him. All of Amazon's forty-seven buildings in downtown Seattle have quirky names. One is christened Fiona, after the prelaunch code name for the Kindle, and another Nessie, named not after the Loch Ness Monster but, rather, a system used to monitor spikes or trends on Amazon.com.

The design of Amazon's campus, while seemingly a haphazard collection of skyscrapers spread throughout the city center, is no accident. Bezos could've moved his headquarters to a single giant corporate campus in the suburbs, as other big tech companies like Microsoft, Google, and Apple have done, but he chose to stay in the buzz of downtown, an attractive place to work for its tens of thousands of young techies. As the company expanded, it would simply build or acquire new skyscrapers.

Bezos's real estate strategy, however, has a deeper purpose than creating a mecca for techies. One of Amazon's great strengths is that it's run like a federation of independent nations, each with its own leader and citizens. While conducting interviews at Amazon, I had to walk blocks each time I saw an executive. There's no central corporate suite for the heads of all the business units. These executives are spread throughout the city, running their own operations. Bezos, of course, is the leader of the federation and his word on important decisions is final, but his lieutenants have more latitude to make decisions and investments and pursue new innovations than is typical in today's corporations.

This setup partly reflects Bezos's strong belief that too much communication and coordination between and within business units slows things down. That idea is antithetical to what professors teach at the Harvard Business School. Communication and coordination are supposed to nurture teamwork and get employees to buy into a company's strategy. Bezos concluded the opposite: that bringing everyone up-to-date on a project lengthens its gestation. In 2002, he instituted his now legendary two-pizza teams for software development. Project teams would include no more than ten people, a group small enough that they could be fed by two pizzas. This kept bureaucracy down and time-wasting corporate communications to a minimum. "Our overall approach to teams has evolved slightly," says Amazon's Greg Hart, "but the basic organizing principle is pushing responsibility and autonomy down to the smallest possible atomic unit, which to as great a degree as possible has complete control over the success or failure of what they're working on."

From the outside, this structure seems like a recipe for disaster. Hundreds of pizza teams operating in separate buildings scattered throughout downtown Seattle. But it works. And for one reason only. Bezos had inculcated his business with the tenets of Bezonomics, which gives these independent groups a beacon in the fog, a set of principles that will guide their work whether they're creating a new reading device called the Kindle, a new video streaming service, a voice recognition assistant named Alexa, or slicker ways to buy on Amazon.com.

Simply put, the foundational principles of the Bezonomics philosophy are customer obsession, extreme innovation, and long-term management. Just about any CEO worth their stock options claims they follow some or most of these principles, so much so that they've become leadership clichés. Most, however, fail to execute them consistently and over long periods. So why is Amazon different? Bezos's secret is what he calls his flywheel, a conceptual engine that drives the three deeply seated values of Bezonomics and keeps the organization true to its principles. It is a way of thinking, a mental model that influences the behavior of Amazonians.

At heart, the flywheel is a metaphor for a virtuous cycle. Rather than focusing on the competition, Amazonians spend their every working moment trying to make their customers' lives better. One way is to lower costs for its shoppers. By lowering costs, Amazon increases the number of customers who visit Amazon.com. That attracts more independent sellers who want to reach the growing traffic on Amazon's platform, which leads to more revenue for Amazon. That leads to economies of scale, which help further lower prices for customers. The lower prices pull in more customers, who attract more sellers, and the flywheel keeps turning and turning and turning.

It is the concept of the flywheel, which every Amazon manager knows by heart, that allows this giant corporation to operate as a federation of independent nations. Employees don't have to wonder what their role is or what to do. Their job is to push the flywheel a little harder every day. It's a true north that gives them the freedom to act autonomously. So integral is the flywheel to Amazon's corporate culture that job candidates are expected to understand the concept and explain how their work there will contribute to spinning it. As a blog on the company's corporate website puts it: "Anyone who has worked at Amazon for more than a couple weeks has heard the term 'flywheel.' In fact, I suspect that many, if not most, people who interview here discuss the flywheel as part of their onsite interviews. So, getting your head around Amazon's concept of the 'virtuous cycle' prior to interviews here is a good idea."

The flywheel was born at an inauspicious time in Amazon's history. In 2001, the company was in a tailspin. The dot-com boom had gone bust, and previously high-flying and overvalued dot-com stocks, such as eToys.com and the delivery service Webvan.com, ended up in the cyber graveyard. From 2000 to 2005, the stocks on the NASDAQ exchange lost $5 trillion in market value. Amazon was no exception. Its stock was in a free fall. In December of 1999, Amazon's stock traded at nearly $107 a share. By September 2001, it was worth only $5.97. A devastating article published on the eve of the meltdown in the business magazine *Barron's* was titled "Amazon.bomb."

In the fall of 2001, in the wake of the 9/11 attacks on New York City's World Trade Center and on the Pentagon, the mood in the nation was somber. At Amazon, the terrible shock of the terrorist attacks was compounded by the fact that the company had lost its way. It was cutting costs and firing employees, and it was under intense scrutiny by a Wall Street analyst who argued that Amazon would run out of cash by the end of that year.

Around the same time, the management book *Good to Great* was published, a seminal work on leadership by Jim Collins. This deeply researched book explored why some companies lasted and thrived and why others failed. It would go on to sell more than 5 million copies worldwide. Amazon invited Collins to fly to Seattle to coach its executive team and to meet with Bezos and the board. While there, Collins talked to them about the need to build a new engine for growth he called the flywheel. "What I told them," recalls Collins, "is that you want to respond in times like this not by reacting to bad news but by building a flywheel."

At the meeting with the board, Collins says Bezos was "really sharp and a good listener." In retrospect, Collins believes that the Amazon CEO had always been an instinctive "flywheel-level thinker" but simply lacked the language for it. When Collins sketched out the concept, it was for Bezos a crystallization of an orientation and discipline he'd already displayed since his founding of the company. "Jeff was like a great student," says Collins, "who just gets stuff and then takes it to a far higher level than you ever imagined."

Collins explained to Bezos and the board that the success of every great company or organization or sports team is never due to a single event or a single idea. Greatness isn't about the person who gets there first, nor is it due to a big acquisition. Instead, success comes from pushing a big flywheel. "When you first start pushing, it takes a lot of effort to get that flywheel going one revolution," says Collins. "And you don't stop, and you keep pushing and you get that second turn and you start building momentum and then it starts to compound upon itself, and you get four turns and eight and sixteen and thirty-two and then thousands and tens of thousands and millions, and that flywheel has its own momentum built in to it. And you keep compounding that momentum." The flywheel for any great company, Collins argues, is not a line of business; it is an underlying architecture of momentum that can be renewed and extended into multiple businesses and activities. New technologies can become powerful flywheel accelerators helping to take the wheel from millions of turns to billions of turns.

Collins pointed out to the group that the flywheel is not just a list of priorities drawn in the shape of a circle. It is a way of thinking. The key to the flywheel is that there is no one big push that makes it go. That would be like asking what was the one investment that made Warren Buffett great. It wasn't a single act or decision but a series of good decisions made with a coherent concept—in Amazon's case it was being "genuinely customer centric"—that over time accumulate one after the other and give a company momentum.

Bezos jumped on the idea. He and his team made a sketch of what Amazon's flywheel should look like. As we've learned, Amazon is fiercely focused on driving down costs for its customers and improving service. So, the first spot on his flywheel sketch was lowering costs for customers. By lowering costs Amazon increases the number of customers who visit Amazon.com. That attracts more third-party sellers who want to reach the growing traffic on Amazon's platform—the second spot on the flywheel—which leads to more revenue for Amazon. That leads to economies of scale that help lower prices for customers—the third spot on the flywheel. This pulls in more customers, and Bezos was right back where he started on his sketch of the flywheel. The circle was complete. He realized that if he could get his employees to focus their attention on any of these components—traffic, sellers, selection, or customer experience—that would distribute

more energy to all of the spots on the flywheel. The whole system grows. Bezos understood these linkages beautifully.

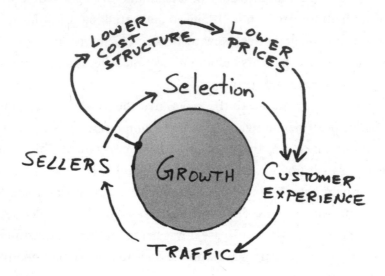

Flywheels are not static. This is where Bezos's second tenet
of Bezonomics—genuinely wanting to invent—fits in. To keep
Amazon's momentum going even faster, he understood that his
company had to continually renew each element of the flywheel
by innovating. This meant Amazonians had to think imagina-
tively, they had to ask constantly what they could do that would
be new and different within the flywheel construct to please customers and to attract more third-party sellers. "We are eager to
pioneer and invent," said Bezos. "This marries well with customer
obsession because customers are always dissatisfied even if they
don't know it, even when they think they're happy. They always
want a better way and they don't know what that will be. I warn
people that customer obsession is not just listening to customers,
it's also inventing on their behalf." Every new innovation—Prime
membership with two-day free shipping, free video and audio
streaming, the Kindle, Fire TV, the Echo, and Alexa was designed

to attract new customers and keep current ones happy, which would attract more third-party sellers, which would boost sales, causing the flywheel to turn faster with a sense of inevitability.

In the years following that fateful meeting with Collins, Bezos ramped up his innovation engine and the flywheel spun faster. He invested heavily in speeding up deliveries, deploying robots in his warehouses, and developing devices like the Kindle and Fire TV and Alexa and services such as AWS and Prime. The flywheel encouraged his workforce to focus every day on how to make the business better and better.

By 2018, Amazon was spending $28.8 billion a year on R&D, more than any other company in the world. That number, however, is somewhat deceiving because it includes not just R&D but what the company's annual report describes as costs for "maintaining its existing products and services, its server farms, stores, website displays"—costs most businesses would report as operating expenses, not R&D. What this means is that Bezos doesn't think about R&D as being separate from the business. R&D *is* the business. This accounting treatment was so odd that the SEC asked Amazon to break out its R&D costs according to accepted accounting standards. Bloomberg's Justin Fox unearthed a December 2017 letter in which Amazon's vice president and worldwide controller Shelley Reynolds argued that the company, because of its relentless focus on innovation and customer obsession, doesn't manage its business by separating activities "typically considered research and development from its other activities." In other words, Amazon innovates better than most other companies because its flywheel generates continuous improvement up and down the organization. Everyone is expected to innovate—not just a handful of scientists in white lab coats.

As for being "genuinely long-term oriented," Bezos knew that building and maintaining a flywheel is a long, hard slog. Many companies try to invent their own flywheel, get bored after a few years, and throw it out in favor of a new one—and then set out on a new strategy or pursue new tactics. This can cause confusion, wasted time, and losses. Bezos realized that building a flywheel takes years and years, not months, and he was willing to stick with it. And he was able to persuade Wall Street to keep supporting Amazon's stock as the company suffered losses or reported lackluster profits from 2001 to the mid-2010s, while it invested heavily in innovations that would please its customers. All of Amazon's major innovations—from the Kindle to AWS to the Echo—were many years in the making. Even when Amazon failed, as in the case of its late-to-market and mediocre Fire Phone, it kept innovating because Bezos felt deeply that no matter the outcome, the effort would pay off in the long run. Some of the learning from the failed Fire Phone, for instance, ended up in Amazon's successful smart speaker, the Echo.

Bezos even applies flywheel thinking to his personal life. At Amazon, the CEO teaches a leadership course for top employees. Given the long hours and highly competitive work environment at the company, he gets questions about work-life balance. He doesn't, however, think the question is framed in the right way. He prefers to think of it as "work-life harmony." He believes that the number of hours a person works a week isn't the real issue. What makes a difference is whether the work gives someone energy or saps it. "I know that if I am energized at work, happy at work, adding value, part of a team, whatever energizes you—that makes me better at home," argues Bezos. "Likewise, if I'm happy at home it makes me a better employee and a better boss. . . . Some people come into a meeting and they add energy to a meeting. Others come in and the whole meeting just deflates. You have to decide which kind of person you're going to be. It's a flywheel, it's a circle, it's not a balance. That's why the metaphor is so dangerous. It implies there's a strict trade-off. You can be out of work and have all the time for your family in the world but really be depressed about your work situation and your family [won't] want to be anywhere near you."

The flywheel has been fairly well known in business circles ever since Jim Collins wrote about it in *Good to Great*. It's what Bezos has done with the idea since then that is truly revolutionary. Over the last decade, Bezos has taken the concept of the flywheel to an entirely new level. He is applying big data, artificial intelligence, and machine learning to the flywheel at an unprecedented rate, to make it spin even faster—on its own. In his 2016 shareholder letter, Bezos explained the power of machine-learning models: "Machine learning drives our algorithms for demand forecasting, product search ranking, deals recommendations, merchandising placements, fraud detection, translations, and much more." Smart algorithms every day, every hour, every second learn how to please Amazon's customers by figuring out ways to lower prices or speed up a delivery or suggest the appropriate songs or movies or have Alexa answer a question correctly in a few milliseconds. Think of this new iteration as the AI flywheel.

The tens of thousands of engineers, data scientists, and programmers whom Bezos has hired have made the AI flywheel a learning machine, a cyber contraption with its own intelligence that takes all the data that Amazon collects on its 300 million customers and then analyzes it in minute detail. The machine makes decisions about what items to purchase, how much to charge for them, and where in the world to stock them. AI software can analyze mountains of data, including customers' previous purchases; items added to carts, but not yet purchased; products saved in the wish list; and even a shoppers' cursor

movements to predict what someone might order. In one hypothetical, say summer is arriving in Myrtle Beach and beachgoers
start searching for a new umbrella or a deal on sun lotion. The
machine will know to stock more of those items in its South
Carolina warehouses so that Amazon's customers won't have to
worry about them being out of stock and will get them, in some
cases, by the next day. And the flywheel keeps spinning.

At first, I found this concept hard to believe. How could
machines be so smart that they could make business decisions in
near real time for the hundreds of millions of products that Amazon sells around the globe? I knew that AI was getting smarter,
and the cost of crunching mind-numbing amounts of data was
falling, but there was a lot of hype surrounding the technology.
Have machines gotten this good? To find out, I talked to Jeff
Wilke, Amazon's CEO of Worldwide Consumer, while I was in
Seattle. Wilke, who started at Amazon in 1999 and helped build
the company into a logistical giant, oversees all e-commerce
globally, a portfolio that includes marketing, operations, physical retail, Amazon Prime, Whole Foods stores, and more.

On the surface Wilke is what you'd expect from a Seattle tech
executive: open-collar shirt, slacks, and a friendly demeanor.
Beneath that friendly exterior is a brilliant logistical mind. Wilke,
who was summa cum laude at Princeton and earned an MBA
and MS in chemical engineering from MIT, ran a pharmaceuti-
cal business for AlliedSignal before joining Amazon at the age of
thirty-two. At the time, Amazon was struggling to fulfill orders
for its growing number of products, and Bezos asked Wilke to
reengineer its warehouse system. The norm in the industry at
the time was for warehouses to ship out small numbers of huge
orders—such as crates with a hundred boxes of cornflakes—
but not to handle millions of small orders a day, which is what
Amazon needed. So instead of hiring only traditional warehouse

managers, Wilke hired operations researchers and data scientists to create a custom system that grew into Amazon's highly flexible warehouse system.

On a summer day, I met with Wilke in his corner office overlooking downtown Seattle. When I asked him whether Amazon's flywheel was now being driven by AI, his eyes lit up. "I've been thinking about this model for a long time," he said. "In the old days we used data to help make decisions, but humans still made the ultimate decisions. Part of what we're doing now with machine learning is taking some of the most repetitive intellectual processes and eliminating the requirement for human decision making."

Take, for example, how Amazon ensures that its customers almost always can find what they want and get it delivered when they want it, no matter where they live in the markets that the retailer serves around the world. Before machine learning came along, Wilke conducted weekly retail reviews with as many as sixty managers—similar to Walmart's famous Saturday-morning meetings. Those who were responsible for supply and those responsible for demand would sit around a table—some would call in from other regions—and negotiate what to buy, how much to buy, and which warehouses needed what amount. The company's computer systems provided lots of useful data about sales trends on which to make their decisions, but it was still human beings making those decisions. Amazon has now taken the most recurring conversations discussed around that table—such as what is the error rate in shipping, what are the shifts in consumer demand, what are the changes in the time to get a product from the factory to the warehouse—and designed machines to make decisions based on those factors. "We were able," says Wilke, "to close the loop so humans no longer have to decide. We place buy orders for millions of items automatically."

Under the old system, Wilke and his managers only had the bandwidth to focus on Amazon's top-selling items, but at the scale it operates today, those conversations wouldn't be possible. Now the original retail buying model that used to be stored in human brains is stored in deep learning algorithms—the thinking process is the same, but Amazon's managers don't have to repeat the same analyses over and over again. The other advantage is that the machines produce more consistent results. In the past, Amazon managers had their own spreadsheets and their unique models for making guesses about supply and demand. Now Amazon has consistent decision-making across all its online businesses everywhere in the world. Everyone is using the same model to get the same insight. This is what makes the AI-driven flywheel so powerful and what makes Amazon such an intimidating competitor.

Any business wading into the new world of AI must be aware of one important caveat: AI isn't easy. It isn't an overnight solution that can be accomplished simply by tacking the latest AI software onto a business model. Amazon spent more than two decades accumulating data on its customers and honing its AI programs to get to the point where the software *is* the business model. It comes as little surprise, then, that a 2019 survey by the research firm IDC found that only 25 percent of global corporations have an enterprise-wide AI strategy.

Even at Amazon, machines are still far from perfect. If there is an aberration, the deep learning algorithms still aren't smart enough to adjust on the fly. Say a hurricane hits New Orleans: the machines won't know to stock more food and water there because it's a random event. And the programs sometimes become outmoded. Wilke and his AI team are constantly evaluating the algorithms to make sure they're maximizing business. "We can decide to turn the machine off—which we get to do because humans built it—if we find it's not serving our purpose or if we have a better model," says Wilke.

His vision of the future is that of a partnership where machines and humans support each other and end up making better decisions. There are some things machines just aren't that good at detecting—yet. An experienced fashion buyer, for example, is better at figuring out what this season's fashion color palette might be or what might be hot at the couture shows in Paris, Milan, and New York. An Amazon buyer attending a fashion show who thinks maroon cashmere sweaters will be all the rage will recommend it, and the website will offer it for sale. The buyer then identifies a similar product in the company's catalog that came out the year before. Here's where AI comes into play: an algorithm measures how the new maroon sweaters sold compared to the older one and uses that difference in sales to train machine models to order more effectively in the future. "Human insights," says Wilke, "make these models better and better."

When it started out as an online bookseller in the mid-1990s, Amazon collected data on which books its customers were buying online and made book recommendations based on the reading habits of people who read similar works. If you liked *The Spy Who Came in from the Cold* by John le Carré, you might consider *Casino Royale* by Ian Fleming. Today that system runs on steroids: every time a customer buys or searches for a product, orders a movie, listens to a song, or reads a book, the action is noted, and the algorithm learns to be smarter the next time around by offering the customer more accurate products, including book, movie, and song recommendations. Today an estimated 35 percent of Amazon's online revenues come from its product recommendations.

The system is so good that it enables Amazon to offer same-day delivery for many products in certain markets and is moving toward delivery within hours. This constant data flow allows the system to track customer behavior, make predictions of future behavior, and then check whether the decision the software made was the correct one. If not, the machine will adjust the next time. This is how a machine learns. Because of such predictions, a customer can order a video-game player on Amazon and receive it eight minutes later. It's almost as if Amazon's software knows what customers will order before they order it. Eerie. Those who understand and can execute such systems will be the big wealth creators of the future.

Bezos has applied—at an unprecedented scale—big data and AI to push his flywheel, and by doing so, he has created a new turbocharged way of thinking that will change the way successful businesses are run in the twenty-first century. He is applying or will apply this turbocharged flywheel not just to retailing but to a long list of industries on Amazon's radar: media, health care, banking, shipping, and more. His model is going to change the world in a way that's more profound than most of us can imagine. Perhaps Alexa will allow us to do doctor visits from home or a robot will deliver packages to our door or we will pay for our online purchases directly from an interest-paying Amazon savings account. Bezonomics embraces customer obsession, extreme innovation, and long-term management, but the AI-driven flywheel is the engine that drives the execution of these principles.

A handful of other companies besides Amazon have built their own version of AI-driven flywheels—although they don't call it that. The list includes Facebook, Google, Netflix, China's Alibaba, and Tencent, with its messaging app, WeChat—and they've applied it mostly with great success. Google, for example, attracts more than a billion people to its search engine because its algorithms are the best at crawling the web to learn which sites have the most reputable people linking to them and therefore which sites are most likely to provide the best search results. The smarter the software gets, the more people it attracts; the more advertising it sells and the more resources it has to make its search engine smarter and thus attract more users. That's an AI flywheel. The exact working details of the flywheels of these big tech companies differ, but what is clear is that this is the business model of the future, and any company that ignores this new way of doing business does so at its peril.

Creating a business model that can compete with Amazon or Alibaba or Google will be an enormous challenge for companies around the globe because the AI-driven flywheel won't work unless it has access to tremendous amounts of data on customers and the brainpower to make sense of all that information. Companies will guard their data zealously and battles will emerge over who controls what information and the winners will be those with the best data scientists. This is why a computer science graduate in the U.S. fresh out of school can command an average starting salary of $110,000 a year.

Amazon has amassed mountains of data on what its 300 million shoppers buy, which gives it a huge advantage in e-commerce. Facebook's algorithms keep getting better at collecting and interpreting data on the habits and preferences of the 2.4 billion people on the company's social media site, which makes it a favorite place for advertisers. Alibaba and its affiliate Ant Financial know so much about their customers' financial habits that they have created one of China's largest money market funds. Tencent's WeChat, which started out as a mobile messaging app, now allows its billion monthly users to hail cabs, book flights, and pay for purchases. It is using the data to move into new industries like health care. All these companies have armies of world-class programmers and data scientists toiling around the world to monetize data.

As these tech platforms move aggressively into new industries, the incumbents will scramble to keep their own data out of the hands of the usurpers. As Amazon, Google, and others move more and more into the health-care field, players such as CVS Health, Kaiser Permanente, and Walgreens will do all they can to protect and monetize their customer information. Traditional companies like these that grew up as pharmacies or hospital providers will have to scramble to try to match the AI firepower of companies like Amazon, Alibaba, or Google. In countries such as the United Kingdom and France that have national health-care systems, Amazon could play a role in making the delivery of medicines and health-care products faster and more convenient and in helping patients answer medical questions. In 2019, Britain's National Health Service announced that Alexa would use information on its website to answer health queries for its patients. If Bezos's AI flywheel ends up providing lower costs and better service to patients, valuable health data will start flowing into Amazon's servers that will make its algorithms smarter, which will help lower costs and improve service. The fast-spinning AI flywheel would then become a serious threat to the incumbents.

The point for Amazon's competitors to keep in mind is that the dividing line between the digital and real economies will become increasingly blurred and will eventually disappear. As Tony Ma, the founder of China's Tencent, put it: "There will be no purely Internet-only companies because the Internet will have spread to cover all social infrastructure; nor will there be purely traditional industries because they will have grafted onto the Internet."

This new business model doesn't come without its societal and ethical challenges. Big data is becoming so big it boggles the imagination. In the two years from 2016 through 2017, more data was collected than in all of previous history. The research group IDC predicts that by 2025 the average person around the globe will interact with connected devices from smartphones to Wi-Fi thermostats to cars that respond to voice commands every eighteen seconds. This, of course, has raised serious privacy concerns. Another issue is the black box phenomenon. When machines make a decision, who will challenge the machine when it makes a mistake? Often those who have invented the software have no way of knowing how a machine decided what it did and why. This could have serious implications as AI infiltrates more of society's crucial decisions, such as diagnosing a patient, granting a mortgage, or deciding who gets into college.

Businesses embracing AI must set new standards of transparency or risk the ire of their customers—not to mention exposing themselves to financial liabilities. And if the rest of the business community fails to master the AI flywheel, the world might very well end up with a handful of global AI oligopolies controlling our purchases, our entertainment, and even our health and finances.

To understand better how Bezos's AI flywheel is spinning a web around our daily lives, we must explore the most vital elements of the flywheel: Amazon Prime.

CHAPTER 6

Earn Your Trident
Every Day

As an experiment, Kashmir Hill, an enterprising reporter at the tech website Gizmodo, spent a week seeing if she could live without Amazon. The challenge wasn't as simple as it sounds. She found that Amazon was so pervasive in her life that she often didn't even realize when she was using it. Giving up shopping was technically easy but emotionally painful. Hill, who has an Amazon Echo, an Echo Dot, two Kindles, two Amazon Prime Chase credit cards, Amazon Prime Video on her TV, and two Prime accounts (one for her and one for her husband), spends around $3,000 a year shopping on Amazon.com. She wrote: "I've become such a loyal shopper that I barely know where else to go online to buy things." When trying to replace a cell phone holder for her car, she ordered it on eBay, only to have the package arrive in a yellow smile envelope with "Fulfillment by Amazon" printed on it. The eBay seller relied on Amazon for its shipping.

As difficult as it was for her, pulling the plug on Amazon.com was easy compared with escaping the company's iron-fisted digital grip. She set up a private network and instructed it to avoid any site that had anything to do with AWS, Amazon's cloud computing system that acts as the backbone for a large swath of the Internet. She soon found that she could no longer access Netflix, HBO Go, Airbnb, and her Slack account at work, crucial for communicating with her colleagues. In all, her private network blocked more than 23 million IP addresses controlled by Amazon. She concluded that: "Ultimately . . . we found Amazon was too huge to conquer."

Amazon's ubiquity is no accident. Everything the company does is part of an effort to build a giant ecosystem that follows us everywhere, whether it's the home, the car, the office, or strolling down the street with our smartphones. The key organizing factor around this ecosystem is Amazon Prime, the company's membership program. Any business wishing to compete with Amazon or thrive within its jungle must understand the power of Prime and its role in Amazon's remarkable growth over the past decade or so.

Amazon, as we've seen, used its AI flywheel to help grow its e-commerce business into the largest in the United States. The AI programs that spin the flywheel faster don't, however, fully explain Amazon's explosive growth. Enter Prime. It is the most powerful force driving Amazon's AI flywheel. The membership program, conceived in 2005, is to this day still pushing the flywheel at increasingly faster speeds. In 2018, Amazon signed up more new Prime members than any year in the program's history, and on Prime Day 2018, where members get special deals on Amazon.com, the company signed up more Prime members than on any other single day in its history. While some of that growth came from entering new markets overseas, the majority of new Prime members came from the U.S. Considering how long and hard Amazon had been pushing its membership program in America, that market, by any normal analysis, should've been slowing, not growing at record rates.

Prime members are gold to Amazon. They spend more than other shoppers, listen to more of its music, watch more of its videos, and read more of its books, and give Amazon $119 a year for the privileges that come with being a member. They're relatively affluent and loyal, rarely dropping out of the program. The most common reason for closing an account is when a couple gets married or starts to live together and therefore no longer needs two accounts. Amazon has spent tens of billions of dollars on the computer systems needed to track Prime members and make sure they get what they want, when they want it, and at a price they can't refuse.

In retrospect, the creation of Prime looks like a no-brainer, but the decision to launch the program was fraught with controversy. In the late 1990s, to attract customers to Amazon.com, the company started to create advertising campaigns, including one in which a chorus of men dressed like the children's television star Mr. Rogers praised the selection of goods on Amazon.com, singing that they'd finished all their Christmas shopping "with 21 days to go." The advertising campaigns didn't generate the response Bezos hoped for. Then a pivotal moment occurred, leading to one of the most powerful innovations in the company's history.

For the 2000 and 2001 holiday seasons, Amazon decided to attract more shoppers by offering free shipping for orders of more than $99. The program was a success, and Bezos believed it generated strong word-of-mouth marketing. In early 2002, Bezos held a meeting in Seattle to discuss whether to make the holiday free-shipping offer available all year. The result was Super Saver Shipping, which offered customers the option of paying for overnight, two-day, or three-day shipping, or free shipping on orders over $99 for those willing to wait longer for their packages to arrive.

Then in 2004, Charlie Ward, an Amazon engineer, dropped a

suggestion into Amazon's Idea Tool Box to create a club for Amazon shoppers who needed items quickly and were willing to pay for it. Bezos loved the concept and set in motion a secret project referred to inside the company as Futurama. Ward suggested that the Free Super Saver Shipping service could be changed to work like an airline club with a monthly fee or annual fee. As he told *Vox*: "So I threw out this problem to the group: 'Wouldn't it be great if customers just gave us a chunk of change at the beginning of the year and we calculated zero for their shipping charges the rest of that year?'" Bezos was hooked and launched his Prime service in February of 2005 for a $79 annual fee.

To this day there's debate over the origin of the Prime name. According to Brad Stone's *The Everything Store*, Bing Gordon—at the time an Amazon board member and a venture capitalist at Kleiner Perkins—claimed credit for the name. Others at the company say that the name derived from the pallets that needed to be shipped first to meet the two-day or one-day delivery requirements because they were in a "prime" position in the warehouse, nearest to the loading gates. Whoever's idea it was, Bezos warmed to the name Prime.

Some at Amazon thought the decision crazy and that it could potentially bankrupt the company. At the time, Amazon charged $9.48 for expedited shipping, so any Prime member who ordered more than eight times a year would cause Amazon to lose money. Cem Sibay, the Amazon vice president who, before he took charge of Prime in 2016, was in business development and was instrumental in acquiring Audible, now the largest audio book service in the world, recalls: "When I first joined Amazon there was a lot of debate around this within the company. Were we going to lose those customers who were willing to pay for two-day shipping, were we going to lose our most profitable customers who were already getting free shipping by spending a minimum of $25 per order? Were we going to give shipping away to them for free?" Bezos decided it was worth the risk. He believed that if Amazon could structure the service in a way that made free shipping not an occasional indulgence but an everyday experience, it would change the shopping habits of its customers. He was dead right. In one move, Bezos had drawn a moat around his best customers and changed the psychology of shoppers. He got them addicted to "free" shipping.

Today, no other retailer anywhere around the globe has anything that comes close to matching Amazon's Prime program. Some, like Walmart.com, offer free shipping with minimum orders, while some others, like Costco and Sam's Club, offer the right to shop for warehouse-priced goods in their stores for an annual fee. Britain's ASOS offers free shipping for a yearly fee of $16. Responding to the power of Prime, Walmart in late 2019 started offering unlimited grocery delivery for a $98 annual fee in two hundred U.S. markets. In China, Alibaba has the invite-only Luxury Pavilion, which offers personalized home pages, product recommendations, VIP awards, exclusive sales, and invites to events. No one, however, offers the breadth of benefits of Prime—benefits that encourage customers to stay on Amazon.com and to spend more and more.

For their $119 fee, Prime members get award-winning movies and TV shows, a music streaming service with 2 million free songs—listeners can upgrade to tens of millions of free songs for $7.99 a month, a $2 discount from what non–Prime members pay—free book downloads on Kindle, and free storage space on Amazon's cloud for family photos. Members also get discounts on groceries at Amazon-owned Whole Foods stores.

After years of deep investment in technology, shipping logistics, and media properties, Prime has grown to the point where it is a stand-alone business within Amazon, with its own profit and loss statement. Prime generates profits (the company doesn't break out exact numbers) and keeps the company's online sales growing, but its importance to the bottom line is greater than that. Many of the perks Amazon offered to its Prime members over the years have turned—or are about to turn—into major businesses of their own. Prime stands as one of the few examples of corporate synergy that actually works. Prime Video, Prime Music, and Amazon Shipping, which soon may become a serious competitor to UPS and FedEx, all grew out of perks offered to Prime members. Amazon's streaming music service is one of the fastest growing in its field and an up-and-coming competitor to Spotify and Apple Music.

So, what's the secret sauce that makes Prime such a success? Amazon deliberately keeps the press and Wall Street in the dark about how Prime actually works and the strategy behind it. The Amazon executives who sat for interviews for this book said that, at its heart, Prime is a way to change consumer shopping patterns, to turn the occasional online shopper into a person locked into the Amazon ecosystem who interacts with the company on a frequent basis. The idea is to make Prime so attractive and so easy to use that customers can't imagine living without it. It's the online equivalent of nicotine—a metaphor that Amazon would never use. It is addictive.

Many members sign up for Prime when going through some major life event such as a wedding, the birth of a child, or buying a first house. These are times of great stress and having a Prime account helps simplify life, allowing a new mother or bride-to-be to feel more in control by ordering whatever they need from one website with fast, free shipping. The genius of this model is that after a while Prime members get addicted to the convenience of one-click buying and free shipping and basically stop browsing other e-commerce sites, which means they stop checking whether they might find an item cheaper elsewhere. Amazon has locked an army of price-insensitive shoppers into their ecosystem.

One thing Prime is not is what management consultants call a breakage model. Under this strategy, a business tries to get people to sign up for a deal and not use the full value of it. All-you-can-eat buffets are one breakage model; streaming music memberships another. Gym memberships are yet another. Every January, health clubs typically get a wave of folks signing up who've made a New Year's resolution to get in shape. Maybe a quarter of those are solid gym rats who show up three or four times a week, another quarter tend to be casual goers who work out once a week or so. The rest? After February rolls around, they don't show up at all. The no-shows are not ready to cancel because they can't admit to their laziness—not yet. The health club keeps the membership money and doesn't have to provide the service. Nice work if you can get it.

Prime is exactly the opposite, says Amazon's Sibay: "The thing that's different about Prime is that it is an all-you-can-eat model, but what's important for us is that our customers engage in all the offers as much as possible and as frequently as they want and need to. The vision we have for Prime is to bring the best of shopping and the best of entertainment and incredible value to our members. It's really about how we can engage more customers every day and how those positive engagements have customers coming back for more." The customer benefits, and it drives the Amazon flywheel as well. It's a true win-win model.

Constantly improving the benefits of Prime isn't easy, which is one reason working at Amazon is so highly demanding and at times stressful. Bezos will not tolerate stagnation, especially when it comes to his crown jewel, Prime. Bezos, in his 2017 shareholder letter, riffed on pleasing Amazon's divinely discontented customers: "Their expectations are never static—they go up. It's human nature. We didn't ascend from our hunter-gatherer days by being satisfied. People have a voracious appetite for a better way, and yesterday's 'wow' quickly becomes today's 'ordinary.'" Amazon's managers believe that complacency isn't an option. They know that if they disappoint even their most loyal customers only once, they have options to go elsewhere. "The Navy SEALs," says Sibay, "have a motto: you have to earn your Trident every day."

If customers are satisfied—always Bezos's main goal—they're more likely to buy more. That's exactly how it has played out. Prime members today on average spend an estimated $1,300 a year on Amazon, compared to $700 for non–Prime members. The company says it sees a big ramp-up in spending right after a customer signs up for Prime. Most people join for fast and free shipping, but once inside the Prime ecosystem they start discovering other benefits, such as downloading their first movie or song or access to video games on Twitch.

Becoming a Prime addict also works the other way around. Some customers buy an Amazon Fire TV for streaming movies and shows, and then realize that if they sign up for Prime they can get Amazon movie and TV originals for free, plus NFL football on Thursday night, as well as unlimited access to much of the company's video and music libraries and slews of discounted books, audio books, and magazines. And once they sign up, they're likely to become shoppers. Says Sibay: "If customers were primarily media purchasers in the past, they might say, hey, because I have Prime I can now buy toothpaste or toilet paper from Amazon and get that in two days. It really improves cross-category discovery by members, which again contributes to the flywheel." As Bezos once summed it up, "Every time we win a Golden Globe award, we sell more shoes."

Amazon tracks the habits of its Prime members at a level of detail that is stunning. Sibay explains that one of the most relevant metrics for him is what he calls the "frequency of touch points." This means Amazon's data analytics can measure how many times each one of its Prime members uses the service, whether it's for shopping, storing family photos on the cloud, gaming, or streaming media. The more relevant Prime becomes to Amazon's customers, the more they use it, chalking up an ever-rising number of Sibay's touch points, a metric that he watches like an osprey circling the bay waters for its next meal. If the touch-point numbers are falling (or not growing fast enough), it means Amazon isn't doing enough to make Prime irresistible to its members. That's a signal for the company's employees to put their shoulders to the flywheel to produce more great movies and TV series, speed up shipping, or give better discounts on, say, grocery purchases from Whole Foods.

While free delivery is the biggest reason most people sign up for Prime—Amazon won't give an exact percentage—free movies and TV shows are also attracting new members in significant numbers. As noted earlier, Amazon in 2019 will spend an estimated $7 billion to create programming for its Prime Video streaming service. That's a lot of money to keep its Prime members happy. Prime Video was launched in 2011 as a benefit for Prime members. It grew over the years and has morphed into a major Hollywood player. Amazon Studios, the company's Hollywood production arm that provides content to Prime Video, is run by Jennifer Salke, formerly the president of NBC Entertainment. In 2018, it reportedly paid $250 million for the rights to a prequel to J. R. R. Tolkien's *The Lord of the Rings*—a project that could approach half a billion dollars when production and marketing costs are added. The streaming service is also paying to attract top-notch talent such as Julia Roberts, who stars in its thriller TV series *Homecoming*, and *Westworld* creators Jonathan Nolan and Lisa Joy, who will produce *The Peripheral*, an apocalyptic sci-fi series based on the work of novelist William Gibson.

To an outsider, it seems that Amazon hires the best Hollywood creative talent, and like all studios, hopes it picks winners. But the company goes much further than that. All the movies and TV shows it produces are designed to help Prime keep the flywheel spinning. Behind the scenes, Amazon meticulously allocates its media production and marketing costs to its Prime members and calculates whether each movie or show is adding to or subtracting from Amazon's bottom line.

In 2018, Reuters obtained confidential Amazon financial documents showing how the company thinks about its Prime Video division. The documents revealed that Prime Video attracted 5 million new Prime members from late 2014 to early 2017, about one-quarter of the total number of people who joined the membership program during that period. The papers also revealed that the viewing audience for Prime Video was about 26 million customers, which is far less than Netflix's 130 million viewers, but an impressive number for a streaming service that simply started as a benefit for Prime members.

What became clear from these confidential documents was that Amazon believes that Prime Video is a formidable and profitable way to attract new Prime members. Here's how it works. The company assumes that if the first thing a Prime member does after signing up is watch a movie or TV show, then Prime Video was the reason the person joined Prime. The example in the documents that best illustrates this point is *The Man in the High Castle*, a fantasy drama set in a universe in which Nazi Germany and Imperial Japan have won World War II and split America into two competing and hostile colonies. The show attracted

8 million U.S. viewers as of early 2017. The crucial metric, however, was that the show worldwide attracted 1.15 million new Prime subscribers whose first interaction with the membership program was to watch *The Man in the High Castle*. Amazon spent $72 million to produce and market the series, which works out to a recruitment cost of $63 per subscriber. At the time, Prime subscribers were paying $99 a year for a Prime membership, which more than covered that cost. Perhaps most important, Prime members spend on average $1,300 a year at Amazon— almost twice as much a year as nonmembers. When viewed from that perspective, investing in *The Man in the High Castle* became a no-brainer.

Conversely, the documents revealed that a well-reviewed show called *Good Girls Revolt*, which was about gender equality, cost $81 million to make but only attracted 52,000 new Prime members who watched it first after signing up. The cost of that show worked out to more than $1,500 per new Prime member, and Amazon canceled it after the first season. Of course, it's impossible to gauge the long-term profitability of shows like *The Man in the High Castle*, because it's not known how long these new Prime members hung around or how much they ended up spending, but the contents of the Reuters-obtained documents do stand as testimony to the granularity at which Amazon measures important segments of its flywheel.

Greg Hart, who runs Prime Video, cautions that the situation is more complicated than the leaked documents suggest. He says that Amazon looks at a number of different metrics; there isn't a single one that results in a thumbs-up or thumbs-down on a piece of content. He argues that Amazon could have, for example, an original show that doesn't attract a lot of new Prime viewers but is appealing to existing members. Those shows in all likelihood wouldn't be killed. Says Hart: "Overall we just want to find shows that engage an audience and make them want to come back—and those can be new members or those can be existing members."

Amazon finds various ways to use AI to make Prime Video as sticky as possible. One of the most effective tools is to tailor suggestions for shows to each individual viewer. By tapping into a member's past viewing habits, the AI algorithm can constantly optimize the list of suggested shows viewers see on their Prime Video home screen. And it does this individually for each of its Prime viewers. If humans tried that task, it would take millions of man-hours and would be prohibitively expensive. Amazon started offering recommendations with books, added merchandise on Amazon.com, and now constantly calculates what each of its members might like to watch next. If someone likes British dramas, that person's Prime Video feed will evolve over time and might recommend a channel like Acorn or BritBox that has a lot of content from the UK and a lot of dramas. Or the recommendation might be PBS's *Masterpiece* because it has *Poldark*, the story of an eighteenth-century British soldier. "We want to introduce you to a show that you might not have been aware of," says Hart, "but that when you find out about it and start watching it, you love it. That saves time for you, it saves friction for you, and it makes the video viewing process better." It doesn't hurt that Fire TV owners can just ask Alexa to find a show or movie. And the flywheel spins a notch faster.

As Bezos has said, consumers are "divinely discontent." The worry is that today's digital lifestyles have raised that discontentment to an unprecedented level, and Amazon's Prime members are at the forefront of that phenomenon. At a tap of a button on a smartphone or by simply asking Alexa, consumers can instantly get prices, reviews, shipping information, and more, whether they're shopping, looking for a movie to watch, or ordering a prescription drug. Customers are more empowered than ever, and they want the best selection, prices, and service—now.

Yes, that kind of service and selection has endeared Amazon to hundreds of millions of shoppers. What, though, does a digital lifestyle portend for us socially and psychologically? As I've pointed out, only about one out of every ten U.S. shopping dollars is spent online, but that number will grow rapidly over the coming decades. What happens when stores become more of a rarity, and we do most of our shopping in our homes and offices?

For many, feelings of social isolation will increase. Already the home is filled with digital distractions to keep us from venturing out into the world. Why go to a movie theater when you can watch great films in HD on a sixty-five-inch screen with a killer surround sound system? Why go to a library when a reader can download a book on Kindle or buy a physical copy from Amazon? Most grocery shopping is still done in markets, but with Amazon and Walmart offering two-hour delivery or curbside pickup, how long before we stop visiting markets and meeting neighbors there, and instead get our tomatoes and salmon delivered to our doorstep? We're becoming a nation of agoraphobics, and the price we will pay is a diminished sense of community. We'll miss meeting friends at a coffee shop—why do that when a drone can deliver a hot cup of coffee to your home, as Google is doing in Australia? Also missing will be the joy of discovering a delicious goat cheese at a small farmer's market or a ripe mango at a big supermarket—items you might not have come across had you been at home asking Alexa to deliver your regular shopping list. The only remedy is for individuals to resist the temptation of doing everything online—no matter how convenient. It will be an uphill battle.

CHAPTER 7

Sexy Alexa

For centuries humans have been obsessed with talking machines. In AD 1000 the polymath Pope Sylvester II, who was said to have traveled to Al-Andalus and stolen a tome of secret knowledge, built a mechanical head of brass that—as myth has it—could answer yes-or-no questions. The brass head told him he would be pope, and when asked whether he would die after he'd sung a mass at Jerusalem, the brass head said yes. Sylvester II died by poisoning while performing mass in a church called Jerusalem.

It took nearly another millennium for talking heads to become more than a myth. The first breakthrough came when Bell Labs in the 1950s created "Audrey," a system that could recognize the numbers one through nine. Around that time a Stanford computer professor, John McCarthy, coined the term "artificial intelligence." He defined it as machines that can perform human tasks, such as understanding language, recognizing objects and sounds, learning, and problem solving.

By the 1980s, talking dolls, such as Worlds of Wonder's Julie, could respond to simple questions from a child, but it wasn't until the next decade that the first serious speech recognition software hit the market. A product called Dragon could process simple speech without the speaker having to pause awkwardly between each word. Despite this progress, over the next two decades, voice recognition as well as other types of AI programming largely disappointed its supporters, periodically entering into what the academic community dubbed AI winters—periods when progress and funding would dry up. The root cause wasn't that scientists didn't know how to write clever programs. It was that these AI programs required tremendous amounts of rare and expensive computing power.

The fortunes of this technology changed as Moore's law—which posits that computer processing power and speed doubles every two years—made crunching the mountains of data necessary for voice AI more affordable. By 2010, computing had gotten cheap enough for Apple to launch its Siri voice assistant mobile app for the iPhone. Smartphones with their miniature keyboards were an ideal device for voice recognition—it's easier to ask your phone to do something than to send your thumbs scrambling over a keyboard. Google soon followed with its Voice Search.

These voice apps could understand most words—even slang—and respond in a very conversational way. Up until this point, however, these pieces of software were only as good as the programmers who wrote them one painstaking line at a time. That's where AI has made a difference. Now these apps could get smarter because they resided not only on the smart device but were also connected through the Internet to massive computer data centers. Here complex mathematical models sift through huge amounts of data—more than could ever be stored on a laptop or cell phone—and become skilled at identifying different speech patterns. Over time, they become more adept at recognizing vocabulary, regional accents, colloquialisms, and the context of conversations by analyzing, for example, recordings of call center conversations with customers. The machines are *learning*.

These rapid developments in voice recognition weren't lost on Jeff Bezos. By the early 2010s, his Prime program had gained traction and was pulling large numbers of customers into the Amazon universe, but he was looking for the next big tool to keep his AI flywheel spinning ever faster. He saw voice as a huge opportunity.

Amazon, a company full of *Star Trek* aficionados—and led by a true Trekkie in Bezos—began dreaming about replicating the talking computer aboard the *Starship Enterprise*. "We imagined a future where you could interact with any service through voice," says Rohit Prasad, Amazon's head scientist for Alexa AI, who has published more than a hundred scientific articles on conversational AI and other topics. What if Amazon's customers could order books and other goods, and download movies and music, just by talking? No sitting at a computer and typing on keyboards, no more reaching into a pocket or searching the house to find a cell phone. In November 2014, Amazon launched its smart speaker, Echo, with its AI voice assistant, Alexa, a device that would help consumers communicate more easily with Amazon.

Alexa and the Echo were hits, and by 2019, more than 100 million Alexa-enabled devices had been sold. So popular was Amazon's device that during the holiday season of 2018, the company sold out of its supply of its $29 Echo Dot smart speakers through January even though it had rush-shipped them on 747s out of Hong Kong as fast as they could be made. Besides the Echo, Amazon now sells hundreds of products with Alexa built in, such as microwave ovens and security cameras. As well, Amazon has persuaded consumer electronics and appliance companies to embed Alexa inside such products as lightbulbs, thermostats, security, and sound systems. Alexa: "Play Nicki

Minaj on Spotify on the living room Sonos speaker." And she obliges.

Amazon's smart speakers use artificial intelligence to listen to human queries, scan millions of words in an Internet-connected database, and provide answers from the profound to the mundane. As of 2019, Amazon's Alexa devices responded to consumers in more than eighty countries, from Albania to Zambia, fielding an average of 500 million questions each day. Alexa will play music, update you on the traffic, and let you turn off your security system. It can add events to the family iCloud calendar. It can tell jokes, respond to trivia questions, and perform prosaic, even sophomoric, tricks. (Ask Alexa for a *blech*, if you must.)

Thanks to the ubiquitous Amazon Echo smart speaker and its Alexa voice recognition engine, Amazon has sparked nothing less than the biggest shift in personal computing and communications since Steve Jobs unveiled the iPhone. In the not so distant future, "smart" home devices like Amazon's Echo will be as important as personal computers or even smartphones. Voice commands, not keyboards or phone screens, will become the most common way we interact with the Internet. "We wanted to remove friction for our customers," says Amazon's Prasad, "and the most natural means was voice. It's not merely a search engine with a bunch of results that says 'Choose one.' It tells you the answer."

To get an idea of how important voice is to Amazon's AI flywheel, consider that the company has invested billions in the technology. Amazon won't release exact numbers, but Gene Munster of the investment firm Loup Ventures estimates that Amazon and the other tech giants are spending a combined 10 percent of their annual research-and-development budgets on voice recognition. If there's still any doubt how seriously Bezos takes Alexa, he has, as noted previously, some ten thousand employees working on Amazon's voice recognition genie and her magic lantern, the Echo. This army of Amazonians toil away at making the AI software behind Alexa faster, smarter, and more conversational, with the aim of having her answer as many questions as possible, accurately the first time asked. Alexa is designed to feel like an ever-present companion so that Prime members who use her will get sucked more deeply into the Amazon vortex.

As voice recognition improves—which it does as computing power gets faster, cheaper, more ubiquitous, and thus more mainstream—Amazon can more easily build a seamless network where voice links its smart home devices with other systems. In geek circles, this is called ambient computing. Everywhere a person is at whatever time of day, the Internet will be lurking. Alexa is built in to "soundbars" from Sonos, headphones from Jabra, and cars from BMW, Ford, and Toyota. Drivers can tell Alexa to turn on the home air-conditioning, deactivate the alarm, turn on the lights, and put in an order to Whole Foods, which they can pick up during their evening commute. In the fall of 2019, Amazon released a bevy of new products designed to make Alexa even more ubiquitous. These include the Echo Frames eyeglasses, the Echo Buds earphones, and the Echo Loop, a titanium ring. These devices all have embedded microphones and connect to a smartphone via Bluetooth, allowing someone walking down the street to find out movie theater times or the location of the nearest Amazon Go store. Says Nick Fox, a Google vice president who oversees product and design for the Google Assistant, a voice system that competes with Amazon's Alexa: "I don't have to open my phone and go to an app. I can just say to the device, 'Show me who's at my front door,' and it will pop right up. It's simplifying by unifying."

Yes, in one sense it is simplifying one's life, but in another way it's *complicating* it, when one spends hair-pulling hours trying to figure out how to set up and connect all these smart devices. And at first many will find talking to the Internet confusing and strange, and it even might make one feel a bit silly. My wife ends up raising her voice at Alexa when she doesn't understand her request the first time around, and then snaps: "I hate Alexa!" At times she seems a bit dense. (Alexa, not my wife.) For some reason she can tell me when low tide will be but sometimes gets confused when I ask her for high tide. Ask Alexa to play Leon Bridges and she will. But leave out the words "in the living room" and Alexa will play the music on the Echo in the kitchen, not on the better-quality Sonos speaker in the living room. Over time the AI in the system will help Alexa get smarter, and perhaps she'll anticipate that most of the time we want to play our music on the better Sonos speaker in the living room.

Or maybe younger generations will know exactly how to communicate with Alexa. Swami Sivasubramanian, who manages machine learning for AWS, said that his three-year-old daughter has grown up in a household where her only interaction with the web is through voice: "My daughter grew up in a world with Alexa. She has only known a world of Alexa. She walks into a room and uses Alexa to turn on the TV or turn on the lights." To her, talking to Alexa is as natural as a millennial double-thumbing a text to a BFF.

Artificial intelligence has long been a staple of dystopian popular culture, notably in films such as *The Terminator* and *The Matrix*, where wickedly clever machines rise up and pose a threat to humankind. Thankfully, we're not there yet. For all the progress made so far with the technology, voice recognition remains in its infancy. Its applications are rudimentary compared with where researchers expect them to go. "With AI voice recognition we've gone from the age of the biplane to the age of the jet plane," says Mari Ostendorf, a professor of electrical engineering at the University of Washington, and one of the world's top scientists on speech and language technology. She notes that computers have gotten good at answering straightforward questions but still are relatively hopeless when it comes to actual dialogue. "It's truly impressive what big tech has done in terms of how many words voice AI can now recognize and the number of commands it can understand. But we're not in the rocket era yet."

To recognize what we say, voice recognition systems rely as much on physics as on computer science. Speech creates vibrations in the air, which voice engines pick up as analog sound waves and then translate into a digital format. Computers can then analyze that digital data for meaning. Artificial intelligence turbocharges the process by first figuring out whether the sound is directed toward them by detecting a "wake word," such as "Alexa." Then machine-learning models, which have trained themselves by listening to what millions of other humans have said to them before, can make highly accurate guesses as to what was said. "A voice recognition system first recognizes the sound, and then it puts the words in context," explains Johan Schalkwyk, an engineering vice president for the Google Assistant. "If I say, 'What's the weather in . . . ,' the AI knows that the next word is a country or a city. We have a five-million-word English vocabulary in our database, and to recognize one word out of five million without context is a super-hard problem. If the AI knows you're asking about a city, then it's only a one-in-thirty-thousand task, which is much easier to get right."

Cheap computing power allows the systems multiple opportunities to learn. To ask Alexa to turn on the microwave—a real example—the voice engine first needs to understand the command. That means learning to decipher thick Southern accents

("MAH-cruhwave"), high-pitched kids' voices, non-native speakers, and so on, while at the same time filtering out background
noise like song lyrics playing on the radio.

The technology has taken off in part because it has gotten so
proficient at translating human commands into action. Google's
Schalkwyk says his company's voice engine now responds with
95 percent accuracy, up from only 80 percent in 2013—about
the same so-so level of accuracy human listeners achieve. This
level of accuracy is reached, however, only when the question
is simple, like, "What time is *Mission: Impossible* playing?" Ask
Alexa for an opinion or try to have an extended back-and-forth
conversation, and the machine is likely to give either a jokey pre-
programmed answer or to simply demur: "Hmm, I don't know
that one."

To consumers, voice-driven gadgets are helpful and sometimes entertaining "assistants." For Amazon and the other tech
giants that make them—and keep them connected to the computers in their data centers—they're tiny but extremely efficient data collectors. Nearly 70 percent of Amazon Echo and
Google Home users have at least one household accessory,
such as a thermostat, security system, or appliance connected
to them, according to Consumer Intelligence Research Partners. A voice-powered home accessory can record endless facts
about a user's daily life. And the more data Amazon, Google, and
Apple can accumulate, the better they can serve those consumers, whether through additional devices, subscription services, or
advertising on behalf of other merchants.

The commercial opportunities are straightforward. A consumer who connects an Echo to his smart thermostat might
be receptive to an offer to buy a smart lighting system. Creepy
though it may sound to privacy advocates, Amazon is sitting
on top of a new treasure trove of personal data, the better with

which to market more efficiently to consumers. Amazon says it only uses data from Alexa to make the software smarter and more useful to its customers. The better Alexa becomes, the company claims, the more customers will see the value of its products and services, including its Prime membership program—and the AI flywheel revs up another notch. Although Amazon is making a big push into digital advertising, a spokesperson says it doesn't currently use Alexa data to sell ads. Given that advertising is one of the fastest-growing and most lucrative new businesses at Amazon, it's hard to image Amazon not finding a way to monetize Alexa without annoying its Prime members. Some consumer products companies are already experimenting with paid content like recipes and cleaning tips as answers to Alexa searches.

Despite one of Amazon's early selling points, what people aren't asking their devices to do is help them shop. Amazon won't comment on how many Echo users shop with the device, but a recent survey of book buyers by the strategy consulting firm the Codex-Group suggests that it's still early days. It found that only 6 percent who had Alexa used it to buy things online. "People are creatures of habit," says Vincent Thielke, an analyst with the research firm Canalys, which focuses on tech. "When you're looking to buy a coffee cup, it's hard to describe what you want to a smart speaker."

Amazon does say it's not overly fixated on the Echo as a shopping aid, especially given how the device ties in with the other services it offers through its Prime subscription, such as music and videos. Still, it holds out hope that the Amazon-optimized computers it has placed in customers' homes will boost its retail business. Says Amazon's Prasad, the natural-language-processing scientist, "If you want to buy double-A batteries, you don't need to see them, and you don't need to remember which ones. If you've never bought batteries before, we will suggest ones for you." That suggestion, of course, often includes Amazon's house brands.

"Amazon is carpet-bombing America with these devices," says Peter Hildick-Smith, president of the Codex-Group. "Behavioral change is the hardest thing, and companies hate to try to do it. But at the point where shoppers realize they can list their groceries and other items on Alexa and get them delivered on the same day, it will become frighteningly disruptive to the industry. By the time competitors figure out that Amazon owns the shopping list, it will be too late. It's a classic Bezos long-term chess game. Something like shopping on Alexa that seems worth nothing today will be worth billions in five years."

A recent study suggests that Alexa and her ilk may indeed scale to Bezonian heights. The research firm OC&C Strategy Consultants predicts that voice shopping sales will reach $40 billion by 2022—up from only $2 billion in 2018. A critical evolution of the speakers helps explain the promise. Both Amazon and Google now offer smart home devices with screens, which make the gadgets feel more like a cross between small computers and television sets and thus better for online shopping. Amazon launched the $230 Echo Show with a ten-inch screen in 2017. Like other Echo devices, the Show has Alexa embedded, but it also enables users to see images. That means shoppers can see the products they are ordering as well as their shopping lists, TV shows, music lyrics, feeds from security cameras, and photos from that vacation in Montana, all without pushing any buttons or manipulating a computer mouse.

The rise of vision recognition technology—voice recognition's AI sibling, long used for matching faces of criminals in a crowd—will make shopping on these devices even more convenient. In late 2018, Amazon announced it was testing with Snapchat an app that enables shoppers to take a picture of a product or a bar code with Snapchat's camera, and then see an Amazon product page on the screen. It's not hard to imagine that the next step for shoppers will be to use the camera embedded in the Echo Show or in their smartphone to snap a picture of something they'd like to buy and then see on-screen the same or similar items along with prices, ratings, and eligibility for Prime shipping.

I put image recognition technology to the test one day while procrastinating in the writing of this book. I downloaded onto my iPhone an app for ASOS, the British fashion site, and snapped a picture of my brown Top Sider boat shoes. On the screen popped a half dozen options in similar colors and styles. All I had to do was click on the picture of the boat shoes I liked, and they were mine. The technology worked well, but I didn't really need another pair of boat shoes. Sorry, ASOS.

Google is fighting back, not willing to leave voice shopping to Amazon. The search giant doesn't sell products directly like Amazon, but its Google Shopping site connects retailers to the Google search engine. Already it is empowering the Google Home device as a shopping tool. It has a partnership with Starbucks, for example, that allows a caffeine-deprived commuter to tell the Google Assistant to order "my usual," and a grande cappuccino will be ready upon arrival. In China, Alibaba has its smart speaker called Tmall Genie, which is being used in cars. (BMW customers in China can use the system, for example, to place online orders, view cinema listings, listen to their favorite playlist, or check the weather at their destination.) Tmall Genie can also be used to order and pay for things in restaurants and stores.

Alibaba's shipping and warehouse division, Cainiao, delivers 25 billion packages a year, and getting them all to the right place at the right time is a monumental challenge. At the Neural Information Processing Systems conference in late 2018,

Alibaba's research institute unveiled a virtual customer service agent designed to make life easier for the company's 3 million couriers. Alibaba estimates that when fully employed the voice recognition software could cut the amount of time its couriers spend on the phone by 160,000 hours a year. The virtual agent handled interruptions from the customer—curveballs like "Who are you?"—and made humanlike inferences about the delivery. When the customer said he wouldn't be at home, the machine knew that it had to come up with another delivery solution. This is how the conversation went:

> Agent: Hello, I am Cainiao's voice assistant. I am—
> Customer: Hello.
> A: Yes, hi, you have a package scheduled for morning delivery to 588 Culture West Road. Is it convenient for you to receive?
> C: Who are you?
> A: I am Cainiao's voice assistant. I'd like to confirm your morning delivery to 588 Culture West Road. Does that work for you?
> C: I'm not home in the morning.
> A: Then do you have another address that you'd like to use?

The virtual agent had to infer from the statement "I'm not home in the morning" that the package needed to be delivered to another address—pretty smart for a machine. Yes, the AI voice agents will certainly make mistakes—just like humans do, but the advantage the machines have is that they keep getting smarter. Because Alibaba keeps feeding its smart voice assistant recordings of the millions of phone calls it receives from its customers, the algorithm can keep learning about accents, ways of asking questions, different delivery requests and how they worked out, or didn't.

All these impressive technological achievements aside, there's a significant ick factor associated with voice. Legitimate concerns linger as to how much the tech companies are eavesdropping on their customers—and how much power they're accumulating in the form of data derived from the spoken information they're collecting. That powerful organizations such as Amazon and Alibaba have control over so much personal data can be disquieting, especially to privacy advocates who worry that these corporations will be able to eavesdrop on our conversations at home, in the car, and in the office. There is some reason for concern. Smart speakers are supposed to click into listen mode only when they detect "wake words," such as "Alexa," or "Hey, Google." In May 2018, Amazon mistakenly sent a conversation about hardwood floors that a Portland executive was having with his wife to one of his employees. Amazon publicly apologized for the snafu, saying Alexa had "misinterpreted" the conversation.

In late 2018, an Amazon customer in Germany requested data about his personal activities—his right under new European privacy laws—and received a computer file with 1,700 Alexa audio recordings of someone he didn't know. The customer, worried that the anonymous person didn't realize his privacy had been violated and should be notified, shared the file with the German magazine *c't*. The *c't* editors listened to the files and were able to piece together a detailed picture of the customer, who owned an Echo and a Fire TV, and his personal habits. As the magazine reported: "We were able to navigate around a complete stranger's private life without his knowledge, and the immoral, almost voyeuristic nature of what we were doing got our hair standing on end. The alarms, Spotify commands, and public transport inquiries included in the data revealed a lot about the victims' personal habits, their jobs, and their taste in music. Using these files, it was fairly easy to identify the person involved and his female companion. Weather queries, first names, and even someone's last name enabled us to quickly zero in on his circle of friends. Public data from Facebook and Twitter rounded out the picture."

When the person was contacted by the magazine, he was shocked. Amazon apologized and said it was a one-off error by an employee.

Privacy isn't the only worry. The spoken word has the potential for errors far beyond that of typed commands, in some cases leading to financial repercussions. In 2017, a six-year-old Dallas girl was talking to Alexa about cookies and dollhouses, and a few days later four pounds of cookies and a $160 dollhouse were delivered to her family's door. Amazon simply said that the parents should've known that Alexa has parental controls that would've quashed the girl's order.

With more than 100 million of these devices already installed and in listening mode, it's only a matter of time before voice becomes the dominant way humans and machines communicate with each other. So Alexa and her competitors prompt certain questions, such as: Are we moving toward a world of short answers, and flea-sized attention spans—one where we've lost track of the written word? Even if Alexa *does* get smart enough to have long, complex conversations—and that is years if not decades off—it will certainly seem odd to be conducting some of our most stimulating interchanges with an algorithm. Linguist John McWhorter, in his book *The Power of Babel*, scarily conjectures that writing may be a temporary blip in human evolution. People, he argues, prefer talking and texting with emojis and shorthand to formal writing.

For many reasons, widespread adoption of voice is likely. For example, voice promises to have a democratizing impact on an industry that has separated novices from experts. Voice enables people who are less literate to use the system. It permits Parkinson's victims who can't type to use the Internet. It helps the blind to be online and command the computer to do things like turn on the home security system. It helps the elderly who are befuddled by technology and lets people interact with the web while driving. In other words, voice expands the number of people who can enter Amazon's world.

CHAPTER 8

Warehouses That Run in the Dark

Throughout much of the history of the Internet, big tech companies mostly dealt in the intangible world of cyberspace. Facebook's and Tencent's social media platforms are nothing more than massive streams of electrons traveling at the speed of light through the companies' myriad server farms. The same can be said of the Google and Baidu search engines. Given the nature of their business models, they don't—relatively speaking—provide work for a large number of people. Compared to Amazon's roughly 650,000 workers, Alphabet, Google's parent company, employs 98,000, while Facebook employs only 36,000—and many of those jobs are highly skilled, well-paid programming and data scientist jobs. For the most part, Alphabet, Facebook, Baidu, and other big tech firms hire the kind of workers whose jobs are not likely to be threatened by automation.

By contrast, Amazon operates not only in cyberspace but also in the realm of the tangible. The company is a leader in the adoption of the Internet of Things—which at its heart is the digitization of much of what we do in the real world. Devices such as cell phones, Amazon Echo smart speakers, Amazon microwaves, earbuds, and thermostats connect to the Internet, making them smarter and easier for us to control. (And as we saw in the previous chapter, easier for the companies that make them to collect data on our buying habits.) In the business arena, warehouse robots, scanners, and self-driving delivery vans also connect to the Internet, thanks to inexpensive sensors and smart algorithms. By 2022, there will be more than 29 billion connected devices worldwide, roughly four times the number of people in the world.

Now tech giants such as Alibaba, JD.com, Tencent, and even Google's parent, Alphabet—with its smart home devices and self-driving cars—are joining Amazon in its quest to infiltrate every corner of our lives with AI. This has dire implications for the global job market. As these companies automate their warehouses, use drones and self-driving trucks for delivery, many solid blue-collar jobs will disappear. Moreover, as Amazon and other global tech giants move into new industries, they'll accelerate the digitization of health care, banking, and other sectors of the economy and have an even bigger impact on jobs.

The tangible nature of Amazon's retail business puts it at the center of a coming, massive disruption of the workplace like society has never seen. Bezos has created one of the most aggressive and successful implementers of robotics, big data, and AI in history, and while the company has so far been creating hundreds of thousands of jobs, that trend will soon reverse itself as AI and robotics improve and more and more companies around the globe begin to adopt Bezonomics.

Think of Bezonomics as the beginning of a new paradigm for doing business. When Henry Ford proved in 1913 that the moving assembly line worked, a handful of other carmakers copied the process and eventually built the largest car industry in the world. Hundreds of small auto shops, filled with skilled craftsmen painstakingly assembling vehicles one at a time, held on for a while, but then closed their doors completely. In 1961, a California start-up named Fairchild Semiconductor started selling the first microchip, an invention that allowed the miniaturization of electronics and led to corporations using computers to expand globally at a level never before seen. That breakthrough eventually put armies of accountants, middle managers, and telephone operators out of work. Tim Berners-Lee, a computer scientist at CERN, a Swiss research organization, created in 1989 the HTTP Internet standards, which facilitated communication on the web between servers and clients. In the following years, more and more companies adopted the web as a business model. That gave us laptops, smartphones, search engines, online shopping, and social media. This revolution also helped put out of business a host of newspaper publishers, booksellers, and retailers.

Now comes artificial intelligence, and Jeff Bezos is showing us how disruptive a force it can be when melded with his flywheel business model. Bezonomics is leaking into everything as companies everywhere try to adapt to an AI world either by trying out Bezonomics in crude form or by discovering their own variations. But one thing is certain: all this progress will come at a heavy cost. Amazon and other tech-driven companies that follow its lead are poised to unleash an unprecedented amount of disruption on society and the economy. Unless you're an Amazon, Alphabet, or Alibaba shareholder, this isn't a good thing.

As Bezonomics spreads, the global wealth gap will widen as the economy becomes even more starkly winner-takes-all. The proliferation of robots with AI brains will dislocate hundreds of millions of workers around the globe, from warehouse stevedores to taxi and truck drivers to checkout clerks. And finally, as companies adopt Bezonomics, the ones that apply it first will have an almost insurmountable competitive advantage, as any retailer that has tried to match Amazon's online pricing, delivery, and service well understands.

Whether it's residents in the streets of Long Island City protesting Amazon's second headquarters or the president of the United States railing against Bezos on Twitter, Amazon gets blamed—in varying combinations—for widening the wealth gap, threatening future jobs, and putting Main Street shops out of business. The company has done some of what its accusers say, and it will surely disrupt society and the global economy even more in the future. Stopping it, however, will not accomplish much. Politicians could shut down Amazon tomorrow, and Bezonomics, fueled by AI, would continue to pose a threat to jobs, widen the wealth gap, and help the most agile businesses to easily crush the competition and amass power. Amazon is only the first company to show that AI can be successfully applied to the tangible world on a massive scale. Others will surely follow.

If a fear of massive job losses has made Bezos the focal point for the anxiety that today's workers feel about the future and for what his critics say is wrong with capitalism, it's not hard to understand why. The consulting firm McKinsey estimates that, under a worst-case scenario, automation will replace 800 million workers—some 30 percent of the global workforce—by 2030. McKinsey is also quick to point out that economic growth is likely to offset the numbers of jobs lost because of increased spending on health care, and growing investment in infrastructure, energy, and technology. It might be true that the economy will eventually replace those jobs, but in the interim a scenario where nearly a third of the world's workers will be forced to seek new jobs is chilling. It stretches the imagination to believe that the legions of warehouse workers, call center agents, grocery cashiers, retail clerks, and truck drivers who lose their jobs to automation will quickly and easily learn to become computer programmers, solar energy installers, or home care providers. The global economy may eventually generate enough new jobs to replace the 800 million lost, but the disruption in the meantime will be immense.

Until now, technology has been about making a worker's job easier. Think of a robotic arm lifting a heavy automobile hood for an assembly worker. Some economists are now beginning to think that technology has gotten so versatile and efficient that it will no longer be used simply to make jobs easier as it has always done, but that it has crossed a threshold and will largely replace labor in manufacturing, trucking, logistics, retail, and administration—sectors that are most vulnerable to disruption from automation. Daniel Susskind of Oxford University has proposed an economic model that is centered on a new kind of capital, which he calls "advanced capital." It is advanced in the sense that it is an investment designed to totally displace labor. His model leads to a scenario in which "wages decline to zero." His thinking is not yet mainstream, but it is chilling just to contemplate.

To better understand how Amazon's automation threatens the future of work, I visited one of its vast warehouses in Kent, Washington. Anyone who has ever spent time at one of Amazon's fulfillment centers—as the company calls them—will find that the work there is anything but fulfilling. The Kent facility on the outskirts of Seattle employs two thousand people and sprawls over 815,000 square feet. But that number is deceiving because the warehouse operates on four stories, meaning that it really covers 2 million square feet, an area that would spread out over 46 acres.

Inside the warehouse, as far as one can see, there are towering white walls topped by ceilings of black latticed girders holding long, bright white operating-room lights. The floors are connected by eighteen miles of conveyor belts constantly speeding Amazon's smiling boxes to the next destination. The massive space is interspersed with webs of safety-yellow metal railings and staircases. From these parapets one can watch swarms of Amazon warehouse workers, dressed in T-shirts, shorts, and running shoes, stowing and picking products from bins or packing them into boxes. The conveyor belts emit a loud constant roar like a jet engine, broken by the occasional warning beep of a forklift or the whoosh of a robotic arm.

Amazon's 175 global fulfillment centers are some of the most automated in the world. After the company bought Kiva robots for $775 million in 2012, it started filling its warehouses with robots, and now some 200,000 of these machines whir around Amazon's facilities doing many jobs that used to be done by humans. In one sense, this is a good thing. Robots now can perform a lot of the backbreaking lifting of packages and bins. Large robotic arms, for instance, can lift heavy pallets laden with products from one floor to the next. Amazon's warehouses that use these robots, according to one estimate, contain on average 50 percent more inventory per square foot than those centers without and have helped cut operating costs by some 20 percent.

AI controls how products flow through Amazon's warehouses, with data scientists running simulations to constantly update the software and optimize how many robots are needed on the floor, which yellow storage bin to grab, and where they need to go so the right worker can pick the right product for packaging. The system has to run like a complicated ballet performance. If the robots aren't moving fast enough, workers stand around twiddling their thumbs. If they move too fast, bins back up, creating congestion on the floor and slowing things down. The key is to optimize the movement. The AI algorithms do just that.

Even after installing all these robots, Amazon still employs 125,000 full-time workers in its fulfillment centers and at least

100,000 more part-timers during the holiday rush. Warehouse and shipping costs are some of the highest costs for Amazon.com, and the company, known for its relentless efficiency, works with its Day 1 mentality to cut expenditures and streamline operations. For the most part, over time, that will mean more robots and fewer people.

For those who move the mountains of merchandise through Amazon's warehouses, the work can be difficult, repetitive, and stressful. Full-time associates toil ten hours a day, four days a week, with a half-hour lunch break and two fifteen-minute breaks. Some workers have complained that they don't have adequate time to take bathroom breaks and that the pace of the work is relentless. To deliver an Amazon package within the promised two days or less requires a dizzying work pace where employees are under constant pressure to meet tough goals. One way to look at it is that Amazon—its industry-leading $15 minimum wage aside—is squeezing the lowest rungs of society to get one's package delivered cheaply and quickly. On top of that, Amazon's high standards drive the rest of the global warehousing and delivery industry faster and faster, putting more stress on workers everywhere.

Some of the most important work at an Amazon warehouse falls into two main tasks: stowing incoming products into bins and then picking the products from the bins to be boxed and shipped. In many of its warehouses the process is already highly automated. Amazon's computers tell the stowers which bins have space to store products. When, say, a carrot peeler arrives from the manufacturer, a stower scans it, and a screen at his workstation suggests which bins are best for placement.

When a customer then orders a carrot peeler, one of Amazon's footstool-sized orange robots knows which bin has it, speeds over to a six-foot-high yellow shelf full of bins, slides under the shelf, lifts it, and carries it to a picker. The screen at the picker's workstation tells the person which bin has the carrot peeler. The picker grabs it, scans it, and places it in a tote that then travels by conveyor belt to a packing station where a worker places the item in a shipping box. Robots then label the boxes and send them on their way to the shipping bay.

This all happens in a dizzying speed reminiscent of Lucille Ball in the episode of *I Love Lucy* where she tries to keep pace with a conveyor belt of chocolate bonbons speeding by, ultimately stuffing them in her pockets and in her hat. The pace of work varies, but some of Amazon's stowers and pickers handle a product every twenty-four seconds on average, which adds up to roughly 1,300 items a day. During my tour of the warehouse, I stopped at random to speak with Joe (not his real name). He wasn't someone PR had arranged for me to meet ahead of time; although I was accompanied by a media person who might've made Joe hesitant to offer any criticism about the company. In his thirties and wearing a blue T-shirt, Joe seemed happy enough, and when I asked him how he handled nine hours of repetitive work each day, he said that it was like playing a video game. In fact, he *was* playing a video game. Amazon had set up a pilot program among pickers around the country to see how they stacked up against each other, and he could track his progress on the screen at his workstation. Joe said he'd made it to the twenty-sixth fastest in the country out of the thousands that were playing.

"Does that impress your boss?" I asked.

"I don't care about my bosses. I care about bragging rights with my friends. I get texts saying, 'Hey, you're number twenty-six. That's great.'"

Joe, of course, is just one satisfied worker, and it's hard to gauge whether his experience is typical. One can get a clearer picture by scrolling through a job site called Indeed.com that, as of 2018, had published 28,000 workplace reviews posted by Amazon warehouse employees. (To post a résumé, job candidates must write a review of their current job, which explains how the site generates so many reviews.) Overall, Amazon warehouse workers give their employer a rating of 3.6 stars out of 5—the same rating that Walmart earns. In other words, workers see Amazon warehouses as an above-average place to work.

Most of the Amazon workers on the Indeed.com site describe a challenging work environment where the company pushes hard for productivity and targets. One stower who was working at an Amazon warehouse in Haslet, Texas, wrote:

> *I have to say that Amazon is a place of opportunity, it has awesome benefits, most managers are fair and have a good judgement towards every employee, the job culture is mostly motivating depending [on] the team you are in.*

That said, that same worker in Haslet described a job that was like being in the army—it's not for everyone and many people won't last long because of the pressure to work at a furiously fast rate:

> *I learned that in this job you need to be very persistent, mentally strong, and have consistency with what you do, I also learned from personal experience that it's not good to show your full potential and I say this because they will take advantage of you to make rate all the time and that will lead you to burn out. . . . The hardest part of the job is to try and stay focused and mentally aware of your job while having [the] management team on your back for being late from your "15 minute break" that is actually a 5 minute break because it takes 5 min to get*

to the break room and 5 to get back because it has to be a scan to scan process which is unfair in all levels. The lunches are 30 minutes and it will feel like you have your food stuck in your throat for a while because that is not enough time to digest the food before getting back to your physical, mentally demanding job.

A former Amazon worker in Jeffersonville, Indiana, writes of how he was constantly afraid of losing his job:

It's a job. That is the only good thing I can say. Middle management is kids out of college who just don't know what they are doing yet. The company lies to associates and is constantly changing the work specifics. It gets confusing. The evaluation process is horrid. There is a lot of machine and technical malfunctions that can affect individual performance. But if you can't prove it, you will be written up or fired. That's a heavy, stressful fact of life there. All of the jobs are physically abusing. 10–12 hours pounding on a concrete floor; up and down flights of stairs, high noise level because of surrounding machinery. It's always "Day One," which is exactly the problem. Doesn't matter if you have been loyal, worked hard and even achieved well in the past. What matters is what happened today. Having a bad day there will cost you your job. I can't think of any time I joyfully came to work. It was just a job. Not a place to stay long at all. It busts your spirit and wrecks your body.

Some paint an even more gruesome picture. James Bloodworth is a British writer, a former member of the Trotskyist group Alliance for Workers' Liberty, and onetime editor of the left-wing website *Left Foot Forward*. His book *Hired: Six Months Undercover in Low-Wage Britain* recounts his working for a three-week stretch in 2016 at an Amazon warehouse in Rugeley, England. He writes that the warehouse employed roughly 1,200 people, most Eastern European immigrants, who worked ten-and-a-half-hour shifts, earned $9 an hour, and had to walk as much as fifteen miles a day to get their jobs done.

He describes a workplace where "decency, respect and dignity were absent," one that resembles a low-security prison where workers don't have enough time for lunch, get penalized for taking sick days, and get punished for missing their productivity goals. He describes how one day, while working as a picker, he came across a Coca-Cola bottle of urine on a shelf, purportedly put there by a worker too scared to take a bathroom break.

Amazon, not surprisingly, strongly disagrees with Bloodworth's account. Ashley Robinson, an Amazon spokesperson, told me that she would state on the record that no one has ever urinated into a bottle in an Amazon warehouse. (Although it is hard to prove a negative.) She adds that workers get adequate time for breaks and if they need extra time for a good reason, they can request extra time.

Amazon says that there are two reasons it gets bad publicity about its warehouses. First, for years it believed that if it took care of its customers everything else would follow, so there was no need to defend itself. As the attacks mounted on its working conditions, however, the company changed tack and finally started to challenge these negative portrayals in the press. Second, Amazon is a non-union shop, and it charges that some labor activists who have vocally criticized the company see its 125,000 full-time warehouse jobs as a ripe target.

Carletta Ooton, who, after a long stint at Coca-Cola, became Amazon's vice president of health, safety, and sustainability, says, "I think we are very misunderstood. I think we are doing a ton of stuff right. I've worked for companies that get it right. I wouldn't be here if I didn't think we're doing the right thing." Ooton says that Amazon's warehouse safety record is on par with other companies and that it has recently installed new safety measures, made changes to the designs of the workstations, and installed new technology to improve safety. Fulfillment center workers in certain areas now wear radio-frequency vests that signal the robots racing around the warehouse floor to avoid them. It installed light curtains around robotic arms. If anyone breaks the plane with their hand, the robot stops. If an employee's badge isn't programmed to show that the worker has received the proper training to drive a forklift, the machine won't start.

Clearly, Amazon could be better at training its managers to deal with workplace issues, and it could be more forgiving at setting stretch targets or at least provide workers with more guidance on how to achieve those targets. What's inarguable is that warehouse jobs in general are intrinsically hard on the body and the soul. Another Amazon spokesperson (warehouse media) told me that the company realizes that working in a fulfillment center is tough, but hopes that people will use these jobs as a stepping-stone to a better life. For example, after an employee is there for a year, Amazon will pay for 95 percent of their training. The only catch is that it has to be for a job that is currently in demand. Tarot card readers need not apply. If you want to train to maintain or program the robots in the warehouse, Amazon will pay for that. Even if you want to leave Amazon and become a nurse or a truck driver at another business, Amazon will pay for those courses. Some 16,000 Amazon employees have taken advantage of the program since its inception in 2012. The idea is that these warehouse jobs, which pay a competitive wage plus benefits, should act as a stepping-stone for people who want to earn some money while pursuing a new career.

Perks aside, most people would concede that these jobs are, for the most part, hard, stressful, and at times dehumanizing, and that it's arguably cheaper and more humane to automate them. It's also good business. Everything Amazon does stems from the benefit to the customer. "One thing I've learned about Amazon is that we're constantly increasing what we sell and how fast we need to get it to people. That means we'll see more and more automation," says Brad Porter, a vice president and distinguished engineer who heads up the company's robotics program.

Porter, an MIT-trained engineer who joined the company in 2007, was in charge of making the software on Amazon.com run smoothly and contributed to the company's delivery drone project and then robotics. He explained to me one day that one key reason robots aren't more pervasive in Amazon's warehouses is because of what he calls the "deep bin picking problem." Machines are ham-fisted oafs when it comes to picking out one odd-shaped object from a jumble of items in a bin. Humans are particularly good at this. Over millions of years of evolution, we've developed remarkable hand-eye coordination. Those ancestors of ours who could climb down from the safety of a tree and pick berries the fastest before the arrival of a predator were more likely to survive. For proof of how hardwired "deep bin picking" is in the human species, just watch a four-year-old reach into a Halloween bag and in a nanosecond pick out the mini Snickers bar among the forty other candies she's collected.

"Finding a single item in a deep bin is quite challenging for robotic manipulation today," says Porter. "You can build a system that's good at picking out fixed items like a cell phone box from a bin, but given the amount and variety of new items coming into Amazon, the algorithms aren't there yet." Because of the daunting need for near–100 percent accuracy, Porter won't say how long it will be before Amazon solves its "deep bin picking problem." Says the engineer, "If you're in a demo lab setting and something doesn't work, it's not a big deal. But if you're in a warehouse setting where 15 percent of the time something is failing, that's just an operational nightmare."

Amazon isn't the only one working on technologically advanced warehouses. Some of the most advanced can be found in Europe and in China. Ocado, a British online-only supermarket, which calls itself an "AI First Organization," offers a glimpse of the future. It opened its Andover, England, facility, which is the size of several football fields, in 2018. Inside the space are metal rails in the shape of a grid that look like a giant chessboard. More than a thousand battery-operated robots, which resemble white washing machines on wheels, travel back and forth on the grid at speeds as fast as nine miles per hour. A 4G network acts as an air traffic controller, sending signals to the robots to keep them from crashing into each other. Under each square of the grid sit bins of grocery items stacked seventeen high. In what seems like rush hour at O'Hare, these units fly around the grid picking up the desired crate with a set of claws that pull it up into its belly. The units then drop the crate off at a dock where humans grab the item and place it into a shopping bag for delivery. In a traditional warehouse with items spread over wide expanses, assembling the right products for an order could take an hour or more. The robots can do it in a matter of minutes. Ocado's system can fill 65,000 grocery orders every week. In February 2019, a fire that started from an electrical fault at a robot recharging station destroyed the warehouse. Ocado is rebuilding.

Ocado isn't just an online grocery. It hopes to sell its robotic system to big retailers around the world. So far it has sealed deals to build warehouses for international retailers, including one signed in 2018 with the U.S. supermarket chain Kroger for twenty automated "customer fulfillment centers." On the day the deal became public, Ocado's shares jumped 45 percent.

Chinese online retailer JD.com, which has designed a warehouse specifically to work smoothly with machines, offers another glimpse of what the future may look like. One of China's largest online retailers with 310 million customers, JD.com opened a warehouse in 2017 that uses robots to pick up packages of a predictable shape and size—like a cell phone or a box of laundry soap. It's the world's most automated facility of its kind. From the outside, the large white building on the outskirts of Shanghai looks like any warehouse in China. What catches the eye— besides the giant red logo of JD.com with its smiling dog—is what's *not* there: a large parking lot for employees. That's because this vast warehouse, which ships approximately 200,000 packages each day, has only *four* employees.

When someone orders, say, a Galaxy cell phone, a light gray plastic bin with the item automatically slides off a shelf and onto a conveyor belt that brings it to a packing area where a six-foot-long, milky-white robotic arm with small green suction cups picks it up. As an unfolded cardboard box slides by, the large white arm drops the phone onto the cardboard. The cardboard is then folded around the item and sealed, and a shipping label is attached.

Next, another arm picks up the box and places it on a robot that looks like a small, red footstool. Scores of these mobile robots then zip over to an open area of the warehouse, speeding around each other like cars maneuvering on the Place de la Concorde at rush hour to find the right opening in the floor to drop their cargo. The package slides down a shoot to a shipping bin that moves automatically to the correct loading bay. No humans to pick and sort packages, no lunch breaks, no sick days, no vacation time, no urinating in bottles. Theoretically, except for those times when JD.com's four workers are doing maintenance on the robots, the warehouse could be run in the dark. Robots don't need to see.

The JD.com warehouse works because it handles only standard-sized packages. Amazon doesn't have that luxury. "Send me something in a poly bag or a plastic clamshell and it gets harder quickly for a robot to recognize it," says Amazon's Porter. Imagine a robot trying to tell the difference between a carrot peeler, an oyster knife, and a pack of ballpoint pens, all in packages of slightly different shapes, colors, and materials. It is a devilishly tricky task.

To crack that problem, the company in 2015 launched the Amazon Robotics Challenge, which offers annual prizes for anyone who can design the best picking robot. It was looking for a robot that can identify items, take them from totes and stow them in storage bins, and then remove them from the bins and place them in boxes. The competing teams won points for the correct placement of items and for speed, and lost points for mistakes like dropping or crushing an item.

In the summer of 2017, sixteen robotic teams from ten countries gathered in Nagoya, Japan, to compete for the prize. The winner was Cartman, a robot from Australia built by a team of engineers from Queensland University of Technology, the University of Adelaide, and the Australian National University. Cartman was made of off-the-shelf parts and cost only $24,000 to build. It moved on a Cartesian grid—back and forth and up and down across three axes at ninety-degree angles. Imagine a three-dimensional chessboard. Cameras identified the object in the bin and then its long arm used a rotating gripper with a suction cup at its end and a two-fingered claw to grab the item. Although it wasn't perfect, Cartman was the best that day, and walked away with an $80,000 prize.

Picking robots, however, might emerge on the scene even sooner than many think. In 2014, a team with members from Harvard, MIT, and Yale that had won a DARPA robot challenge formed a company named RightHand Robotics and opened an office in Somerville, Massachusetts. One of its founders, Leif Jentoft, says that the company has figured out how to make robots distinguish and pick out items from a jumble of different-sized, -shaped, and -colored packages. "We looked at how the human hand works," says Jentoft. "We put mechanical intelligence into the robot using 3-D camera data and sensors to identify the right object and then just like [people] do, the robot bends its hand to the shape of the object. If it tries to pick up an object and fails, the robot learns and tries to pick it up in another way."

Jentoft says his robot picker is accurate enough for commercial use. Paltac, the largest Japanese convenience store wholesaler for consumer packaged goods like soaps and toothbrushes, used one of RightHand Robotics' machines during the 2018 holiday season to process tens of thousands of packages. "The technology is already there," claims Jentoft. "It's still in the opening innings but moving forward with more speed than we expected."

Warehouse jobs aren't the only part of the workforce being disrupted by Amazon's automation. With its acquisition of the Whole Foods grocery chain and the opening of a handful of smaller stores, the company is moving into traditional retailing, which just about any industry expert says is long overdue for an overhaul. In its relentless drive for efficiencies and cost savings, Amazon has the job of checkout cashier fully in its sights. After all, who likes waiting in line, unloading items onto a counter, standing by while the checkout person scans and bags the items, then pulling out a credit card to pay before leaving the store?

To remedy that inconvenience, Bezos in 2018 opened the first Amazon Go store in its Day 1 Seattle headquarters building. From the sidewalk, the store looks like any upscale urban market café, with its tall plate-glass windows revealing inviting shelves of premade quinoa and kale salads, Mediterranean chicken wraps, Middle Eastern veggie flat bread sandwiches, lavender-flavored sparkling water, and Fran's chocolate bars.

When I visited on a late-summer day, the store, which by then had received huge press attention, was buzzing with customers. The remarkable thing is that checkout isn't required. Once customers download the Amazon Go app, they need only take their phone and swipe at a turnstile to enter the store. After shoppers pick out what they want, and pop it in a bag, they simply walk out of the store and the amount will be charged to their Amazon account. The app tells the store's system who is entering. Cameras in the ceiling track customers as they move around the floor. For privacy reasons, the system is designed not to make out any personal features; to the cameras, customers look like black blobs.

When a customer picks a sandwich off the shelf, two things happen: the ceiling cameras track the blob grabbing the item, and, to help ensure accuracy, a scale under each shelf measures the change in weight of its items and informs the system whether, say, one and not two sandwiches have been taken. When the customers walk back out through the turnstiles, their Amazon account gets charged. Humans still work in the store preparing food and wandering the floor answering questions. Amazon offers beer and wine, and by state law a person has to check for IDs (a task that wouldn't be hard to automate), but there are no cash registers and no cashiers. On the day I visited the store, I picked a chocolate chip cookie off the shelf and walked out the door—it felt like shoplifting until I noticed later on my cell phone that $4 had been charged to my Amazon account.

Customers seem to enjoy the store. Late in 2018, on the consumer rating site Yelp, 173 customers gave it 4.5 out of 5 stars—with the most common complaint being that the Amazon Go location had turned into a crowded tourist attraction. Hurdles, however, lie ahead. The technology is expensive and some local governments have pushed back, arguing that cashless shops discriminate against the poor who don't have bank (or Amazon) accounts. Nonetheless, Amazon seems to love the stores—it has opened new ones in Chicago, New York, and San Francisco. The technology is more than just another Amazon effort to please its customers. It could allow the company to better understand foot traffic patterns in the store and to get data quickly on which items sell the most at which price. It could also build a profile of each shopper's preferences and habits.

For the tens of millions of cashiers in stores around the world, this isn't good news. In America, there are 3.6 million cashiers, one of the largest categories of jobs in the country. As Amazon spreads its Go technology to other locations, including possibly hundreds of Whole Foods, these workers' jobs are threatened. Other big retailers like Walmart and Kroger pose an additional threat. In 2019, Walmart opened a cashier-less Sam's Club store in Texas.

While the outlook for warehouse workers, truck drivers, and checkout clerks is dire, economies historically create new opportunities for displaced workers. When America shifted from an agriculture society to an industrial one in the late nineteenth and early twentieth centuries, millions of farm jobs disappeared, but the sons and daughters of displaced farmers migrated to towns and cities and eventually found new kinds of work in textile, shoe, and automobile factories and as clerks in stores. Such worries lived on through the modern industrial age. The "Triple Revolution Report," which was written by a group of brilliant people, including two Nobel Laureates, argued that the U.S. was on the brink of economic and social upheaval because industrial automation would destroy millions of jobs. That report was delivered to President Lyndon Johnson in March of 1964. No one showed up for that revolution.

In the years ahead, as automation displaces hundreds of millions of jobs, some humans will work alongside robots as "cobots"—a term to describe how humans working with robots will be more efficient than humans or robots alone. A warehouse worker who previously lifted and stacked objects could become a robot operator, monitoring the flow of work, maintaining and operating drones, and fixing things when the machines make a mistake. And new creative vocations will arise. "There are a ton of things humans can do better than machines," says MIT professor Erik Brynjolfsson. "The new jobs will be more on the creative side. Humans can do more connecting with people, and more thinking. I don't think there is any shortage of work in our economy that can only be done by humans, and I think that will hold true for decades. There will be massive disruption, but there's no shortage of work for humans."

Yes, there will be new jobs, but what is different this time is the scale and pace of the disruption. It won't be a Verhoevenian dystopia where robots take all the jobs, and hordes of the unemployed wander the land scavenging for food and seeking shelter. But this time around the disruption will be at such a scale that it will take affected economies decades to handle the masses of displaced workers—either by creating types of jobs we can't imagine or by having the government pay people a living wage.

Consider that, globally, some 3 million industrial robots will be in use in factories by 2020, more than double the number from just seven years earlier. That doesn't bode well for factory and warehouse workers. Pundits have long worried that self-driving vehicles will steal jobs from America's 3.5 million truck drivers and countless more millions of taxi drivers. Amazon's partnership with Toyota to develop a self-driving delivery van will only hasten the transformation. In the hotel industry, Amazon in 2018 started supplying Marriott with its Alexa-powered Echo smart speakers so guests can order a hamburger from room service, request fresh towels from housekeeping, or get a dinner recommendation—all without the help of a human. And how long before those towels get delivered to the room on a robotic cart?

AI, however, could do even far more damage. It is getting smart enough to replace jobs that one might think would be invulnerable to technology. For example, AI programs can now do some of the work usually reserved for first-year lawyers, bankers, writers of press releases, and, even in some cases, doctors. Stanford University researchers developed an algorithm that can diagnose chest X-rays for pneumonia better than radiologists. Deutsche Bank CEO John Cryan predicted in 2017 that eventually half of his firm's 97,000 employees could lose their jobs to machines. In 2017, Tencent's Dreamwriter, a news-writing robot, generated two thousand finance or sports-related news articles each day.

Even artists and musicians have a target on their backs. AIVA Technologies, a Luxembourg start-up, has created AI software that composes jazz, pop, and classical music that is being used in soundtracks for films, video games, and advertisements. By reading through, say, a large database of classical pieces written by Bach, Beethoven, Mozart, and other greats, the software captures concepts of music theory and then composes on sheet music. Does it work? The company says that when it asked a number of professional musicians to listen to AIVA's pieces, none guessed the music was composed by a computer. So, what's an out-of-work composer to do? Train to be a radiologist only to find that that skill, too, has been usurped by a computer?

So far, the Amazon Go store, automated warehouses, and

self-driving delivery vans are just early warning signs of a wave of new technologies that will make hundreds of millions of jobs obsolete around the world. For most people, the pink-slip-bearing robots haven't arrived yet. But all signs point to the fact that they're coming, except for those who exist in certain insulated professions—often ones that are high-touch or have an emotional component.

Some of the dispossessed will find new jobs, others will survive on a universal basic income provided by their government, and others still will turn to the gig economy, trying to eke out a living any way they can. One way to do this, of course, is to start a business that sells stuff on Amazon.

That, however, would mean having to compete directly with Amazon's relentless AI flywheel.

CHAPTER 9

Dancing with the Devil

John Morgan looks back wistfully on his days running a kite-surfing shop on the coast of Spain. His biggest worries during his twelve sun-filled years as a small retailer were making sure he had the right selection of North Face and Patagonia gear in stock and that the waves were big enough to attract surfers to his beachfront store. One day, a friend sent Morgan (who asked not to use his real name for fear of getting on Amazon's wrong side) information about a course on how to sell on Amazon. It all seemed so easy. Just pick a Top 100 selling product on Amazon, do some small design tweaks, find a manufacturer in China to make it cheaply, and then sell it under your own brand name on Amazon.com. After that, spend a little time experimenting with online search terms to drive customers to your product page and watch the money roll in. Morgan was hooked.

He shuttered his surf shop and returned to his native London and in 2013 started selling travel gear on Amazon. He was one of the 2 million or so third-party sellers on Amazon, small retailers who peddle their goods on the site and pay the company a fee for the privilege. At first everything was going as Morgan expected. By 2016, he was profitably selling a million dollars a year's worth of his travel cubes, handy plastic containers in which to pack clothes and toiletries and that allow travelers to jam about a third more stuff into their suitcases.

Morgan's success didn't go unnoticed by Amazon's ever-watchful AI algorithms. The company's critics charge that it constantly monitors which category of products is selling well on its site, and if it likes what it sees, it creates its own brand of the item to compete. (Amazon has denied that it does this.) Morgan woke up one day that year and discovered that Amazon had started selling its own travel toiletry kit for $22. Morgan's sold for $35. "Overnight they killed my product line," recalls Morgan. It cost the entrepreneur $15 to make each bag. If he sold his at $22 to match Amazon's price, his profits would disappear because he had to pay the online giant around $7 in fees for the right to sell each of his bags on Amazon.com and for the company to handle his warehousing and Prime shipping.

The entrepreneur's troubles were only beginning. When Amazon offered its own line of travel cases, it featured them at the top of Morgan's product page—his most valuable real estate. The placement would inevitably attract the attention of shoppers away from Morgan's products to Amazon's. To stay visible at all on Amazon's site, Morgan had to pay Amazon thousands of dollars to own online search terms such as "travel pouch," "toilet kits," "suitcase space saver," etc. That meant that when a shopper typed in one of these terms, they'd see a page that featured Morgan's product near the top. By contrast, Amazon could give its own products great listings for free. It's hard to compete with a seller who has that kind of edge. "They have all of the data," says Morgan. "They know what factory in China you're using, and they have all your shipping data. They know how many products you sell every day in which markets. And they have their own advertising platform, which they can use to outposition and outbid you on. They are basically harvesting off your traffic."

To stay alive, Morgan did what every gutsy entrepreneur does when faced with doom—he doubled down. He cut the costs of his bags dramatically by outsourcing his customer service to two people manning phones in the Philippines—whom he paid half what he had been paying—and by hiring less-expensive designers in Eastern Europe to create his web graphics. He also switched his strategy, trying to make up with volume what he lost to Amazon in profits. So, to buy more inventory, he borrowed $300,000 from Amazon—the company acts as a bank for its third-party sellers, lending more than $1 billion in 2018—and it worked. Morgan's sales rose from $1 million in 2016 to $2.5 million in 2017, and he was making money again. Then in January of 2018, Amazon's algorithm suddenly decided that Morgan was no longer credit worthy and, without notice, refused to extend his loan. It was a decision made by a machine in a black box, and it couldn't be appealed. "I have no idea why the algorithm made that decision, and there is no one to talk to—that's what's crazy," says Morgan. "They completely screwed me—again."

In what he describes as an incredibly stressful year, the Londoner spent most of 2018 scrambling to pay back the Amazon loan, which carried a hefty 12 percent interest rate. Because he was using most of the money flowing into his business to pay off the loan, he didn't have the cash to buy the new inventory he needed to keep sales growing. His story, however, doesn't end with him turning the lights off. It took him nine months to pay off the Amazon loan and then Morgan was able to secure a $500,000 line of credit from a friend—another Amazon third-party seller. His business was back on the path to prosperity.

"What I can't stand," says Morgan, "is when Amazon becomes the playground bully, because you can't compete with that. They have an unfair advantage." Yet the entrepreneur says he loves his business—where else can a small business get access to 300 million customers around the globe?—and wouldn't trade it in for another surf shop on the sunny shores of Spain. He summed up his experience, saying that selling on Amazon is like "dancing with the devil."

Morgan's experience lies at the heart of a raging debate over whether Amazon is killing off small businesses. Because Amazon is the biggest online kid on the block, it often gets blamed for the woes of mom-and-pop enterprises. President Trump in March of 2018 tweeted that Amazon is putting many thousands of retailers out of business. The Institute for Local Self-Reliance, a leftist think tank that argues for stronger local communities, compares Bezos to a "19th-century railroad baron controlling which businesses get to market and what they have to pay to get there," and argues that Amazon is fueling a sharp decline in the number of independent retail businesses.

It is difficult to prove or disprove that argument by looking at the statistics. Some studies show that the number of small businesses in America is growing—although that data is from several years ago. And those studies don't break out the small Main Street retailers competing with Amazon.

Anecdotal evidence, however, suggests that some small businesses do indeed get hurt by the e-commerce giant. East Hampton, a seaside resort for New York's one-percenters, has plenty of well-heeled shoppers, but Sneakerology, a shop on Main Street selling fashionable casual and sporting footwear, couldn't attract enough customers and closed its doors in late 2018. When asked what happened, the store's manager said Sneakerology couldn't compete with Internet sales, plus manufacturers wouldn't send them the hottest shoe models because their volume wasn't big enough. This is the plight that many Main Street stores have suffered. If these businesses fail to differentiate themselves and have no strong web presence, their fate is likely doomed.

On the other end of the spectrum is Reader's Hardware store in Dobbs Ferry, New York, a thriving family business that has served its community for decades. Reader's is located only a few miles away from a Home Depot and shoppers can certainly buy most of Reader's inventory items on Amazon for less, but the small local hardware store offers something that the superstore and Amazon can't: knowledgeable service. Ask a clerk—if one can be found—at that Home Depot for advice, and the best that can be expected is a vague wave of the arm toward some crowded aisle where the product you mentioned might or might not reside. At Reader's, the friendly clerks will not only walk with you to find the items you need, but also patiently give advice on the right kind of washer needed to fix a leaky faucet or the best texture of paint for kitchen cabinets and how to apply it. Although the prices at Reader's are generally slightly higher than at Home Depot or Amazon, the small store's loyal customers are willing to pay the premium for a good experience.

Small businesses that have an edge—whether it's knowledgeable service or a craft product like farm-made cheese that can't be easily sold at scale on Amazon—should do just fine, even as Amazon continues to grow and take more oxygen out of the retail environment. Some service businesses, too, will be immune—try getting a haircut or a tattoo on Amazon. With Amazon controlling nearly 40 percent of all online commerce, though, most small retailers who want to survive will have to figure out how to sell on the retail giant's platform. But this, as John Morgan found out the hard way, is a cutthroat game. Businesses not only have to compete against Amazon, but also against more than 2 million small businesses around the world that sell their goods on Amazon.com.

In its defense, Amazon likes to point out that the more than

2 million small- and medium-sized businesses that sell on its site have created, as noted before, 1.6 million jobs worldwide, and 25,000 of these firms had revenues of $1 million or higher. To say that these sellers have become an important part of Amazon's online business is an understatement. In his 2018 shareholder letter, Bezos wrote that since 1999 the sales of third-party sellers have grown twice as fast as Amazon's own online revenues. With numbers like those, it's hard to argue that Amazon is killing off small businesses to the degree that its critics charge. And what these same critics don't understand is that killing these small merchants is the last thing Amazon wants because they generate better profit margins for the corporation than its own traditional e-commerce business. That's because Amazon charges merchants like John Morgan hefty fees for most items—on average, 15 percent of a product's retail price and then roughly another 15 percent for those that use its "fulfilled by Amazon" warehousing and shipping service. One private equity investor, who wishes to remain anonymous, says that the business of letting independent merchants sell on Amazon is one of Bezos's biggest growth businesses and predicts that it will grow more than tenfold over the next decade.

For third-party sellers, those fees are a steep price to pay, but in exchange they gain access to a massive number of customers plus the credibility that the Amazon name delivers. I once ordered a cedar gate for my garden on Amazon, and when it arrived, I realized it wasn't what I'd wanted. It was sold by a third-party merchant on Amazon, and when I tried to return it the seller said the $140 gate wasn't returnable. I called Amazon, and they confirmed that the merchant wouldn't accept returns, but then asked me what was wrong with the gate. I said I didn't like it. Without a pause, the Amazon rep said she'd credit my American Express card with $140 and added that I could keep the gate, which to this day still sits in my basement. (If anyone wants a cedar gate, I'm accepting offers.)

Some small businesses find that Amazon can make or break a product. Robert Wang, the inventor of the Instant Pot, an electric multicooker that can steam, pressure-cook, and sauté, watched his sales languish until in 2010 he listed his product on Amazon. Food writers and cooks started writing positive reviews of the device, which could shave hours off the time it takes to prepare meat or beans. Sales began to climb, and the Instant Pot eventually became a megahit. As of early 2019, the product had garnered 31,021 reviews with an average rating of 4.5 stars. At one point, some 90 percent of the product's sales flowed through Amazon. As CEO Wang told the *New York Times*: "Without Amazon, we wouldn't be here."

Yet for every Wang there are hundreds of entrepreneurs who don't make it on Amazon. More typical are hopeful entrepreneurs who keep their day jobs while selling products on Amazon in their spare time. Some get crushed when Amazon decides to compete with them directly by launching a similar product. Others get caught in a Wild West world where merchants do anything it takes to compete with each other—sometimes ethically and sometimes not. It is a world rife with fake reviews, counterfeit products, and hijacked websites. Some unscrupulous third-party sellers have made trumped-up complaints to Amazon about their competitor, causing the e-commerce giant to suspend the victim's account until the grievance is settled. For many sellers, having their accounts suspended by Amazon was a death sentence.

What many small businesses selling on Amazon also come to realize is that they're competing not only with the more than 2 million other third-party sellers already on its site, but with an endless array of look-alike Amazon-created products, such as household goods, clothing, food, and electronics. These appear under various names, so, often, shoppers don't even realize they're buying a product made and sold by Amazon.

The advantage Amazon has—and this factor feeds some of the biggest complaints about its power—is that it owns all the product and pricing data flowing through its e-commerce platform. Its AI software crunches data in near real time, and sets prices and inventory of its own products according to competitors' pricing, product availability, item preferences, order history, expected profit margin, and other factors.

Amazon claims that it doesn't use an individual seller's data to gain a competitive advantage. That doesn't mean, however, that it doesn't take a hard look at the data in different product categories—how are AAA batteries selling? What about gray hoodie sweatshirts for men? It has other advantages, too. In late 2018, Amazon started promoting its own brands at the bottom of a competitor's page under the headline "Similar Item from Our Brands." Clicking on the link brings the shopper to the product page for Amazon's own private label offering. So far Amazon's private label products only amount to a small fraction of its sales, but the category is growing and poses a threat.

In addition to its private label products, Amazon, of course, sells products it buys directly from manufacturers and wholesalers. This is its core retail business. In this arena, the company also competes with independent sellers, and, as some have charged, unfairly. In 2016, the nonprofit publication *ProPublica* conducted an investigation of Amazon's pricing algorithm. It tracked 250 frequently purchased products over several weeks to see which ones were selected for the most prominent placement on Amazon's virtual shelves—the so-called buy box that pops up first as a suggested purchase. The buy box is the most valuable piece of retail real estate on the Internet today. *ProPublica* found that in three out of four cases Amazon favored the products it was selling directly over those of independent sellers on its site. In one instance, a tube of Loctite glue sold directly by Amazon popped up in the "buy box" for $7.80, although third-party sellers were offering the same product for about 10 percent less with free shipping. When a shopper clicked to buy the Amazon glue, the deal got worse because shipping amounted to $6.51 *unless* you were a Prime member. *ProPublica* concluded that Amazon's algorithms aren't objective, but are slanted toward the products Amazon is selling directly. They also seem designed to drive more people to buy Prime memberships. Amazon told *ProPublica* that a lot more than just price goes into the "buy box" algorithm to make sure that "customers have the best overall experience."

Because selling on Amazon is so complicated and treacherous, it's not surprising that an entire industry of Amazon consultants and law firms has emerged to advise sellers on how to survive in the Amazon jungle. Chris McCabe worked at Amazon for six years advising third-party sellers before starting his Boston-based Amazon consulting firm. Business has been brisk because of the sheer number of sellers who run afoul of the e-commerce giant's rules. If Amazon gets a complaint about a seller dealing in counterfeit goods, shipping the wrong or dangerous products, or running fake reviews—whether the charge is true or not—the giant e-tailer suspends the seller's account until the case is resolved. "With Amazon it is you are guilty until you're proven innocent, and oftentimes that means that you are out of business," says McCabe. "It should be innocent until proven guilty." Amazon shoots first and asks questions later because it's protecting the customer—its holy crusade. Unfortunately, good actors end up getting abused by bad actors who make false reports to Amazon to cripple a competitor.

According to J. C. Hewitt of the Vaughn Law group, which advises third-party sellers, Amazon once shut down a multimillion-dollar cosmetics seller with no communication or explanation. "It turned out," said Hewitt, "that it was because the business had multiple accounts—presumably a no-no under Amazon's rules." The company had to go to its local legislator for help. Complaints about Amazon's capricious closings became so widespread that in the summer of 2019, Germany's Federal Cartel Office reached an agreement with Amazon in which the company promised to give all its third-party sellers worldwide a thirty-day notice before closing down a site. That should certainly help alleviate the problem of innocent sellers being closed down, but it will also allow unscrupulous sellers to exploit that thirty-day period and rip off consumers with counterfeit goods or bait-and-switch products.

When sellers have a problem, they have to call Amazon's customer support, but the results aren't always happy. One seller who wished to remain anonymous for fear of angering Amazon describes the experience this way: "When you have any problem, you have to deal with someone at Amazon who works offshore, and they have no idea what they're talking about. And normally you know more than they do, and you're telling them what to do and hope that they will do it. They are abusing us through their lack of competence."

Only the most successful sellers can afford great customer service from Amazon. By paying as much as $5,000 a month, sellers get access to a knowledgeable customer service rep on the phone who speaks decent English and theoretically knows what's going on. It's a tidy little side business for Amazon. Say the company pays one of these agents $50,000 a year, and each one on average handles twenty-five seller accounts. That's more than $1 million in revenue a year for each $50,000 agent. Nice margins. As the frustrated seller put it: "Amazon is charging us thousands of dollars a month for what they should do for free."

Why are sellers willing to pay these steep fees? They look at it as an insurance policy. If a big account gets shut down even for a few weeks, it could lose hundreds of thousands in revenue.

The rise in the number of Chinese merchants on Amazon has made these insurance policies all the more valuable. Bad players can come from all corners of the world, and the vast majority of Chinese people are honest and hardworking, but many Amazon sellers and consultants interviewed for this book say that China's third-party sellers are notorious for cutting corners. Some sellers say the Chinese can be lawless and unaccountable and proactively use black hat technologies to attack other sellers on Amazon. China even holds massive conferences for sellers to learn the tricks—some of them shady—of selling on Amazon.

Many of the conference attendees are owners of well-funded Chinese factories who used to make products for American and European Amazon sellers, but once they saw how well many were doing, they decided to cut out the middleman, sell directly on Amazon, and make more money. Amazon actively recruits these sellers. As previously mentioned, the company offers them an exclusive shipping service to bring their products to the U.S. called Dragon Boat that is cheaper than what American sellers have to pay for traditional shipping lines. Why the white-glove service? Bezos wants to be the platform of choice for the massive number of Chinese sellers who want to reach the American market. Amazon's main competitor here is China's online giant Alibaba, which sells in the U.S. through a platform called AliExpress.

Bezos's strategy is working to the delight of Chinese sellers and to the dismay of many American and European sellers who are seeing their markets invaded by China. The Chinese, after some false starts, have become sophisticated about the designs of their products, online search, and product differentiation. As of 2019, they've become a force to contend with, launching brands on Amazon backed by millions of dollars. As of 2018, about a third of all sellers on Amazon were Chinese, as were four of the top ten sellers. In 2017 alone, more than 250,000 new Chinese businesses started selling on the site.

Amazon seller forums in the U.S. and Europe, which are private online gatherings where sellers can trade stories and tips, are full of complaints about some Chinese actors who are bending the rules. There are also complaints about cutthroat American and European sellers, but the vast majority of complaints are about China. One of the most common complaints is hijacking. Here a seller hacks a competitor's account and takes over its page on Amazon. It might look like the seller's page but it's not. The hackers steal the other person's web design, its images photos, and product description. The hacker controls it. When Amazon customers buy on that page, they don't know the true identity of the seller.

When one seller realized he'd been hijacked by a Chinese seller, he wrote them to complain. "They just laughed at me and said come and find me in China," he recalls. Why didn't he contact Amazon and have them take down the fake Chinese site? He could certainly do that, but he was terrified of retribution. "All they have to do," he says, "is report to Amazon that I'm selling counterfeit products—which isn't true—but Amazon will take me down. [The company] shoots first and asks questions later. They would have suspended my account immediately for two to four weeks while I go through a review process." It's a scary thought. The equivalent in the brick-and-mortar world would be running a thriving store on Main Street until some inspector comes along and says you're being shut down until a certain complaint is resolved.

The main reason the hackers are taking over a competitor's site isn't to steal sales. (Although, in fact, they're doing just that.) The ultimate goal is to pirate the other seller's sales data, which is gold in the Amazon universe. They can see how much the hacked product sells for, which colors or styles of the product sell best, and what advertising search words work the best. Rather than spending tremendous amounts of time and money to formulate a successful online advertising strategy, the unscrupulous sellers just steal the data by hijacking a site.

If that doesn't work, some shady sellers have paid Amazon employees to get that data. In Shenzhen, Amazon fired a group of workers who were selling data for bribes ranging from $80 to $2,000 paid by Chinese sellers who wanted to use the data to outrank and crush their competition. The data sold included internal sales metrics and reviewers' email addresses. Among other things, the purloined data allows sellers to know exactly how much their competition is spending on key advertising words so they can outbid a competitor by pennies and get the key words for themselves. By doing this, the data thieves can severely damage a thriving Amazon competitor.

One European Amazon seller saw her business shrink by half when her Chinese competitors attacked her site with bots. These cyber saboteurs constantly searched with her key advertising words (for which she had paid top dollar), then clicked on her site but did not buy her product. Her rivals would also buy large numbers of her products and then return them. Amazon's ever-watchful algorithms concluded, "Hey, this seller bought these key search words and a lot of shoppers are clicking on her site but no one is buying so her product must stink." Always putting the customer first, the algorithms dropped her product down to page three of the rankings where few go to shop. "Once you're on page three," she says, "you might as well roll down the shutters and move on."

To compete on Amazon, sellers need to have reviews and

they're hard to come by—unless they're bought. Some merchants purchase fake five-star reviews for their products—there are plenty of black hat operations dwelling on Freelancer.com, Fiverr.com, and Facebook that are more than happy to serve up praise for a fee. An FTC complaint about a dietary supplement seller on Amazon cited an email in which the owner of the company offered a black-ops shop $1,000 to create thirty fake positive reviews and suggested a longer-term partnership to keep his product's rating above 4.3 stars.

The most damaging fake reviews falsely charge that a competitor is selling a counterfeit product. In many instances, Amazon would close down the site accused of counterfeiting until the unwitting seller could prove that they're the real McCoy. Amazon has sued freelancers who write fake reviews, but the practice is still a major problem for the company.

Then there are the review exchange clubs where sellers give reviewers free products in exchange for a write-up. Some of these reviewers are conscientious, but many are in it for the loot and get so many free products that they can't possibly properly evaluate them. Also, these reviewers tend to give only positive reviews because if they earn a reputation for negative ones, the pipeline of free products will dry up.

In one particularly odd twist, some crooked sellers will hijack another seller's site to steal their reviews. Clint Hedin is a successful third-party seller who has peddled everything from lawn aerator shoes, to garden hose nozzles, to nutritional supplements. One day he woke up to find that a Chinese seller had obtained permission from Amazon to switch the photos and product descriptions on his nozzle site to ones pitching HD antennas. "When the Chinese take over a page, they want to hijack your reviews. I had 590 reviews for my garden hose at 4.5 and 5 stars. What that means is if you want to sell antennas, you will be more successful with 600 reviews. No need to grind out a marketing campaign to customers. It's crazy—they were selling HD antennas, but the video reviews and photos were of garden nozzles." Apparently, many shoppers just look at the number of stars and the number of reviews and never scroll down to check that the reviews are really about garden nozzles, not HD antennas.

The hijacking caused confusion. Some customers who thought they were buying antennas got nozzles, which hurt Hedin's reputation as a seller. He tried to get Amazon to fix the problem, but nothing happened. Even if Amazon had shut down the black hat site, Hedin says the Chinese operate on ghost accounts that just disappear and then pop up the next day under a different name. Ultimately, he decided to delist his product, but then Amazon said it would charge him for keeping the unsold inventory in its warehouses. Hedin paid to have his nozzles shipped back to him and donated them to a local charity, losing thousands of dollars on the mishap.

The problem of fake reviews has gotten so bad that Saoud Khalifah, a former Goldman Sachs trader, has built a business around it. He started his company FakeSpot after ordering some exercise equipment that had earned five stars on Amazon and then seeing the gear break after one week of use. He went back and looked at the reviews and noticed that they contained broken language and odd phrases, much like those emails from Nigerian princes who want you to send them money so they can retrieve their fortune and share it with you. In 2015, Khalifah set up a site for himself and his friends that would analyze Amazon reviews for awkward language and other fraud signifiers—for example, one-line, five-star reviews have a high probability of being phony. When shopping on Amazon, Khalifah would cut and paste the URL of a given review page into his software program to determine if it was likely a fake.

Khalifah's site went viral and, as of 2019, it has analyzed more than 4 billion reviews on Amazon and other online retailers. From what he's observed so far, he estimates that about 30 percent of the reviews on Amazon are suspect. Amazon uses machine learning to weed out fakes, but the volume of reviews posted each day on its site is growing so rapidly that they're hard to police. What can be done? Savvy consumers should be suspicious if a product gets too many five-star reviews or if many of the reviews are very short and have similar fawning language. One strategy is to look at the three-star reviews, which probably give the most honest assessment of a product's pros and cons. A dishonest seller is unlikely to pay a review factory for mediocre three-star reviews, and one-star reviews are often written by cranks apt to complain that the cardboard shipping box is dented or that the product isn't the shade of blue they expected—whatever that means.

Of course, sometimes reviews accusing a seller of peddling fake goods are actually true. Counterfeiting has gotten so bad that for the first time in its 2018 financial filings, Amazon mentioned that it had become a significant issue on its site. A number of businesses are suing Amazon for not doing enough to prevent counterfeits. The luxury carmaker Daimler, which produces Mercedes-Benz automobiles, sued Amazon for allowing wheels to be sold on its site that violated the company's design patents. And a Tennessee family sued Amazon because it bought what it claimed was a fake hoverboard, which caught fire and burned down their house. Amazon is working on AI algorithms that can more easily detect fakes sold on its site, but until those programs get smarter, honest merchants and customers remain in danger of getting blindsided by counterfeiters.

While Amazon certainly poses a threat to small businesses that don't have a web presence, it has created a robust marketplace for the more than 2 million firms that sell on its site. Those enterprises may face growing competition not only from Amazon itself but from each other, but their numbers continue to grow, and many are thriving. To claim that Amazon is putting many thousands of mom-and-pop retailers out of business—as America's president Donald Trump did a couple years into office—without placing in context how the company interacts with its wide variety of client sellers is at the very least distorting.

The larger and more immediate threat is the one Amazon poses to big, traditional brick-and-mortar retailers.

CHAPTER 10

The Game of Drones

Amazon's announcement on June 16, 2017, that it was buying the Whole Foods grocery chain for $13.7 billion sent tremors throughout the industry. Retail stocks sank, CEOs fretted, and the cognoscenti started debating which shoe would fall next. Amazon had spent more than two decades building itself into the world's most powerful online retailer, so why would it even want to invest in brick-and-mortar retail, a musty industry with paper-thin profit margins? And besides, what does Amazon know about that end of the industry?

The answers to those two questions are obvious to those inside Amazon. First, the growth rate of Amazon's online business in the U.S. is slowing—as is inevitable for a company that controls such a large share of the market—and therefore it can't keep expanding at its rapid pace without entering traditional retail, one of its next big frontiers. Amazon is an online behemoth, but retailing in general is so huge—$4 trillion a year in the U.S.—that the company accounts for only a small share of the total market. Globally, the industry is even larger at $25 trillion annually, and Amazon's share of that is even smaller at around 1 percent.

Second, Bezos and his lieutenants love trying new things. Jeff

Wilke, the Amazon executive who runs e-commerce, Prime, and Whole Foods globally, tells a self-effacing story about how little Amazon knew about the grocery business before buying the high-end grocery chain. After the acquisition was announced, he flew to Austin for an all-hands meeting with Whole Foods employees to explain the thinking behind the deal. Wilke, who was onstage with Whole Foods CEO John Mackey, was saying how much he respected the high-end grocery chain for inventing the organic food category, adding that he'd probably get to live longer because of its food, while thanking Mackey and the employees in the audience. At one point, he turned to Mackey and said that at his hotel he had a quinoa vegetable dish and that no way would that have been an option in Texas fifteen years ago. Mackey turned to him and said, "Jeff, quinoa is not a vegetable."

Looking back on the incident, Wilke, during my interview with him, smiled and admitted that Amazon had a lot to learn about brick-and-mortar retail and that the acquisition of Whole Foods will help it climb that steep learning curve. In online retailing, the number of items sold can almost be limitless. It costs very little for Amazon to list the hundreds of millions of products on its site. But brick-and-mortar stores have limited shelf space and can stock only thousands of items, not millions. Managers have to decide what to put on the shelves. Make the wrong decisions, and sales suffer. "I can tell you now that we've owned Whole Foods for a year," said Wilke in my August 2018 interview, "that there's an enormous amount of expertise in merchandising and in the layout of physical stores and in buying things properly and deciding what to put on limited shelf space."

Traditional retailing is undergoing a titanic shift, the biggest change the industry has faced since Walmart put masses of mom-and-pop shops out of business and ushered in the age of the superstore after founder Sam Walton opened his first location in Rogers, Arkansas, in 1962. Today, being an online merchant isn't enough. Being a brick-and-mortar store isn't enough. The edge will go to those businesses that can combine the best of online shopping with the best of brick-and-mortar retail. It's a kind of boundary-less retail model that merges physical stores with cyberspace and creates multiple, convenient ways for consumers to shop. It is Bezos's next big push on his retailing AI flywheel.

Behind this emerging trend are hordes of customers who want convenient options. They want to be able to buy online, buy online and pick up at a store, buy online and have the store deliver, or just plain, old-fashioned shop in the store. And it seems that customers can't get their orders filled fast enough. A 2018 survey from the fraud prevention start-up Trustev found that 56 percent of eighteen- to thirty-four-year-old shoppers expect same-day delivery as an option. That means when and where the customer wants it—with no cracked eggs, missing items, or melted ice cream. No retailer wants to face the wrath of a hungry family, upset because the organic chicken breasts were missing from their order. It's an easy way to inflict lasting damage on a brand.

"No customer that I know wakes up in the morning and says, 'Where am I going to buy today?'" says Amazon's Wilke. "They just wake up and say, 'What do I need?' If I happen to be near my computer or phone, I might order it there. If I happen to be driving near the store, I'll pick it up there. What's happening is that our stores over time look more and more like other retailers' stores, and theirs are coming toward us. Customers will decide." While some like to spend time in stores looking for new shoes or cool sporting gear, most of us don't like spending more time than we need to buying boring commodity products like milk, cereal, and laundry detergent. This is why retailers think boundary-less shopping will be a hit.

This new model of retail, in which the online and the physical worlds meet, will likely trigger an even further shakeout of retailers. First off, America—the country that, in the near term, will feel the changes most acutely—has too many stores, roughly four times as much retail floor space per capita as other rich nations. At the same time millennials, rather than heading for the mall, are spending a large share of their discretionary income on cell phones, streaming media, health care, and student loans. And they also like to shop online, which means that fewer and fewer stores are needed. Second, most traditional retailers don't have the computer expertise to build the kind of slick online presence and fast delivery needed for hybrid retail and thus compete with Amazon. And even if they wanted to, many couldn't afford to build such an expertise—in recent years some of the big retailers have been taken over by private equity firms or hedge funds that have loaded the businesses with debt. That was one of the key contributing factors in the failures of longtime retailing behemoths Sears and Toys "R" Us. In 2017, more than six thousand U.S. stores announced closures, and at least fifty retailers filed for bankruptcy. As of 2019, a number of prominent retailers, including Neiman Marcus, the Gap, GNC, and Guitar Center were struggling under heavy debt loads.

While many traditional retailers were swimming against a tide of debt and coping with fickle, price-conscious consumers, Amazon, almost two years after its purchase of Whole Foods, again shocked the industry when the *Wall Street Journal* on March 3, 2019, leaked the news that the e-commerce giant planned to launch a *new* grocery store chain in dozens of locations in major cities, including Los Angeles, Chicago, and Washington, D.C. Because Whole Foods sells mostly healthy foods, its line of products is limited. "Hey, where are the Oreos?" might be the complaint of a customer not familiar with Whole Foods' ethos. In answer, Amazon's new grocery line will offer a wide variety of goods, including foods that might be tasty but not so good for us, and beauty products, which tend to have better margins than food.

The move sent a strong signal that Amazon isn't going to cede the grocery business to Walmart without a fight. As the king of online moves its forces into brick-and-mortar, Walmart, the largest grocer in the U.S. and the largest retailer in the world, is spending billions building up its digital retail business to compete with Amazon online, as will be chronicled in the following chapter.

As it girds for battle in the brick-and-mortar world, Amazon has ambitions beyond groceries. As of 2019, Amazon operated forty-two small retail stores under the names Amazon Go, Amazon 4-star, and Amazon Books. It has been a bumpy start. Running a store in a way that dazzles customers is a different game from running the world's largest online bazaar. When the company opened in New York's fashionable SoHo neighborhood an Amazon 4-star store—which featured items that earned online customer review ratings of four stars or better—the *New York Times* was scathing: "It is grim. A permanent store with the harried, colorless mood of a hastily assembled clearance-sale pop-up. Lot-Less Closeouts stores have more vim and charm."

As of 2019, Amazon had opened only fifteen Go stores, where shoppers can buy prepared foods such as sandwiches, salads, and drinks without checking out, but they seem more popular with consumers than the 4-star stores, and there's no reason why the company couldn't roll out more quickly. Analysts at RBC Capital Markets calculated that each Go store could generate $1.5 million a year in revenue. If Bloomberg is correct in reporting that Amazon by 2021 will open as many as three thousand Go stores, that could amount to $4.5 billion in annual revenue.

Amazon's biggest bet so far in brick-and-mortar, however, is in groceries because that's where the money is. In 2017, Americans bought more than $700 billion worth of food and other items from supermarkets. Online sales account for only a small fraction of those revenues, but the market-research firm Kantar Worldpanel projects that U.S. e-commerce sales of food and alcohol will reach roughly $40 billion by 2021, up from $14.1 billion in 2017.

So far, Walmart is the king of the U.S. grocery industry, accounting for 56 percent of all sales. Kroger comes in second with a 17 percent share. Amazon's Whole Foods is a rounding error with a little more than a 2 percent share. So why did Bezos buy this welterweight grocery chain? With the acquisition of Whole Foods' five-hundred-plus stores, Amazon gets much-needed real estate in prime urban and suburban areas. It also gets a high-end grocery whose customers fit nicely into the demographics of its Prime members. At the time of the takeover, roughly half of Whole Foods' shoppers were already Prime members, and eight out of ten Whole Foods customers also shopped on Amazon. Amazon began offering its Prime members discounts at Whole Foods—another way to lock shoppers into the Amazon ecosystem. From Whole Foods' point of view, the marriage with Amazon saved it from a hostile takeover threat from the activist hedge fund JANA Partners. It also got access to the capital and the kind of technological expertise that it would need in order to compete in the increasingly cutthroat grocery industry, where Walmart dominates.

Those in the retail industry who fret about Amazon and point to its staggering, technological prowess are right to worry. The battle for the grocery market will be won by those who can deliver the freshest food the fastest and with the fewest mistakes. Bezos plans to disrupt the grocery business by making ordering food as fast and simple as saying, "Hey, Alexa, I need milk and bananas," and then having the order arrive at a person's home within a few hours. That sounds simple, but to pull it off is anything but. It will take a lot of AI muscle.

In the race to speed up delivery, Amazon is innovating along every step of a product's journey. Every item the company sells has to be moved from a farm, a dairy, or a manufacturer to one of its warehouses—and sometimes Amazon's algorithms decide that a product then needs to be shipped to another warehouse nearer to where the demand is. As Amazon builds out its retail business, it's essentially becoming, as noted earlier, a giant shipping company, and if it keeps growing its delivery fleet at its current rate, it could become a major and disruptive player in that industry as well.

The motivating factor is cost savings. Consider that in 2018, the company delivered an estimated 4.4 billion packages worldwide. To lower the cost of getting all that merchandise from producers in China, India, and elsewhere to its warehouses in the U.S. and Europe, Amazon is amassing its own fleet of container ships, jumbo cargo jets, and tractor-trailer trucks. (Are you listening UPS, FedEx, and DHL?) By taking control of the packages it ships long distances, Amazon could, according to Citigroup, save $1.1 billion annually, compared to using UPS or FedEx.

Amazon understands that math well and is investing heavily to achieve those savings. As of 2019, it operated more than 10,000 trucks with the Amazon smile painted on their sides. It's renting cargo space on container ships to handle shipments from Asia, and it says that by 2021 it will have 70 cargo jets in operation. (To put that in perspective, FedEx owns or leases 681 aircraft.) Amazon is opening regional air hubs in Texas, Illinois, Ohio, and northern Kentucky. It is undeniable that the Amazon fleet keeps gaining headway.

Some shipping experts are skeptical that the company can build a delivery system to rival FedEx and UPS, which have invested heavily for decades to build their vast networks. And for the most part, the shipping industry had ignored the threat. In an investor call in late 2018, FedEx CEO Fred Smith told investors, "We don't see them as a peer competitor at this point." Yet big book chains such as Borders and Barnes & Noble were skeptical that Amazon could disrupt the book market and look what happened. Amazon is a logistical powerhouse driven by AI, and it's not inconceivable that it could figure out how to ship items long-distance cheaper than the incumbents and start offering its shipping services to other companies, in much the same way it built out its cloud computing business, AWS.

In a signal that it finally appreciated Amazon as a serious threat, FedEx in mid-2019 announced that it would no longer distribute Amazon packages in the U.S. Indeed, it disclosed in its 10-K SEC filing that given the significant capital Amazon has invested over the years in its shipping fleet, it now considers the e-commerce giant to be a competitor.

When a shopper orders groceries online, getting those goods to that person's home—known in the industry as "the last mile"—is complicated and expensive. For years, numerous companies including Amazon have tried to fill grocery orders from centralized warehouses and, with the exception of the delivery giant FreshDirect, have had little success. A warehouse doesn't have the fast turnover that a giant supermarket does, and fresh foods might not be so fresh when they arrive. Webvan, which tried this model, went bankrupt in 2001 and was absorbed by Amazon, whose own delivery service, AmazonFresh, is struggling. The online grocery service, which charges $14.99 a month, operates in twenty-three cities, including New York, Chicago, Dallas, London, Tokyo, and Berlin. The service has failed to deliver the stellar customer service of its sister businesses. Some customers complain of poor quality or spoiled produce, orders being packed incorrectly, canceled or late deliveries, and regularly missing items, according to *Business Insider*. In the 2018 Temkin Experience Ratings, which measures customer satisfaction, AmazonFresh lost thirteen percentage points, putting it in last place among grocers.

Whole Foods is one solution to Amazon's food delivery problems. Its stores are within an hour's drive of 40 percent of the U.S. population. In the future, these locations are likely to do double duty as warehouses. Because Whole Foods stores have a high turnover of vegetables, fruits, and other perishables, the odds are good that a delivery will arrive on time and with the kind of fresh items shoppers expect. Prime Now, the delivery service Amazon uses for Whole Foods, promises a two-hour window for deliveries, which is free for those Prime members (except for a required tip for the delivery person) who order at least $35 worth of groceries. In some markets, customers can order online and have the groceries put in their trunks when they pull up to a Whole Foods store.

The challenge for Amazon and all other grocers is that delivering food is expensive. Make no mistake: while Bezos accepts high shipping fees as unavoidable to keep the Amazon AI flywheel running, shipping is costing the company a fortune. In 2018, Amazon spent $27 billion on shipping—a 23 percent increase from the previous year. The cost of a single delivery can range on the high end from $7 to $10. The last mile is where the costs pile up. It can account for more than half of the total cost of shipping a package.

Grocery deliveries add an entirely new level of costs. It's expensive to train and hire someone to pick fresh produce, pack it, and deliver it. This is where technology—Amazon's main strength—comes in. The robot technology that Amazon is developing can be used for food orders, eliminating some labor costs. Challenges exist, however, especially in picking out orders. If a customer likes perfectly ripe strawberries, how can a robot distinguish them from those that aren't yet ripe? In Amazon's secretive research labs, a machine-learning team came up with a way to identify whether some strawberries are fresher than others. The solution uses visual recognition technology that allows the machine to learn which strawberries are perfect for eating. It recognizes the reddest, ripest strawberries in the same way face recognition software can pick a particular person out of a crowd.

To lower costs and boost speed, Amazon over the years has tried to outsource some of its local deliveries to smaller, independent couriers that charge less than FedEx or UPS. Amazon Flex is its same-day delivery service, which operates in some ways like Uber, using independent contractors who drive their own cars and get paid by the delivery. In fact, some Amazon Flex drivers are actually moonlighting Uber drivers. As is the case with many gig economy workers, these drivers find it hard to make a living. They might get paid $18 to $24 an hour for delivering Amazon packages to homes and apartment buildings, but after deducting gas, insurance, and maintenance costs, their pay ends up much less than that. Also, the Flex drivers, because they're independent contractors, don't receive corporate benefits, even though some wear Amazon uniforms and report to an Amazon manager.

And the work is tough. Alana Semuels, a staff writer for *The Atlantic*, spent a day in San Francisco as an Amazon Flex driver. She describes how parking in downtown was a nightmare for noncommercial vehicles and she ended up walking two blocks with a thirty-pound package, having to stop and catch her breath every one hundred steps or so. She described how she was "battling a growing rage as I lugged parcels to offices of tech companies that offered free food and impressive salaries to their employees, who seemed to spend their days ordering stuff online. Technology was allowing these people a good life, but it was just making me stressed and cranky. 'NOT. A. GOOD. DEAL,' I scrawled in my notebook after having walked down nine flights of stairs, sick of waiting for a freight elevator that may or may not have been broken, and returned to my car for another armful of packages."

In addition to the swarms of gig economy workers racing around neighborhoods delivering packages, Amazon hires small trucking companies that help handle the ever-increasing number of same-day deliveries. This approach saves Amazon money, but it comes with a slew of headaches. In 2018, *Business Insider* reported that some drivers who worked for these companies drove in trucks with "broken windows, cracked mirrors, jammed doors, faulty brakes, and tires with poor traction." Around the same time, more than two hundred delivery drivers sued Amazon and one of its outsourced courier companies over claims of unpaid wages. Amazon said it would make major changes to how delivery drivers are paid to ensure more transparency and fairness.

In the wake of all the bad press about its couriers, Amazon announced in 2018 a new program called Delivery Service Partners, another step in its effort to build a delivery powerhouse. Here's how it works. Amazon said it would purchase twenty thousand Mercedes Sprinter vans and take applications from entrepreneurs who want to start their own local delivery business. By 2019, more than a hundred budding entrepreneurs had signed up, some of them Amazon employees.

For its new delivery program, Amazon said that it was looking for "a customer-obsessed people person who loves coaching teams in a high-speed, ever-changing environment." Those who qualify could start with as little as a $10,000 investment. (For employees who want to be owners, Amazon will fund their costs up to $10,000 and provide three months of salary to help them get the business off the ground.) These entrepreneurs can each manage a fleet of as many as forty vans. If successful, they can earn between $75,000 and $300,000 a year. It's too early to tell whether the program will work, but it's designed to solve the problem of vans with bald tires and shattered windows, and because Amazon is leasing the Sprinter vans and is helping set up the couriers' operations—which doubtless includes using Amazon's technology—the company can keep close tabs on the business to help prevent any shenanigans over pay or safety.

Despite these changes, Amazon will still have a cost problem. By reducing what they have to pay to firms like FedEx and UPS, the company will save some money, but the last mile remains expensive. Those business owners have to pay for their Mercedes vans, hire and train a workforce, pay employee benefits, and keep some profit for themselves. That's why Amazon is investing billions in new technologies that promise in the longer term to revolutionize last-mile delivery, including self-driving vans, robots that drop off packages at the door, and drones that can drop a box of new Bose headphones in your backyard. Potentially, the payoff is impressive. The consultancy McKinsey & Company predicts that autonomous deliveries will allow retailers to slash shipping costs by more than 40 percent. That means Amazon could save more than $10 billion a year, giving it yet another edge over its competitors. Bezos will in all likelihood use the savings to drop prices for his customers, which will in turn attract more sellers, which will lower costs and attract more customers. And his AI flywheel will spin faster and faster.

With visions of those savings dangling before him, Bezos has jumped headlong into the autonomous vehicle race. Amazon's vast computing power and machine-learning expertise make it a potentially formidable player in the field. In 2016, the company earned a patent for a system that helps autonomous cars figure out which direction traffic is traveling in any particular lane to help a vehicle safely enter the proper lane. In its partnership with Toyota, Amazon is developing a self-driving concept vehicle called the e-Palette, a minivan that can move people or packages, and the two companies plan to unveil it at the 2020 summer Olympic games in Tokyo.

In early 2019, Amazon led a $700 million investment round in Rivian, a Michigan company that is developing a battery-powered pickup truck and a sport utility vehicle. Ford later that year invested another $500 million in the company. Around the same time, Amazon led a $530 million investment round for Aurora, a Silicon Valley self-driving vehicle start-up founded by three stars of this emerging industry: Sterling Anderson, Drew Bagnell, and Chris Urmson. Anderson ran Tesla's autopilot program, Bagnell headed the autonomy and perception team at Uber, and Urmson was the former head of Google's self-driving project, which has morphed into one of the leading self-driving car companies: Waymo. Aurora will not build cars but is developing the AI brains behind autonomous vehicles and plans to partner with retailers like Amazon and major automakers to create state-of-the-art autonomous vehicles.

Amazon is far from alone in the race for self-driving vehicles. According to the research firm CB Insights, at least forty-six companies around the world are working on self-driving vehicle technology. The ranks include major automakers such as GM, Ford, BMW, and Audi; tech companies such as Alphabet, Baidu, Microsoft, and Cisco; Internet car services such as Uber and Didi in China; retailers such as Walmart, Kroger, and Alibaba; and a slew of start-ups like Aurora and Udelv.

One thing that's almost certain is that when autonomous vehicles do first appear in significant numbers, they'll be delivery vans. That's because carrying packages rather than humans greatly reduces the risk posed by self-driving vehicles. If an order of Dr. Bronner's castile soap gets crushed in a fender bender, that's unfortunate but not a tragedy. In an accident, the vans will be programmed to self-sacrifice themselves to avoid harm to pedestrians, bicyclists, or drivers of other vehicles. In other words, they'll crash into a tree rather than collide with a pedestrian or other car. Also favoring delivery vans in this first-mover role is that, for the most part, they have predictable routes and therefore can more easily learn the ins and outs of complex cityscapes—reducing the chance of navigation errors and accidents.

A number of innovative companies, working with big retailers, are already running pilot programs with autonomous delivery vans. On January 30, 2018, the Silicon Valley start-up Udelv made what it claims to have been the first self-driving delivery for Draeger's Market in San Mateo, California. The brains of the vehicle were built on the Apollo software platform, created by the Chinese search engine company Baidu. Baidu is in competition with Alphabet's Waymo and others to create an industry standard—sort of like Android for self-driving vehicles. Subsequently, Udelv partnered with Walmart to deliver goods in Arizona. In 2019, a start-up named Nuro launched a delivery service for Kroger in Scottsdale, Arizona, with autonomous vans that weigh 1,500 pounds, can carry 250 pounds of groceries, and look like shrunken VW minibuses from the 1960s. Delivery costs $5.95, with no minimum order.

All these companies have taken a slightly different approach to autonomous delivery, but the basic concept is that a customer uses a smart app to request a delivery for a certain window of time. Much as Uber does, the app can track the location of the vehicle as it makes its way toward its destination. When the van rolls up to the home, it texts the customer a code and a notice that the package—whether it is groceries, dry cleaning, or prescription drugs—has arrived. The person walks up to the van and punches the code into a screen on the side of the vehicle that pops open a door to a storage compartment. Once the package has been retrieved, the door closes and the van drives to the next destination.

Self-driving delivery vehicles come in all shapes and sizes. In early 2019, Amazon let loose six Scout delivery vehicles on the sidewalks of Snohomish County, Washington. The two-toned, baby blue and black, battery-powered devices look like small coolers on wheels. They can travel the sidewalks at a walking pace and avoid pedestrians and pets. The Scouts use an array of sensors to navigate their way across streets and around obstacles. The self-driving delivery bot stops when it recognizes its destination, alerts the shopper by text, and pops open its top. When the person picks up the package, Scout closes its lid and heads back for its next job. So far, Amazon likes how Scout rolls, and in the summer of 2019 the company decided to expand the program into Southern California.

While the Scout seems to make sense for simple deliveries, it's not yet a good substitution for humans. A robot—at least not yet—can't open gates, climb stairs, ring doorbells, or slide a small package safely between a storm door and front door to keep it dry on a rainy day. These vehicles only work when the customer is at home, which limits their usefulness. What if the customer is a no-show? How long does the car wait? Amazon and others believe part of the solution will be to build personal lockboxes where robots can drop packages, but rolling out such an infrastructure will take years if not decades. And what happens when some mischievous kid tips a Scout over? Or when armies of Scouts jam up city sidewalks? These vehicles might solve the last-mile problem, but they will create a last-fifty-feet problem.

Not all autonomous delivery vehicles roll along the ground. In 2013, Bezos appeared on CBS's *60 Minutes* and explained to correspondent Charlie Rose how Amazon's drones could deliver a five-pound package to customers within a half hour. The significance is that, according to Bezos, some 86 percent of all packages that Amazon delivers weigh five pounds or less. Drone deliveries could save Amazon additional billions by, again, eliminating the human element.

Drones have many positive attributes. Theoretically, they emit less greenhouse gas than gasoline-powered delivery trucks, and they can reach remote areas to deliver crucial medicines. They can help monitor utility lines and bring crucial supplies to disaster areas. They can also be used to bring consumers in rural areas more choice at better prices. In China, online retailer JD.com has used a drone to cut the delivery time to a remote mountain village from days to minutes, while slicing the cost dramatically. And that's just the start for drones and other delivery technology. JD.com CEO Richard Liu says that in the next ten years the evolution of drones and other AI technology will move faster than in the last one hundred years.

In the *60 Minutes* interview, Bezos said that drone technology was in a very early stage, but that he was optimistic it would be in use by 2019. That date has rolled over on the calendar, and delivery drones are still not commonplace in the U.S. In 2018, the Federal Aviation Administration (FAA) slowed down their adoption by requiring a two-and-a-half-year pilot project to collect data and learn about the impact drones will have on airspace. That a civilian drone that year could shut down Gatwick Airport in England for hours underscores the FAA's concern. But the agency is moving ahead. In April 2019, it let Alphabet, the parent company of Google, start a test drone delivery service in Virginia, the first of its kind in the U.S. Amazon soon followed.

Amazon is doing all it can to speed the process along. Bob Roth, a director with Amazon Prime Air, the division building drones, is working on a traffic management system aimed at making low-altitude air travel—below four hundred feet—safe. At Amazon Prime Air, which has offices in Seattle, Tel Aviv, Cambridge, England, and Paris, Roth and his team are building a wholly automated system—no air traffic controllers—to keep the drones out of the way of planes and helicopters and other drones. The system will also allow the FAA to track the drones and to create no-fly zones during emergencies.

If drones start frequenting the skies, Amazon can expect serious blowback from local communities. Some worry about privacy—are the cameras on the drones being used to spy on people? Drone makers say the cameras are low resolution and only meant to aid in navigation and to improve the drone's performance. That might be the case now, but there's no guarantee that the cameras won't get better and nosier.

The bigger worry is noise. A 2017 NASA study found that heavy road traffic in residential areas is much less annoying than the back-and-forth high-pitched buzz of drones. When Alphabet's Wing division started using drones to deliver hot coffee and hot food in three minutes or less to customers in the Australian suburb of Bonython, Canberra, the buzzing didn't go over well. Jane Gillespie, a local resident and a member of Bonython Against Drones (BAD), says the drone's loud, high-pitched whirrs sound like a "Formula One racing car." The community group filed a petition with the local government to curtail drone deliveries. Gillespie and other members of BAD have a point. The noise is horrible. But that wasn't enough of a reason to stop these machines: the Canberra government in early 2019 officially approved drone deliveries despite noise complaints from many constituents.

Drone supporters say that people just aren't used to the kind of noise a drone makes, but that offers scant comfort. It's not hard to imagine a dystopian future in which scores of nerve-jangling drones shatter the peace of many a suburban or rural area. Victims of noisy drones in the U.S. shouldn't count on the FAA for help. The federal agency both regulates air travel and promotes it. Once it approves commercial drones, which is likely, there'll be no turning back.

Whether it's a drone, a Scout delivery bot, or a full-sized autonomous delivery van, autonomous delivery conveyances make more economic sense than human drivers. That means the future lies in self-driving delivery vehicles, and people will need to get used to them plying the streets. At first, these machines will make for some bizarre encounters. In a pilot program in Ann Arbor, Michigan, an autonomous Ford Fusion hybrid was used to deliver Domino's pizza to the front doors of suburban homes. After getting their pizza, some customers, caught on videotape, would say "Thank you" to the car. It's hard to understand why anyone would do this. Perhaps they were afraid that when our robot overlords take over, the first thing they'll do is check the old log files to see who was nice to the robots and who wasn't.

Amazon with its expertise in robotics, machine learning, and autonomous delivery will lead the way in hybrid retailing where consumers can shop in stores, online, or use some combination of the two. This is where the retail industry is headed, and Amazon is using its technological might to change the rules of the game in a fundamental way. By morphing into a hybrid retailer, Amazon will not only find growth in new markets such as groceries but will discover new efficiencies that will unlock more capital for investment. The $10 billion–plus that McKinsey says Amazon will save by moving to autonomous vehicles is a case in point. Those savings and ones like them will give Amazon even more capital to drive down prices for its customers and build and buy more brick-and-mortar stores. Perhaps, as rumor has it, they'll even acquire Target—which would keep Bezos's AI flywheel spinning faster and faster.

So far, only one company in the U.S. is big enough and smart enough to compete on Amazon's scale.

CHAPTER 11

Godzilla Versus Mothra

In the summer of 2016, Marc Lore, like so many other entrepreneurs before him, came to the realization that his company
lacked the firepower to compete with Amazon. His e-commerce
start-up, Jet.com, sold hip, upscale products such as Yes to grape-
fruit face masks and Fitbit Ionic smart watches to millennials,
and it was growing fast with $1 billion in gross revenues. Like
other leaders in his field, Lore knew the retail game was morphing toward a boundaryless customer experience. No longer
was it enough to just own stores, nor was it enough to just be
online. Successful retailers had to offer their customers a mul-
titude of robust choices—either buy at the store, order online
and pick up at the store, or buy online and have the order arrive
in a few days or hours, whatever the preference. The idea had
been around for some time, but it was devilishly hard to execute.
To be able to offer that kind of hybrid experience, Lore knew
he needed scale, which takes a mountain of capital. He'd raised
$225 million in venture funds, but it wasn't nearly enough, so he
turned to Amazon's archrival: Walmart.

In the fall of that year, Walmart bought Jet.com (and Lore
along with it) for $3.3 billion. At the time, Jet.com had been val-
ued by some analysts at about $1 billion, so one way of looking

at the deal was that Walmart paid $2 billion to buy Lore. The world's largest retailer saw in Lore someone who had the online savvy to dig into Amazon's dominance in e-commerce. With nearly 40 percent of all U.S. online sales in 2018, Amazon was ten times the size of Walmart in that market. One pundit quipped that Walmart's purchasing a hip, online company was like a middle-aged man in a midlife crisis buying expensive hair plugs.

Lore saw in Walmart the scale and capital he needed to go after Amazon. The Bentonville, Arkansas, company operates roughly 4,700 U.S. stores, and those locations put it within ten miles of 90 percent of the U.S. population—an ideal setup for same-day shipping. In an attempt to match Amazon Prime's free shipping, Walmart started to offer free one-day shipping for orders over $35, but the key was the company's ubiquitous stores. Lore saw that they could be used as giant local warehouses where products can be picked up curbside by online shoppers or delivered hours after an order is placed. "We have 1.2 million associates in our stores across the country who can do this," Lore says. "That allows us to deliver fresh, frozen and general merchandise in two hours or on the same day cheaper than anybody else." Walmart customers can also order groceries online and drive to a nearby Super Store to pick them up curbside. According to Cowen analysts, in January 2019, some 11 percent of Walmart shoppers used its curbside pickup program. They simply drove to a Super Store, and an employee stashed their order in the trunk.

Lore well knows what he's up against with Amazon—as noted earlier, he used to work there. In 2005, he and Vinit Bharara founded an online retailer in New Jersey called Quidsi—the name combines the two Latin words *quid* and *si*, which mean "what if." The company created Diapers.com, which promised free overnight shipping of diapers and other baby supplies for harried parents. Venture capital firms backed the start-up with a $50 million investment. The two founders relished their independence. Still, from afar, they admired Bezos's online skills and named him "sensei," the Japanese term for a martial arts master.

New moms and dads loved Diapers.com, and Quidsi's annual revenues by 2008 had grown to $300 million a year. According to Brad Stone's *The Everything Store*, Quidsi came under Bezos's radar, and Amazon started dropping its diaper prices dramatically to undercut Diapers.com. At one point, Lore and his team did the math and found that Amazon was on track to lose $100 million on diapers over a three-month period. Seeing a dim future, Lore and his partner began negotiations with both Walmart and Amazon to be acquired. When Bezos learned of Walmart's interest, Amazon executives, as Stone wrote, "ratcheted up the pressure even further, threatening the Quidsi founders that 'sensei,' being such a serious competitor, would drive diaper prices to zero if they went with Walmart." In 2010, Lore and his partner capitulated and sold Quidsi to Amazon for $550 million. Looking back on the deal, Lore says that the reason he felt compelled to sell wasn't so much Amazon's fierce cost-cutting but that, once Bezos targeted his company, investors shied away from providing Quidsi with the capital it would need to sustain a long price war with the e-commerce giant.

Lore's tenure with Amazon didn't last long. As part of the deal, Quidsi was supposed to operate as an independent unit within Amazon, but Amazon eventually absorbed the business into its own operations, and the Diapers.com name eventually disappeared.

After Walmart acquired Jet.com, CEO Doug McMillon put Lore in charge of e-commerce in the U.S., overseeing both Walmart.com and Jet.com, and gave him free rein to build an entrepreneurial, fast-growing online business that could match

Amazon's logistics. Walmart's CEO also wanted to make sure Lore would be well compensated for the tough fight ahead. According to a 2016 *Women's Wear Daily* study, Lore that year was the highest-paid executive in retail, fashion, and beauty, pulling in a salary and bonus of $1.4 million and a stock award package worth $242 million. For its money, Walmart expected this former entrepreneur to take Walmart's stores, its logistical prowess, and its troves of capital and position it as an Amazon beater.

Walmart first started selling online in 1999, just a few years after Bezos launched Amazon. The reason Walmart embraced the Internet at that point was to create a hybrid shopping experience for its customers. Sound familiar? In a 2011 analyst call, then-CEO of Walmart.com Joel Anderson explained that the strategy would be "about building a multi-channel approach." What he meant is that Walmart would use the web to broaden its assortment of products, to provide next-day delivery for online shoppers with items shipped from its stores, and to offer three free shipping options, which Anderson labeled as "fast, faster, and fastest." That strategy might have made sense to Walmart's management at the time, but it didn't to customers, and the program went nowhere.

Lore admits that Walmart was late to the online retailing game, and that it underinvested in technology and therefore had a lot of catching up to do. Walmart.com doesn't have the selection, intuitive ease of use, and customer-friendly features of Amazon.com. Nor does it have a membership club that offers the benefits Prime members receive, such as movies, TV, books, and music, and free two-day or less shipping. For Walmart, the Internet presented the classic innovator's dilemma—it was hard for the retailer to make a big push into e-commerce because doing so would disrupt its successful brick-and-mortar business.

As Lore girds for battle with Amazon, Walmart has one distinct advantage: its expertise in brick-and-mortar—a crucial element in making hybrid retailing a reality. Just as Amazon is racing to build a brick-and-mortar empire, Walmart is striving to meld an attractive online shopping experience with its already formidable brick-and-mortar presence. It's hiring truckload after truckload of data scientists, expanding the number of products available on Walmart.com, inviting small retailers to sell on its site, trying to integrate AI and machine learning to give its customers a better shopping experience, and experimenting with ways to speed up delivery. It's the only company in America that has the expertise and deep pockets to take on Amazon head-on.

In the midst of all the buzz about Amazon taking over the world, it's easy to forget that Walmart is nearly twice the size of Amazon. Its sales hit $500 billion in 2018, making it not only the largest retailer in the world but the largest business in the world. Walmart's 4,700 U.S. stores dwarf Amazon's 550, and it owns another 6,000 internationally, compared to only a handful for Amazon. That's a daunting lead. The question is: Can Walmart transform itself quickly enough into a hybrid retailer to keep Amazon from outstripping its business and making a serious dent in its profitable grocery line? Although Walmart, of anyone, has the best chance of competing with Amazon, Wall Street isn't betting that way. Even though Walmart is twice the size of Amazon, its stock market value in 2019 was only half that of Amazon's.

Walmart believes it can beat Amazon by doing what it does best—smashmouth retailing—and doing it faster and smarter. "If you want to talk about why Amazon is successful," says Lore, "forget about tech, forget about its AWS cloud business and digital entertainment and all these other things that people talk about. At the end of the day it is the core retail business."

In Lore's mind that means getting anything you want at great prices and getting it in a fast and predictable fashion. "That's great, because for us that's a game we know how to play really well. Logistics and merchandising."

The two giants will clash, and the competition will be fierce, but that doesn't mean one has to die on the battlefield. Both Amazon and Walmart have the expertise, capital, and strong balance sheets to transform themselves into hybrid retailers. One can imagine a scenario in which, in the U.S., Amazon and Walmart become the two dominating shopping platforms with the giants splitting the country into spheres of influence.

As Lore explains: "At the end of the day—if I had to guess how it would shake out—Amazon would be more coasts and urban, and Walmart more heartland. That's pretty much the way it is playing out today, where Amazon prevails in the more urban areas, and Walmart in Middle America." Walmart generally has better pricing than Amazon—a plus when selling to middle- and low-income shoppers in rural areas. And its stores and warehouses are also nearer to those customers than Amazon's warehouses, which tend to be near big cities. That means, in the middle of the country, it can sometimes take Amazon longer to deliver to some places with the kind of goods often requested in those areas.

Consider that Walmart has no stores in New York City (although it announced in 2019 that it would open a warehouse in the Bronx for grocery deliveries). Whole Foods has thirteen stores in the area. The two companies—with their selection of goods, speed of delivery, and massive geographic footprints— would make it difficult for other retailers to compete. Internationally, the competition will play out differently. You can imagine a scenario in which a handful of retail giants act like colonial powers splitting up the globe into spheres of influence.

Alibaba and JD.com would be the prevalent platforms in China. Amazon would prevail in Europe along with perhaps Tesco in Britain, Carrefour in France, and the Schwarz Group or Aldi in Germany. Amazon plus Alibaba plus Walmart would battle it out over India, with its 1.3 billion consumers.

Despite all the hype about boundaryless retailing, as of 2019 only a small percentage of shoppers bought groceries online. Ordering food and having it arrive in good shape is much harder to do than with other goods. As discussed in the previous chapter, fruits, vegetables, fish, meats, and other perishables have a short shelf life; some can bruise easily or spoil as they sit in a warehouse. Walmart's advantage over Amazon is that it can use its vastly more numerous and larger stores to ship fresh groceries to more locations, more quickly than can Whole Foods. The immense volume and fast turnover in a Walmart Super Store also mean the company experiences less food waste, a particularly thorny problem for retailers.

Because Walmart's Super Stores are profitable, when someone orders groceries online, the overhead is covered. A business like FreshDirect or AmazonFresh that stores groceries in a warehouse for home delivery has to pay for its overhead, putting it at a cost disadvantage. "The combination of in-store foot traffic and home delivery is the magic," says Lore. In his vision, the store of the future has a smaller area where customers shop and a big warehouse room in the back for online deliveries and curbside pickups. That, however, isn't stopping Amazon from doubling down. As mentioned earlier, Amazon's rumored bid to build a national chain grocery store, supposedly with a greater selection and lower prices than Whole Foods, would compete directly with Walmart.

Despite the fevered activity and heavy investments by both players, Walmart and Amazon still have a long way to go in home grocery delivery. One issue is that it's hard for online shoppers to know exactly what they're ordering. When browsing the Whole Foods site, a customer can see small pictures of items with prices, sizes, and weights, but the experience can be confusing. When I ordered what looked like a small container of coleslaw from Whole Foods, what got delivered was a large plastic container of coleslaw "mix," which is sliced cabbage and carrots, but with no mayonnaise or seasoning. Who knew? I'm sure Whole Foods would've compensated me for the mistake, but who wants to bother contacting them and straightening it all out? There will be a learning curve with shoppers over time. Eventually, the store's systems will know one's likes and dislikes better. Maybe in the future Alexa will tell me, "Are you sure you want the slaw mix? It is just a big box of tasteless sliced cabbage and carrots."

Both companies are working to reduce such confusion through AI and machine learning. Amazon has the advantage here. For years it has had access to the shopping habits of the hundreds of millions who shop on its site. A brick-and-mortar retailer like Walmart that was late to e-commerce doesn't have nearly the depth of data. Walmart hopes to fix that with a pilot project, currently under way in New York City, called JetBlack. For a $600 annual membership fee, JetBlack customers get product recommendations, quick delivery, and the ability to order anything they want, whether it's from Walmart, Gucci, Tiffany, or Lululemon, and get it the same day. Walmart employees visit JetBlack members in their homes and interview them about their likes and dislikes to get a better sense of their shopping habits so that the next time members order milk online, Walmart knows they mean a half gallon of Horizon organic 2 percent milk. Lore says that 80 percent of the time the customer will take its recommendation.

The idea of JetBlack isn't for Walmart to visit every one of its customers, but for it to learn more about their habits and to translate that into AI algorithms. Over time, the system will become more and more automated. "This is a long-term play," says Lore. "The idea is that in the future there is no human interaction. It's just a machine that knows you and what you're asking and what you like." When the algorithms get that good, voice shopping will be all the more accurate and easier. That said, Amazon is light-years ahead of Walmart in perfecting voice recognition technology. Smart devices with Alexa are spreading fast throughout the world, outpacing the competition by far. Walmart uses the Google Assistant for voice shopping. That places it one step removed from their customers and makes it harder for it to collect valuable purchasing data.

Like Amazon, Walmart is also working on the last-mile problem for grocery deliveries. The retailer is partnering with tech companies including Baidu, Waymo, and Udelv to develop self-driving delivery vans. Until autonomous vans become a reality, it's trying to optimize its existing delivery system. In one project rolled out in 2019, Walmart is using its store workers to deliver online grocery orders right to a customer's refrigerator. The delivery people, who wear cameras, type in a onetime code into the customer's smart lock on the front door, walk into the house, and stuff perishables such as milk, ice cream, fruits, and vegetables into the icebox. To prevent theft or vandalism, customers have apps on their phones that let them see the delivery person enter and drop off the bags of groceries in real time or on tape delay. At first, consumers will balk at letting strangers into their homes when they're not there, but many will get used to it in the same way that homeowners have gotten used to giving strangers access to their apartments through Airbnb. So far, Walmart has had no complaints, although the day will come when an unfriendly rottweiler takes a dislike to an unsuspecting delivery person.

Lore believes that direct deliveries to the refrigerator will save costs. No longer will the company have to pack milk and ice cream in insulated boxes, and the arrangement gives Walmart much more flexibility on the timing of deliveries. Typically, the company experiences a bottleneck of deliveries between 4:00 and 8:00 p.m., when people want their groceries to arrive after they get home from work. Walmart's new system will allow it to deliver when people *aren't* home, meaning it can batch its deliveries in ways that make more logistical sense, reducing the number of trips and saving money. As of 2019, the project was being tested in one market. "But we have big plans," says Lore. "It is the future. We will attract early adopters first and then we will scale."

While Walmart and Amazon battle to carve up the U.S. retail market with their hybrid shopping model, the fate of other retailers looks dim. A spirited group of retailers are finding ways, though, to make an end run around these giants.

CHAPTER 12

Amazon-Proofing
Your Business

The days when a store could simply open its doors and expect customers to walk in and buy are over. Retailers today are grappling with an existential debate over what constitutes a store. Is it a marketing platform? A place to hang out? A spot to pick up stuff ordered online? A 2019 *New Yorker* cartoon, showing a young couple leaving a store empty-handed, sums up this predicament. The man says to the woman: "It warms my heart to see their look of hope that we might not just buy it online."

As bleak as this situation looks for many cookie-cutter retailers, the future is bright for those who, instead of trying to confront Amazon head-on, figure out how to outflank it. If a company can't match Amazon's vast assortment of products, low prices, and speedy delivery, it must differentiate itself in other ways. It needs to pursue strategies that Amazon would be hard put to match. The common thread? The retailers of the future will focus their efforts in four major areas: creating an amazing in-store experience that digitally merges with an amazing online one; offering a highly curated selection of exclusive products; investing heavily in technology, including mastering social media; and doubling down on a social mission in a way that makes customers feel good about buying from them.

The businesses featured in this chapter are thriving because they've mastered one of these four tenets. In the long run, however, with Amazon's invasion of brick-and-mortar retailing well under way, it won't be enough to compete by mastering just one of these four strategies. Anyone who wants to keep up in an Amazonian world must eventually master at least two or three or even all four, because it's certain that Amazon will be trying to master them as well in the empire of brick-and-mortar stores it's building.

Some companies like Nike and Sephora have seamlessly integrated the online and in-store experience to make shopping more rewarding for their customers. Others like Williams-Sonoma carry high-end cookware and kitchen equipment that often can't be found elsewhere. Fashion retailers such as Stitch Fix, ASOS, and Lulus have harnessed technology to make their customers feel special in a way that Amazon can't. Stitch Fix hires squadrons of data scientists who can dramatically increase the chances of its online customers finding clothes with the look they favor *and* the right fit. Britain's ASOS is on a fast growth track because it has digitally targeted a global community of twentysomething fashion lovers. It strives to develop an emotional connection with its customers by publishing daily fashion and lifestyle content and by carefully curating its products. Lulus has earned huge pools of fervid fans through the creative manipulation of Instagram and other social media. By giving a pair of eyeglasses to someone in the developing world for every pair it sells and making sure there's a lot of visibility around this social mission, Warby Parker has built a fast-growing business. While each of these companies implements their strategy in a unique way, underlying the strategies is sound advice applicable to any business worried about cultivating exceptional online and in-store experiences.

In competing with Amazon, it often makes sense to ponder what Amazon is *not* good at doing. Yes, the e-commerce giant provides great selection, service, attractive prices, and fast delivery, but think of it more as a highly efficient utility providing commodities to shoppers when and where they want them. With the exception of a Walmart or Alibaba, most businesses will have a hard time besting Amazon on both price and speed. What the company *isn't* good at is building a strong brand identity—who can name the brand of Amazon's chinos or its line of midcentury furniture?—and making its customers feel special. At the scale at which Amazon operates, if the company tried to offer customized products and creative experiences for the masses of customers it serves, it would in all likelihood collapse under its own weight.

One company gaining ground in the Amazon jungle is Nike, the Beaverton, Oregon, shoe and apparel maker. The company has created an in-store experience that links to its online experience in a way that allows customers to smoothly transition between the two worlds. This requires a seamless integration of an individual's personal data, whether one is shopping online at home, on a smartphone, or in the store. Managing data in this fashion creates a highly personalized experience, like the one that can be had at the company's state-of-the-art flagship store on New York City's Fifth Avenue, which opened in 2018. The store isn't just a store but a "House of Innovation 000," with the zeros standing for "origin" or a starting point for, as Nike puts it, "what a flagship store can be for its city."

The 68,000-square-foot emporium sprawls over six floors, and clerks, wearing white scientific lab coats, scurry around the floor to attend to customers. Nike says the idea is for its staff to get to know the members of the community so it can follow their shifting tastes and desires. To that end, Nike's Fifth Avenue store has an entire floor called the Nike Speed Shop that uses local marketing data and feedback from social media to stock its shelves, and quickly restock them based on what neighborhood shoppers want. Customers can get advice from well-informed employees, dubbed store "athletes," or be guided by a digital readout in the store showing what other weekend warriors in the community have been buying. The company offers a membership program called NikePlus in which shoppers can reserve items via a cell phone app and have them held in an in-store locker, ready to try on or pick up whenever it's convenient. They can also check out on their phones, avoiding the cashier's line.

To make sneakers more than just a commodity, Nike lets shoppers order custom versions where they're allowed to pre-designate such aspects as material for the upper shell and lace color, and even add a swoosh in the shape of angel wings. Only NikePlus members get to enter (by appointment only) the top floor of the store, called the Nike Expert Studio. These shoppers get VIP treatment, including exclusive products, personal styling sessions, or advice for the best gear to run a marathon. With that kind of attention and choice, it almost feels good to shell out $200 for a pair of sneakers. So far, Nike's hybrid strategy has worked. Over a five-year period ending in early 2019, Nike's stock rose more than twice as fast as the S&P 500 stock index.

Nike isn't the only pioneer exploring the growing trend of experiential retailing—the idea that stores should provide entertainment or capture the essence of lifestyles. Not to be outdone by its rival, the California shoe and apparel maker Vans opened the House of Vans in London, a 30,000-square-foot entertainment emporium where BMX bikers and skaters can hang and watch movies, listen to live rock bands, get a power drink at the café, sign up for a drawing workshop with street artist Tom Newman, and learn how to sketch iconic Vans skate images from the glory days of yore. The main attractions, though, are concrete ramps, and a bowl, which the company says was designed for skaters by skaters. The activity at the House of Vans generates a heavy flow of posts on Instagram, Tumblr, and Facebook, which creates closely knit communities and lures new customers into the store.

The New York City bedding maker Casper decided that it wasn't in the business of selling mattresses, but rather that it was selling a better night's sleep. In its stores the company has built the Dreamery, nine sleep pods in which, for $25, shoppers can take a forty-five-minute nap—the time the company says is optimal for refreshing oneself without feeling groggy—on a Casper mattress, sheets, and pillows. Customers can reserve a spot in the Dreamery online. A bathrobe, sleep mask, and earplugs are included. After snoozing, the customer is brought into a lounge for a cup of coffee and, of course, a chat with a salesperson. Does it work? According to the company, in its first three years of existence its total revenue grew to more than $600 million.

Retailers like Casper, Nike, and others have created a compelling experience for customers in their stores. In the very near future, retail technology will become even more sophisticated, offering a further merging of online and offline shopping. A start-up named FaceFirst, for example, demonstrated a new system at the 2019 Shoptalk conference in Las Vegas that uses facial recognition to identify customers entering a store. The store asks permission by text to allow a salesclerk to download the customer's shopping history, which includes how many times the person has been at the store, the amount of time spent shopping on the last trip, what was bought, and a list of the products the customer purchased on the store's website. In exchange for sharing this personal history with the store, the customer might get electronic coupons or access to special sales. Every time a customer walks into a store, a camera identifies the person, and their shopping history pops up on clerks' phones. FaceFirst's CEO, Peter Trepp, said in an eMarketer podcast that he was working with a large retailer that had found that 4 percent of its customers made up 55 percent of its revenue. "They didn't know when that 4 percent walked through their doors," said Trepp. Facial recognition could help solve that problem.

In China, where the assumption of personal privacy is practically nonexistent, Alibaba is already using facial recognition to make it easier for shoppers to pay—and also for the giant online retailer to collect valuable customer data. Alibaba's payment arm, Ant Financial, launched in late 2017 a system called Smile to Pay that is being used, among other places, in a Chinese KFC restaurant in Hangzhou. Ant Financial is an investor in Yum China, which owns KFC in China. This is how it works. The diner walks up to a kiosk that has a screen the size of a refrigerator and scrolls down the menu, choosing fried chicken, Coca-Cola, or whatever the taste buds desire. When ready to pay, the customer looks at a circle on the screen and smiles. The amount for the meal gets charged to the diner's account. No wallet, no credit card, no cash, no smartphone, just a KFC meal delivered to the hungry customer.

At first, most people will resent being surveyed by cameras. A 2018 survey of shoppers by the research firm RichRelevance found that 61 percent of respondents found stores' use of facial recognition to identify them as "creepy." The fear is twofold. One common complaint is that it's an invasion of privacy for a business to be able to identify an individual by facial features and then have access to mounds of personal data. The other concern is that these systems aren't secure. A cyber crook could steal an image of someone from Facebook and show it to a facial recognition screen and get a free meal from KFC or, worse yet, steal money from a bank's ATM.

Most consumers will eventually get over the privacy issues raised by facial recognition. Businesses and governments already know pretty much everything about everyone, and a business downloading one's shopping history is a lot less sinister than an insurance company or an employer knowing someone's intimate medical history. As happens with most new technologies, early adopters will use facial recognition for shopping, tell their friends how convenient it is, and the masses will soon follow—just as owners of iPhone Xs have warmed quickly to the device's face recognition password system.

As for peace of mind, facial recognition systems promise to be more secure than other forms of payment. Credit card numbers, driver's license information, and passports can be stolen or forged, leading to identity theft and billions a year in losses. It turns out that it's very hard to fool a face recognition payment system. Alibaba tried to beat its system at the KFC fast-food joint by having a young Chinese woman put on a blond wig, then wear heavy makeup, and then stand in a group with four similar-looking youths wearing pink and blue wigs. Each time, the camera picked out the right person. As for the ploy of holding up purloined Facebook photos, the system uses a 3-D camera that can pick up whether the person is the real thing or a two-dimensional image. The cameras are also programmed to watch for signs of life such as a blink or a turn of the head. If that still doesn't instill confidence, when diners pick up their bucket of KFC chicken, they can type in their cell phone numbers for an extra level of security. Soon car keys, house keys, and computer passwords will be replaced by facial recognition systems. When that day arrives, the desktop file with scores of maddeningly different, hard-to-remember passwords for banking, cable bills, and shopping accounts can be tossed into the trash.

Experiential retailing will help attract customers to stores, and emerging technologies such as facial recognition will help retailers better track and serve customers once they've walked through their doors. That doesn't mean, however, that traditional retailers can ignore online sales. Some brick-and-mortar retailers with the right kind of products, such as luxury goods or custom clothing or high-end furniture and kitchen gear, can thrive by selling directly online to consumers. You can now buy on Amazon a men's Cartier Tank stainless-steel watch for $2,726 from a third-party seller. Yet, part of the luxury experience is how a shopper feels when purchasing an item and, frankly, how great can anyone feel buying a luxury watch on the same site where a can of Penn tennis balls can be bought for $2.99? On the Amazon page there's very little explanation about the watch, how it works, and its pedigree. Customers can't compare it to other Cartier watches. They can, however, save $54 if they buy it on Amazon rather than on the Cartier site. Plus, it's not clear whether this independent seller is even authorized to sell Cartier watches on Amazon, or on any other site for that matter. Is it counterfeit? Or perhaps it's gray market and comes without the manufacturer's warranty.

Compagnie Financière Richemont, the Swiss luxury group that owns Cartier, has grown to prominence by offering the world's wealthiest consumers the highest-quality products. It's now working hard to make buying luxury goods online a rewarding experience—while keeping Amazon at bay. Besides Cartier, Richemont's brands include, among others, IWC, Montblanc, and Van Cleef & Arpels. The company does most of its business in ultra-luxury stores on the grand avenues of New York, Paris, Tokyo, and Shanghai, but, as Richemont is learning, the shopping habits of the well-heeled are changing. These days, time-starved one-percenters want their shopping to be quick and easy, doable with just a tap of the screen on their smartphones. To meet this shift in the market, in 2018 Richemont announced that it was ramping up its investments in high-end Internet retail by purchasing full control of the online luxury fashion retailer Yoox Net-a-Porter for $3.4 billion. Yoox Net-a-Porter owns and operates the Internet retailers Net-a-Porter, Mr Porter, the Outnet, and Yoox, and operates e-commerce sites for more than thirty luxury brands, including Stella McCartney, Dolce & Gabbana, and Chloé.

Richemont's heavy investments in technology, logistics, and online marketing suggest that e-commerce is becoming increasingly important in the luxury market. According to a study by the consultancy Bain & Company, online sales of luxury goods rose 24 percent in 2017 and now account for 9 percent of the total market. Bain estimates that share will rise to 25 percent of the market by 2025. "With this new step, we intend to strengthen Richemont's presence and focus on the digital channel, which is becoming critically important in meeting luxury consumers' needs," said Johann Rupert, Richemont's chairman.

Of course, Bezos won't let these luxury makers expand online without a fight. Amazon has been investing heavily in the high-end fashion industry. It opened large fashion photo studios in Brooklyn, Tokyo, New Delhi, and Hoxton, UK; started its own line of fashion; and sponsored glittering events such as the Met Ball at the Metropolitan Museum of Art. It also created a "luxury beauty storefront" within its site to draw customers looking for high-end brands. More recently, Amazon cut a deal with Miami Heat shooting guard Dwyane Wade to run his own boutique of high-end active wear and sneakers on the site. But Bezos will be hard put to create a highly successful bespoke luxury experience on Amazon.com, given the company's broader and generally more down-market vibe. Ultimately, those luxury retailers that can distinguish themselves by creating online the same kind of posh and pampered experience found in their glittering stores, and by making their customers feel special in ways Amazon can't, will prevail.

Just because Amazon offers hundreds of millions of products, that doesn't mean a shopper can find everything there. Another way a business can compete with the online giant is to delight customers by offering a special, often hard-to-find selection of high-end goods. That's exactly what Williams-Sonoma does, allowing it to become the thirteenth-largest online seller in America as of 2017.

Type in "pots and pans" on Amazon and the first thing that comes up is a fifteen-piece Vremi nonstick cookware set for $43.99—yes, that's for the entire set. A group of 2,227 reviewers gave it 4.5 stars. Great deal. Go to the Williams-Sonoma site and type in the same thing, and a page appears that includes a de Buyer Prima Matera copper stockpot retailing for $800. The pot is made by a French company that was established in 1810. The key is that Williams-Sonoma controls its own inventory, ensuring that much of it is exclusive to its own channel and its own brand.

Some customers will go straight for the $43.99 set, but those interested in unique, high-end goods aren't likely to shop on Amazon. Williams-Sonoma has differentiated itself with one of the most robust Internet operations in retail, bringing in over half its revenue online, and has assembled a database of 60 million customers. Its brick-and-mortar stores, which the company calls "billboards for our brands," along with glossy catalogs, help drive online sales where margins are significantly higher than at the stores.

A custom selection of products also helps retailers avoid the kind of race-to-the-bottom price wars for which Amazon is famous. In other words, one way to compete with Amazon on price is not to compete on price. That's a lesson that Crate & Barrel CEO Neela Montgomery has taken to heart as she works to upgrade this upscale German furniture chain by modernizing stores and investing heavily in social media. Amazon sells furniture online, as do other retailers such as Wayfair and Overstock. Montgomery, however, believes she can charge a premium compared to those retailers by providing a buying experience that is all about good design and great customer service. As Montgomery explained to the *Wall Street Journal*: "Customers tell us that's something they really value about us and expect from us—a more differentiated level of service, a more personalized experience." That kind of customer obsession has served Montgomery well.

One reason that Crate & Barrel can charge more is that 95 percent of its products are unique, and when customers see something special, they generally are willing to pay more. The retailer has to be competitive on the prices of commodity items like wineglasses and silverware, but, says Montgomery, "what we've recognized is we really need to focus on differentiation and rewarding loyalty, rather than necessarily trying to outprice somebody else in the market." The company can also justify a higher price because of their 125 worldwide stores, where customers can sit in the furniture and feel the drapes and rugs. The company has built design studios in its stores to help customers get the look they want—a feature Amazon lacks. Furniture retailers that sell online only don't have that advantage, which results in a higher level of returns—and the hassles involved in returning, say, a couch—and therefore more dissatisfied customers.

So far, Montgomery's formula is working. Comparable store

sales at Crate & Barrel rose nearly 8 percent in 2017. The challenge for retailers such as Crate & Barrel arises when Amazon begins to penetrate more of the market by cutting out retailers and going directly to manufacturers. Bezos is now offering furniture makers white-glove delivery service of their products, which includes a no-hassle returns policy. Furniture makers simply sell on Amazon and leave the rest of the delivery and all the paperwork and complexity of returns to the giant.

Another way to avoid a race to the bottom with Amazon is to sell products that need a lot of hand-holding. Best Buy, the consumer electronics retailer, is one business that by all rights should've been crushed by Amazon. In the early 2000s, the Minnesota company had stores in malls with shrinking traffic, and carried TVs, small appliances, and computers—for the most part commodity products that can be bought on Amazon for less and delivered faster. Customers would engage in what the retail industry called "showrooming," where they'd go to Best Buy, find the TV screen that looked the best, and then return home to order it online for less. The company's sales and profits suffered.

CEO Hubert Joly, who ran the company from 2012 to 2019, cleverly outmaneuvered Amazon by implementing a strategy called Renew Blue. It marries an improved online experience with a store strategy that entails a massive shift to products requiring advice and installation, such as complicated home theater hookups and home Wi-Fi and security systems. Best Buy's Geek Squad, its service and installation arm, travels to homes and offices to help with such complex installations. As Rodney Zemmel, the global head of McKinsey's Digital and Analytics practice, explains about retailing in general: "You have to ask yourself: What do you have that is really defensible? What have you got that is store or human being dependent? How do you compete on quality of customer experience?"

Of course, Best Buy had to keep prices down to compete with Amazon. It started to match prices and offer free delivery and store pickup. One way it keeps expenses low is by having stores within stores. Google, Microsoft, Samsung, and other makers of consumer electronics have opened boutiques within Best Buy stores, which lowers the cost of the retailer's floor space. Over a three-year period starting in early 2016, Best Buy's stock more than doubled—far outpacing the S&P 500 stock index.

Crate & Barrel, Williams-Sonoma, Best Buy, and Richemont have found a balance between selling directly online and through their stores, and it's a formula that in the future should be a winner. Yet if these and other companies want to keep pace with Amazon, they must up their technological expertise. Amazon's mastery of technology is legendary: its customer-friendly platform makes shopping fast, easy, and intuitive. As Amazon cranks its AI flywheel to increase its online domination, retailers that want to compete will need to become, essentially, tech companies with the proper mind-set—the algorithm is king. The key is to offer one's own unique brand of technological superiority.

One business that's using technology to great advantage is Sephora, the global beauty chain owned by the Parisian luxury conglomerate LVMH. In 2017, the cosmetics retailer was gaining market share and hitting record revenue growth. Headquartered in San Francisco, the home of Twitter, Salesforce.com, and Uber, Sephora is as much a tech company as it is a beauty retailer.

The company constantly experiments with different tech systems to engender customer delight. At its more than 1,100 locations across the Americas, a program called Color IQ uses digital devices to scan a shopper's face, capture the exact skin tone, and calculate the best shades for lipstick, powders, eyeliners, and foundations. Once customers find the right combination, that information is recorded in a database and more of the item can be ordered later online. It has also created a social net-work called Beauty Insider Community that allows members of Sephora's loyalty program to share reviews, photos, and get pro-duction recommendations. It reaches its fans on Facebook with interactive catalogs. It even has an app dubbed Sephora Virtual Artist that lets a customer pull up a 3-D live view of their face on a smartphone and virtually try on makeup products. Like a mir-ror, the view of the face moves as the user moves. Shoppers can digitally try on different products and learn better techniques from step-by-step tutorials. The company has garnered all this technology to create a seamless experience between their brick-and-mortar and online stores.

One key advantage that Sephora has over Amazon is that it designs its algorithms to keep consumers fenced within its own apps and sites. This gives the beauty company the data to be able to recommend the right products to their customers and to make sure it's a Sephora product. Compare that to Amazon or one of its third-party merchants trying to sell a beauty prod-uct on Amazon. They must compete with the dozens of other brands that pop up on the site.

Another retailer that has figured out how to outfox Amazon is the women's online clothing store Stitch Fix. Katrina Lake launched her start-up from her Cambridge, Massachusetts, apartment in 2011 while attending the Harvard Business School. The company went public in late 2017 and today has a market cap of $2 billion. Her secret? Marshaling data to provide her online customers with the kind of hands-on service Amazon can only dream of.

Selling clothing has always been a tough business, and Ama-zon is a formidable competitor. In 2018, Morgan Stanley said that Amazon would grab nearly 10 percent of the U.S. clothing market, beating out Walmart and Target to become the biggest garment retailer in the U.S. With its hard-to-beat combination of wide selection, great prices, and hassle-free returns, the company saw its clothing sales grow double digits that year while sales at other retailers such as Macy's, Nordstrom, and JCPenney actually declined. It's tough to compete with Amazon on price and selection alone, and they're right to consider customer service one of their great strengths. However, even though customer obsession is a key tenet of Bezonomics, what Amazon *can't* do is create a highly personalized customer experience that resonates with people. As one private equity executive told me: "In the world of conventional retail we talk about the eye of the merchant. Merchants who have it can predict fashions. That's not Amazon. If you open up an Amazon page, it's ugly. When Bezos talks about customer obsession it's very narrow. It's about being the best utility, not about being good at fashion or hands-on service." Indeed. Amazon operates at such a scale that it doesn't make financial sense for it to hire armies of humans who can provide personalized advice to customers.

That shortcoming opens up an opportunity for businesses both large and small and in any industry to differentiate themselves. Realizing that retailers can no longer offer up a generic user experience and still win, Lake is spearheading a retailing movement driven by mass customization and obsession for brands. Her research told her that people don't necessarily enjoy going into stores and sorting through hundreds of items of clothing in search of something they like. It also showed that many find online shopping tedious. As she told the *Los Angeles Times*: "As a consumer, you don't want to choose from a million pairs of jeans. You just want the one pair that's going to fit you and look great on you. There was such a great opportunity there. What consumers wanted was not reflected in the marketplace." Lake decided to fill that gap with a new, uber-personalized service.

Here's how Stitch Fix works. Customers fill out a detailed profile—their budget, measurements, what styles, colors, and labels they like, how they plan to use the clothes, etc.—and receive a box of five pieces of clothing, shoes, or jewelry monthly, bimonthly, or quarterly. The items are handpicked by Stitch Fix's stylists, who use data they collect from customers' profiles to find clothes most likely to please. Stitch Fix charges a $20 fee for each box, which goes toward any purchases the customer makes. Clients pay for the clothing they keep and can easily return what they don't want.

Lake's secret weapon is combining data analytics (she has one hundred computer scientists on staff) with a well-trained staff of fashion advisors who hand-select clothes to increase the odds that people will like what they order. "Fundamentally what we're offering," Lake said in an interview with MarketWatch, "is personalization. Our data can say, for example, this client has a 50% chance of keeping this denim."

What Amazon can't match is Stitch Fix's highly personalized experience. Amazon's business model is driven by algorithms rather than people. Its goal is to eliminate as many humans as possible from the retail equation to keep its costs low. That's an opening that gives Stitch Fix an advantage. Lake's promise is to provide her customers with a personal shopper armed with smart data analytics, no matter their budget—something that would be impossible to do economically in a brick-and-mortar store and tough to do online, especially at the scale and the low-price points where Amazon operates. Her formula has propelled the monumental growth of Stitch Fix. The San Francisco company had sales of $1.2 billion in fiscal 2018, and was employing some 3,500 full- and part-time stylists to suit customers' tastes.

Like all entrepreneurs and business leaders who compete with Amazon, Lake realizes that Jeff Bezos doesn't stand still. In early 2018, the e-commerce giant launched a new service called Prime Wardrobe that lets customers try on clothing before buying it. (Sound familiar?) Customers can order multiple items and then decide whether they want to keep any of the clothing or send it back. With Prime Wardrobe, customers can also take advantage of a new style assistant called Echo Look, an Alexa-driven camera that takes pictures or videos of the outfit the person is wearing, showing the clothes from all angles, and allowing the images to be shared with friends to get opinions on what works and what doesn't for that important meeting or upcoming date.

With Amazon nipping at its heels, Stitch Fix needs to up its game, and it's doing just that. The company keeps reinvesting in its business, hiring more data scientists, improving its algorithms, and expanding into new markets, such as the UK. In 2018, it added 3 million new customers.

Another small company that figured out how to avoid the Amazon trap is women's fashion seller Lulus. Founded by the mother-daughter team Debra Cannon and Colleen Winter, this online retailer sells everything from bohemian blouses to suede mules to pink sequined maxi dresses at reasonable prices. Says Winter: "If you search for a black dress on Amazon, you might get 10,000 choices. We have a very curated selection, and we give our customers what they want when they want it. We deliver a very consistent brand. If they order a 'small' size from us, they know it will probably fit." Lulus, which is based in California and sells in seventy-six countries, mostly targets fashion-forward teens and millennials. It is, however, the company's shrewd social media strategy that is helping to drive growth and helped it attract in 2018 an additional $120 million in venture capital.

What Winter understands is that to get out from under the Amazon shadow a retailer has to meet its customers where they're most likely to be, making it more convenient and fun for them to shop. This means keeping on top of social media trends, moving quickly to different platforms when your customers do, and making sure the company's user interface is extremely customer friendly. In Winter's case, she knew her customers were millennials who did much of their socializing—and shopping—on their Instagram app.

Winter depends on thousands of social influencers she calls ambassadors to spread the word about its clothing online. Some receive payment from Lulus to create online content, others are just enthusiastic fans of the brand who like to post the latest fashions. The beautiful photos and comments that the ambassadors post on sites such as Pinterest and Instagram help reinforce brand awareness and attract new customers. Does it work? Winter says it's more art than science. She does measure how much she paid for a post and then looks at how many "likes" and comments the post received, but that doesn't tell the entire story. Social media is hard to quantify by looking at overnight numbers on the posts, says Winter. "If we have fifteen posts go live on Instagram every day, what's the return? You just have to believe in it because in the long run you get results." She claims that #Lulus has become one of the top retail hashtags up there with Chanel and Gucci. As Noelle Sadler, Lulus's vice president of marketing, told *Adweek*, "An overwhelming majority of Lulus' customers originally discovered our brand through word-of-mouth—either directly from a friend or through social media—and Instagram continues to be a key discovery platform for us." Sadler claims that nearly 33 percent of the people on Instagram who tapped to learn more about Lulus's products ended up visiting its site. And that makes for good business. As of 2019, Lulus had 1.3 million followers.

Lulus is taking full advantage of a new feature offered by

Instagram that lets retailers sell directly to the 800 million users of the photo-sharing site. When someone sees one of Lulus's carefully curated ads on Instagram, they can now start shopping directly within the app. They can click on the "tap to view" icon to find out more details and prices and then select "Shop Now" to buy the Lulus item.

Amazon is many things, but one thing in particular it's not known for is its social conscience. The company has been criticized for working conditions in its warehouses and has come late to the game on promises to convert its massive, energy-hogging server farms to zero carbon. A start-up named Warby Parker figured it could thrive in an Amazon world by building a business that appeals to people's best instincts. Since its founding in 2010, Warby Parker, the fashion-forward eyeglasses maker, has sold more than a million pairs. For every pair it sells, it gives one away to the poor in the developing world. (Amazon sells prescription eyeglasses, but the customer has to bring them to an optometrist for the lenses.)

What kind of business model gives away its product? Founders Neil Blumenthal and David Gilboa told me that it's a smart one, because being part of a social cause helps strengthen both its brand image and its customer service. Warby Parker manufactures and sells high-quality eyeglasses for around $100, or a small fraction of what a traditional pair costs. It does this by making its own glasses, selling the bulk of them online, and cutting out optometrist shops that mark up eyeglasses tenfold or more. Known for its superior customer service and its cool stores, the rapidly growing New York City company raised $300 million in capital and as of 2018 was valued at $1.8 billion.

Because of the persuasiveness of social media and the expectations of a socially woke millennial generation, every company is totally exposed when it comes to corporate values. That's a lesson that Warby Parker has been well aware of since its inception. Its company is designed not only to make a profit but also to achieve social good in a way that will be embraced by its customers. This gives it an advantage over Amazon, which, while it's trying to improve its social and environmental reputation, doesn't really have a strong identity when it comes to those issues.

When the founders of Warby Parker were business school students at UPenn, they came up with the idea for their eyeglasses company during a conversation over the kitchen table. David Gilboa had lost a pair and couldn't believe he'd have to shell out $700 for a replacement. He discussed with friend Neil Blumenthal whether there wasn't room for a business that could sell fashionable specs for less.

The plan for the business included social philanthropy from the start. As Blumenthal explained to me: "Our social mission was never an add-on. Core to our thinking was we wanted to build the kind of organization that when our alarm went off in the morning we didn't want to roll over and hit the snooze button."

But how does an entrepreneur make a positive impact on the world without getting distracted? Their first priority was to create a stakeholder-centric model, which means the company would serve its customers, investors, and the community at large. Warby Parker would serve customers by selling them affordable glasses and providing great service, and please their investors by doing so at a profit.

The company then used its social mission to help create a motivated team of workers who could provide superb in-store and online service—a hallmark of their brand. "The biggest benefit we've seen is on the employee side," says Blumenthal, "where we've been able to attract some of the most talented and passionate people in the world." To help keep the passion going, Warby Parker sends employees who've worked at the company for three years on a trip to the developing world so that they can see the difference its eyeglass giveaway program is making among the poor.

"What gets us psyched now," says Blumenthal, "is that we want to demonstrate to the world that we can scale a business while doing good in the world, without charging a premium for our product." Given the company's sales growth, it's clear that consumers are responding to Warby Parker's social missions and its enthusiastic salespeople. It has found a good way to compete against Amazon and make the world a better place.

Each of the companies profiled in this chapter reflects a different critical strength. Nike, Vans, and Casper offer a remarkable in-store experience linked to a compelling online experience. Williams-Sonoma and Crate & Barrel provide a highly curated selection of products. Sephora and Stitch Fix and Lulus are leaders in retail technology and social media. Warby Parker profits from having a strong and clear social mission.

Many of these strategies apply most obviously to retailers, but they're just as relevant to other industries about to be attacked by Amazon. Industries such as health care, banking, and advertising are vulnerable. Companies in these industries would all do well to understand how Bezonomics works, because Amazon will soon be applying its low prices, great service, and mighty AI flywheel to conquering their realm, too.

And it's happening faster than most think.

CHAPTER 13

Amazon Unbound

One brilliant fall day, I was strolling up Madison Avenue for a meeting at the Council on Foreign Relations building with a colleague who is a managing director at McKinsey, the largest and arguably the most influential global consulting firm. My friend has the ear of some of the most prominent CEOs in the world. As a longtime journalist and writer of business books, I have a pretty good grasp of the C-suite zeitgeist, and on our walk we concurred that the hot topic these days is Amazon. CEOs, directors, and investors are all abuzz about how the e-commerce giant is threatening to swallow up markets like a Category 5 hurricane. Clothing. Groceries. Consumer electronics. Media. The Cloud. Health care. Shipping. Finance could be next. *Jeff Bezos is moving into my industry, what are we going to do? We can't compete against its prices. We can't match its speed, its deep pockets, or the brand recognition of its smiling A-to-Z logo. How do we Amazon-proof our company?* Everywhere you turn, businesses are reeling from Amazon shock.

On that walk, I asked my McKinsey colleague if he'd be interested in writing a book about how to compete with Amazon. He replied that McKinsey was making so much money advising its clients on that very topic, why give away its secrets?

As that conversation with my friend suggests, an entire industry of consultants is emerging to advise businesses on how to compete with Amazon. Why do so many business leaders see Amazon as a threat? After all, the company is a highly successful e-tailer, but what does it know about other industries?

Those who don't fear Amazon—yet—argue that history is littered with companies that strayed outside of their field of expertise and failed. The conglomerates of the 1960s and 1970s such as Harold Geneen's ITT, which at one point controlled 350 companies in 80 countries, and Charlie Bluhdorn's Gulf and Western, which became known as "Engulf and Devour," started out as stars in a single industry or two but eventually collapsed under their own weight. No one CEO, no matter how skilled, can handle the kind of complexity presented by scores of starkly different markets, customers, and technologies. On top of that, the original savings and efficiencies that come from putting these businesses together eventually disappear as encroaching, complex bureaucracies cause the collective enterprise to lose focus.

At least, that's the argument.

One can almost hear the leaders of industries threatened by Bezos breathe a collective sigh of relief, but not so fast. Amazon is different in one crucial way. With the exception of Whole Foods, it doesn't acquire big businesses in different industries and try to run them. Instead it organically builds businesses in new sectors, sometimes making a relatively small (under $1 billion each) strategic acquisition to acquire the talent or technology it needs to get its invasion armies rolling. Think of Twitch, the online gaming channel; Ring, the digital doorbell start-up; and the online pharmacy PillPack. Amazon then has the patience and capital to make a new business work no matter how long it takes. It's willing to lose money for years on a new business, and it has been given permission by Wall Street to do so. It can

keep prices artificially low until it has attracted enough customers to become a leader in whatever field it's targeting. These tactics from the Bezonomics playbook are applied across swaths of
industries.

What is particularly worrisome about this strategy to Amazon's competitors is that Bezos has a strong record when it comes
to picking industry-disrupting technologies. Over the years
Bezos personally was an early investor in Google, Uber, Twitter,
Airbnb, and Juno Therapeutics. Another worry is that Amazon
has unparalleled technological firepower, which it can apply to
any sector it invades. Better than any company, it can scan transactions on its site and learn who its potential customers are as
well as their desires and habits. Once Amazon targets a sector
of the economy, it applies its AI flywheel—driven by massive
amounts of customer data—and starts pushing slowly, offering
above and beyond what's expected to attract more customers,
which gives it the revenues it needs to provide better products
and services at lower prices, which in turn attracts more and
more customers—and the flywheel turns faster and faster.

This is exactly what Amazon did to the book industry when
it launched in 1995. It underpriced the book chains and lost
money doing so until it became the dominant seller of books
in the U.S. When Amazon thought that readers might want a
more convenient way to read books it launched the Kindle in
2007 and, after years of losses and some false starts, grabbed 80
percent of the e-reader market, in the process becoming a consumer electronics company. Its latest hit product, the Amazon
Echo with Alexa—which the company offered at a loss or at best
breakeven—has obtained a dominant position worldwide. Now
the e-tailer is expanding into the smart home industry, making
its own Wi-Fi-linked microwaves, clocks, and security cameras,
and the list goes on. In early 2018, it even invested in a small pre-

fab housing manufacturer, suggesting that the company might someday build homes that feature Amazon's growing selection of smart appliances. Along those lines, Amazon already has a deal with Lennar, the nation's largest homebuilder, to preinstall Alexa in all the company's new homes.

Another way that Amazon invades a new industry is to take something that it does well internally and then offer that service to others. The computer expertise that Amazon acquired while selling books online was impressive. Why not share that capability with other businesses? In 2006, Amazon Web Services was born. After a decade of building web applications, Amazon realized it had developed a core competency in operating computer infrastructure and data centers at a massive scale and that it could offer cloud services for customers at a great price. Today, AWS is the largest cloud computing company in the world by a wide margin. And since the folks at AWS were also really good at AI and machine learning, why not sell that knowledge to customers at an attractive price? Swami Sivasubramanian, who manages machine learning for AWS, says, "All the expertise we've learned over the last twenty years at Amazon we've packaged up and now offer to our customers." Amazon's Machine Learning service business now offers tools to help other businesses develop voice and facial recognition, speech to text, and other machine-learning skills. The offering is now a small but fast-growing part of AWS.

All this is familiar history. The crucial question is: Which industries will Bezos target next? Imagine a software program that can screen for which new targets are on Amazon's radar screen. The imaginary algorithm would produce a list of industries that share some vulnerabilities that Amazon can easily breech—for example, they sell to a mass market, their service is meh, or their products or services cost a lot. As Bezos once quipped, "Your margin is my opportunity." Over this initial screen, the algorithm would place another screen, selecting for industries that to greater or lesser extent are ripe for disruption through AI—for example, businesses where costly human labor (and thinking) can be replaced by smart machines.

The industries that most closely match those characteristics are advertising, health care, banking, and insurance. Amazon has already made some very early moves into these sectors, suggesting that these industries are already in its sights—although the secretive company does not comment on these initiatives. Heavy manufacturing companies like Airbus or Boeing or Nucor Steel can rest easy. So can businesses that rely heavily on the human touch, such as restaurants and home health-care providers, or ones that perform highly skilled work, such as law firms and strategy consultancies. All others pay heed.

Of the new industries Amazon is invading, it has gained the most traction so far in advertising. Anyone who visits Amazon.com today is confronted with a clutter of sponsored products at the top of the page—digital ads begging shoppers to buy an air cooker or one of a dozen look-alike hoodie sweatshirts. However, it wasn't always this way. For years Bezos's rock-solid tenet of always pleasing customers made the company wary of annoying them or overwhelming them with ads on its site. That has changed. As Jeff Wilke, who runs the company's global e-commerce business, put it: "We started out by selling one item at a time, making a small profit on each of those transactions. We were so focused on making sure the customer experience was great, we were nervous that if we introduced ads it might distract from the customer experience. We just took our time. We experimented with ways to reveal ad placements that were useful to customers, and that manufacturers and brands wanted to bid on. . . . And we happened to, over the last couple of years, have hit on some placements that are really working. And that just compounds it. We think of ads as something that, if it can enhance the customer or the seller experience in a way, why not try it?"

Wilke makes Amazon's foray into advertising seem like a modest undertaking, just a natural extension of giving customers what they want. The truth is that Amazon, drawing on the digital expertise and ruthlessness it applies to most of what it does, is now hard bent on disrupting the $327 billion global digital ad market. Its targets? Google, Facebook, and Alibaba—three companies that account for two-thirds of the total market. In the mid-2010s, Amazon generated little or no advertising revenue from its site. When it realized it could sell display space on Amazon.com without losing customers, it geared up that business and by 2018 recorded roughly $10 billion in advertising revenue. Amazon, however, is still a distant third in the $129 billion U.S. digital ad market, behind Google and Facebook, which together control nearly two-thirds of that market. But Amazon's ad revenues are growing fast. A 2019 report by Juniper Research predicts that Amazon's advertising revenues will reach $40 billion by 2023. And because Amazon's retail business already pays for the huge server farms it needs to operate, a huge chunk of the company's ad revenue falls right to the bottom line, making it a highly profitable business. Morgan Stanley estimated in 2019 that Amazon's advertising business was worth $125 billion, more than the stock market value of Nike or IBM, making it a potential third pillar at the company along with e-commerce and cloud computing.

Amazon knows things about its customers that most marketers can only dream about. It tracks who has bought Tom's toothpaste in the last month, whether someone prefers Nike to Reebok, where they live—Amazon has their shipping addresses, of course—what they watch on Prime Video or listen to on Prime Music, how old their kids are from the kinds of toys bought, and so on. All these data allow Amazon to have a pretty good idea of what customers want. It's no surprise, then, that more than half of all shopping searches now start on Amazon, displacing Google, which used to be the place shoppers went to first to search for goods.

Amazon's main advantage over its rivals, though, is that it can reach people just when they're in a buying state of mind. Google can locate people who—based on their search history—might be interested in buying a pair of tennis shoes. But could it be that these folks have simply been researching how to improve their backhand and have no interest in buying shoes? Facebook can direct advertisers to people who might be talking on the social network about the U.S. Open or Roger Federer's serving technique. While the capacities Google and Facebook have are powerful, it's difficult for these tech giants to track which people, once shown an ad, buy a product or don't. Amazon, though, can place an ad for tennis shoes in front of someone who is actually shopping for tennis shoes, and it has the technology to track whether the ad actually generates a sale. One advertiser found that 20 percent of the Amazon shoppers that clicked on its ad purchased the product, compared to an industry average of about 1 percent.

As Amazon builds its U.S. advertising business, it hopes to grab up much of the international market as well. In China, Alibaba, the Amazon of the East, already has established a formidable ad business. In 2018, according to eMarketer, Alibaba's China retail business chalked up $22 billion in digital ad revenue, about a third of the total Chinese market. While Amazon in 2019 announced it would close down its site in China, it will wage a fierce battle with Alibaba over the global ad market in places such as Europe and India. The point is that Amazon has the scale, the technical know-how, and the loyal customers to become a major force in the global advertising market. It's only a matter of time before Amazon's ad operation reaches critical mass and starts to put serious heat on its rivals.

While the advertising market is one of Amazon's fastest-growing new segments, in the long run that business could pale next to another of the company's undertakings—revolutionizing the health-care industry.

John Doerr is one of the world's most successful venture capitalists. As a partner at the Sand Hill Road powerhouse Kleiner Perkins, he was an early investor in both Google and Amazon. Doerr served on the Amazon board from 1995 to 2010 and is a friend of Bezos's. In late 2018, he made a stunning prediction at a *Forbes* health-care conference in New York City. When asked about disruption in the health-care industry, he said: "Amazon has assembled an amazing asset with 120 million people who are Prime subscribers. Imagine what it's going to be like when Bezos rolls out Prime Health, which I'm convinced he will."

Doerr was onto something. The venture capitalist didn't delve into details, but it's easy to imagine—based on Amazon's nascent activity in this field—that Prime Health could offer customers prescription drugs, home health-care products, access to health records, and remote monitoring by doctors and nurses. This is what is making industry leaders jittery. A 2018 survey of senior health-care executives conducted by Reaction Data asked which new entrant into the field will have the biggest impact. Some 59 percent pointed to Amazon. Apple (with its iWatch that monitors a person's health) followed with 14 percent. Every other potential interloper scored single digits.

The same survey found that 29 percent of health-care executives believed telemedicine will have the biggest impact on their industry, followed by artificial intelligence at 20 percent. Those two areas are perfectly suited for Amazon. It's a leader in AI, and its Alexa—combined with the Echo Show device with a built-in screen—places it in a perfect position to offer home care via the Internet. Amazon has another advantage here. Trust is a crucial element in health care—who wants to put one's well-being in the hands of some fly-by-night operator—and Amazon is the most trusted brand in America.

As of the writing of this book, Amazon hadn't announced a Prime Health initiative for the general public, but early signs point in that direction, suggesting that the company has painted a target on the back of the $3.5 trillion health-care market in the U.S. and an even bigger market internationally. Besides its acquisition in 2018 of the online pharmacy company PillPack, Amazon in late 2018 signed a deal with the Arcadia Group to create a line of home health-care products, including blood pressure cuffs and glucose monitors under the brand Choice that will be sold exclusively on its site. Over the years, Amazon has acquired licenses to sell medical supplies in forty-seven states. As for the very long view, Amazon is working with Seattle's Fred Hutchinson Cancer Research Center to use machine learning to help prevent and cure cancers.

Bringing about real change in the calcified health-care sector won't be easy, and few know that better than Bezos. Over the years, Amazon has tried to enter the field with little to show for it. In the late 1990s, the company invested in Drugstore.com and Bezos became a director, but the online pharmacy supplier was eventually sold to Walgreens, which in the end closed it down. Amazon likes to move fast and to operate on the cheap, but the pharmacy business is the exact opposite. It's burdened by regulations, the need for state licenses, and other hurdles. And let's face it: delivering medicine to customers can be complicated. Some medicine, for instance, needs refrigeration or insulated packaging, which increases cost and complexity. The health-care industry also operates inside an intricate web of long-standing contracts between hospitals, suppliers, drug benefit managers, insurers, and physicians that's hard for an outsider like Amazon to infiltrate.

Despite the long odds, Bezos has decided to double down on health care. The company's logistics have become more sophisticated and its pockets deeper—and, besides, if Amazon wants to maintain its rapid growth pace, it will need new markets to penetrate. As a first step, Bezos in 2014 hired Babak Parviz, an Iranian immigrant who previously headed Google X, a respected research facility (now a division of Alphabet called X) that worked on various moonshot projects, including kites that gather wind energy, the Google Glass virtual-reality headset, and self-driving cars—an initiative that eventually became the Alphabet subsidiary Waymo. Just as at Google, Parviz's innovation lab at Amazon, which is named Grand Challenge, will have, as its name suggests, a broad mandate to take the long view and to tinker creatively on some of the world's biggest problems. A job posting for the lab cited astronomer Carl Sagan: "Somewhere, something incredible is waiting to be known." One of Parviz's key areas of interest is health care.

Yes, Grand Challenge has a broad mandate, but it's interesting to note that many of Parviz's direct reports have deep experience in health care, suggesting that's where the team will place a great deal of its focus. There's Adam Siegel, a cofounder of Skye Health, a health solution start-up that came out of Stanford; David Heckerman, a twenty-plus-year veteran of Microsoft and later the chief data scientist at a genomics start-up called Human Longevity; and Douglas Weibel, who has a PhD in chemistry and cofounded two health-care companies. Of Parviz's twelve direct reports, half have backgrounds in medicine.

One of Parviz's projects, code-named Hera, is working in partnership with AWS, the company's cloud service, to make medical records more accurate and accessible. For example, it's using AI to clean up a patient's history. The first-known product emerging from these labs is a piece of software that scrubs employee health records to unearth coding mistakes, inaccuracies, and pertinent information. Its market is health insurers who want to more accurately assess the risks of the population they cover.

One big opportunity for Amazon is to make medical records as easy to use as an app on a smartphone. Today in the U.S. most medical records reside in two big software systems: Epic and Cerner. Some of the patient data is inaccurate, and most of it is siloed—doctors, hospitals, and the patients themselves don't have easy access to all the information in one place. Anyone who has spent time trying to transfer medical records from one doctor's office to another knows the hassle involved. Doctors complain of spending an intolerable amount of time entering data and searching through databases for a particular test result or piece of family history—time that could be spent providing quality care for patients. Anyone who has sat in an examination room while the doctor has eyes glued to a computer screen is familiar with this irksome situation.

All that medical data needs to be liberated, which won't be easy given privacy regulations both in the U.S. and abroad. But if health-care platforms can be open in the same way that Apple's iOS and Google's Android smartphone platforms are open to developers, companies like Amazon, Google, and Apple along with a host of entrepreneurial start-ups can unleash a wave of innovation in health care.

Perhaps Bezos's steepest challenge will be breaking in to the U.S. pharmacy business. In May 2017, Amazon put together a team to explore ways to capitalize on this $400-billion-a-year industry, and a little more than a year later the company announced the acquisition of the online drug seller PillPack. That company's specialty is to deliver to patients packets that contain the right daily doses of their medicine—especially useful for seniors who get confused about which pills to take when. Bezos picked Nader Kabbani, who helped put the Kindle e-reader on the map, to run Amazon's new pharmacy business—suggesting that the company is looking for fresh thinking in that area. Kabbani has no experience in health care, but is a seasoned Amazon executive who has gained Bezos's trust. This assignment highlights the power of Bezonomics and its AI flywheel, which allows Bezos to pick executives to run businesses they know little about. In 2011, he assigned Greg Hart to oversee the Alexa program even though he had no experience in voice recognition or in consumer electronics. By applying the rock-solid principles of the AI flywheel— start with the customer first, find ways to drive down costs, which frees capital to invest in more features, which attracts more customers, which allows for economies of scale to drive down costs, and so on—he made Alexa a huge success.

PillPack is tiny compared to pharmacy giants such as CVS Health, Walgreens, and Walmart. Its revenues in 2018 were $100 million compared to the $134 billion that CVS Health chalked up in pharmacy sales. At this point, size isn't the issue. Amazon sees the acquisition as a way to get its Prime members used to buying health-care products from Amazon. (In early 2019 it started sending emails to some of its Prime members urging them to sign up for PillPack.) Patients could take advantage of Amazon's same-day delivery to get their medicines, and it's not inconceivable that the company could open up pharmacies in its Whole Foods stores as well as in its chain of new, lower-cost grocery stores that sources say it will open.

Around the same time as the 2018 PillPack acquisition, Amazon announced that it would join Berkshire Hathaway—run by legendary investor Warren Buffett—and JPMorgan Chase—run by banking's highest-profile CEO, Jamie Dimon—to form a nonprofit partnership, later dubbed Haven. The idea is to shake up the broken U.S. health-care system. The organization appointed Atul Gawande as CEO. If anyone has a shot at draining the health-care swamp, it's Gawande. He's a surgeon at the prestigious Brigham and Women's Hospital in Boston and a professor at Harvard Medical School and has written four bestselling books on health care, including *Complications*, which was a finalist for the National Book Award. He's also a longtime staff writer at *The New Yorker*, where in the fall of 2018 he wrote a memorable article titled "Why Doctors Hate Their Computers," which argued that health-care software was so dysfunctional that some doctors were becoming depressed or even suicidal.

Combined, Amazon, Berkshire, and Chase have 1.2 million employees, and the mandate of Haven is to make health care for them better, easier to navigate, and more affordable. This nonprofit isn't just a think tank. If Haven works, it would in the long run save these giants hundreds of millions in health-care costs. Haven won't talk about its strategy, but a federal court case brought against it and its three corporate backers by Optum, a division of the giant insurer UnitedHealth Group, shed some light on the nonprofit's mission.

Optum sued to keep one of its former executives, David Smith, who'd joined Haven in 2018, from working there. The giant insurer charged that Smith had removed confidential, proprietary information that could benefit his new employer. Smith denied the charges. In its complaint, Optum argued that Haven "will very soon be a direct competitor, if it is not already." If anything, this characterization of Haven certainly exposed how nervous mainstream health-care insurers have become about Amazon entering their market in any guise.

A transcript of a trial hearing gave a glimpse of Haven's intentions. In it, Jack Stoddard, Haven's chief operating officer at the time, said the venture was exploring whether it could "reinvent what insurance looks like in terms of benefit design." He said that health insurance is complex, and employees get confused about their coverage. He also said that Haven would be conducting small tests to make primary-care access easier and chronic-care drugs cheaper. The COO added that Haven wants to "make it easier for doctors to do good care and to spend more time, not less time" providing care. One can imagine Optum executives worrying that Amazon will use its formidable data analytics to figure out which treatments are truly cost-effective, and which doctors are getting positive results, and then build easy-to-use digital health tools that will steal patients from Optum.

How much of a threat *does* Amazon pose to giant health-care incumbents such as UnitedHealth, CVS Health, and Walgreens? In the short run, not much. Health care is a tough industry to crack with its complexity, regulation, and politicization—and baked in to it is the need for a highly hands-on and localized treatment of patients. That doesn't mean the industry isn't worried. In 2018, CVS Health, partly in response to Amazon's health-care moves, bought the giant insurer Aetna. The combined company now provides health insurance and pharmaceuticals to roughly 116 million Americans, and it's working hard to reinvent the way health care is delivered. CVS stores, for example, now contain 1,100 mini-clinics where patients can receive basic health services and pick up their prescriptions. Those 50 million customers give CVS Health a much bigger playing field than the 1.2 million Haven has to work with. One CVS Health director told me in a not-for-attribution conversation that Haven was basically "a toy for two rich guys and their banker."

Notwithstanding these headwinds and an entrenched industry possessing billions of dollars to protect its turf, Amazon *does* pose a major threat in the long term. It likely won't unfold, though, in the way most people think. Rather than look at the PillPack acquisition as a direct assault on the giant pharmacy companies, it makes more sense to see it as a Trojan horse designed to help Amazon become a leading player in telemedicine. Put simply, "telemedicine" means diagnosing patients and delivering drugs to them in the home, office, or just about wherever they happen to be. This is the area where Amazon is likely to have the biggest impact on health-care systems both in the U.S. and abroad.

Whether it's named Prime Health, as John Doerr predicted, or something else, an Amazon Health membership program could be pitched to the company's more than 300 million customers globally. The company's massive customer database, combined with its unparalleled data diagnostics and AI capabilities, could allow it to become the gatekeeper for medical services and purchases. Instead of displacing health-care giants like CVS Health or UnitedHealth, Amazon in some instances might act in partnership with them. This, however, poses a threat to the profits of these health-care giants, which is one reason the stocks of major health-care providers took a substantial dip on the day Amazon announced it was buying PillPack.

Signaling that it's dead serious about becoming a telemedicine provider, Amazon announced in the spring of 2019 that it had met the requirements under the Health Insurance Portability and Accountability Act, known as HIPAA, a stringent, federal health privacy law. That means it can now transmit sensitive patient information through Alexa and other pieces of its software. So far, six companies—including insurer Cigna, the diabetes-management company Livongo Health, and three major hospital systems—

have developed HIPPA-compliant Alexa apps for, among other things, scheduling appointments, tracking drug shipments, and reading blood-sugar results.

Here is how Prime Health could work. As an add-on feature to a Prime membership, a customer could sign up for Prime Health for an annual fee. In exchange, customers—let's think of them now as *members*—could get access to Amazon's health services, which might include discounts on a range of health-care products—everything from over-the-counter and prescription drugs to glucose and blood pressure monitors. Members would opt in, allowing Amazon access to their personal medical records. Amazon could use its data analytics and AI to recommend simple treatments or which doctors to see for particular maladies. Say a member uses an online blood pressure monitor and gets a high reading. Amazon could not only recommend that the person see a doctor but also offer a list of physicians who offer the best outcomes for the lowest cost. The patient and provider work that Haven has undertaken could help inform these decisions.

As a preview of what such a system might look like, Amazon in the fall of 2019 launched an app called Amazon Care for its employees in Seattle. The app connects employees to a nurse who can provide advice; can arrange videoconferences with doctors and nurses for diagnoses, treatments, and referrals; and can request a home visit from a nurse for exams, testing, and treatment. The app can also be used to order drugs for delivery right to one's door. The future potential of such a service is huge. Feeling down in the dumps? Alexa might suggest that the member contact their doctor. (Amazon has filed a patent for Alexa to pick up the sound of sniffles or a cough, and Alexa already offers simple first-aid advice.) When the member asks Alexa to set up an appointment with an Amazon-recommended doctor (five stars!), a time and day is downloaded to his or her calendar. At the appointed time, a doctor pops up on the screen and conducts the exam. If the member has a sore throat, a positive do-it-yourself strep test—$32.49 for a pack of twenty-five tests on Amazon— would allow the doctor to prescribe antibiotics, which would be delivered to the member's home a few hours later by, of course, Amazon. In cases of serious illness, nothing replaces an office visit, but telemedicine could cut down on costly visits to a doctor's office or to an emergency room just to treat a sore throat or a minor flu.

A service like Prime Health is likely to appeal to millions because as health insurance deductibles rise, patients are paying closer attention to the cost of health care. A survey by the Commonwealth Fund found that a third of Americans over sixty-five said they had either skipped going to the doctor when sick or failed to fill prescriptions because they couldn't afford the out-of-pocket costs. If Amazon could apply the same extreme cost-cutting techniques to medicine as it does to e-commerce, the savings could be significant.

In the spring of 2019, a little-noticed and seemingly insignificant corporate announcement provided another revealing glimpse of where Amazon is headed. The company said that it would start accepting Health Savings Account debit cards, which under U.S. federal law allow patients to use pretax dollars to pay for valid medical expenses. The significance of this move is far greater than just Amazon offering another convenience for its shoppers who want to buy a blood pressure monitor or a knee brace. Amazon is creating an all-encompassing ecosystem that not only includes shopping, media, cloud computing, and health care, but also the means to pay for all those services. Amazon, in other words, is beginning to look like a bank.

Amazon isn't normally thought of as a finance company, but

one brainstorm by Bezos early in the company's history set the foundation for his quest to become a major player in the finance industry. A few years after Bezos launched Amazon, he was looking for ways to bolster growth.

At one point in early 1997, he was mulling over a common e-commerce problem. Many shoppers simply disappeared when it was time to check out of their shopping carts. The trouble, Bezos realized, was that there was too much friction in the system. Shoppers had to stop and enter their credit card, billing, and shipping details and then double-check to make sure it was correct. That year, Bezos appeared as an inventor on the "411 patent," which described an online purchasing system that was to become the "Buy now with 1-Click" button on Amazon.com. The project took nearly six months and 3,500 person-hours of work before the feature was ready to launch in September of 1997.

Amazon soon found that the 1-Click button dramatically increased the likelihood that its consumers would complete their purchases. The software revolutionized online retailing by allowing shoppers to buy without really having to think about it. Because customers loved the convenience of 1-Click, Amazon began to increase the rate at which it signed up customers, amassing millions of new ones every year. The 1-Click button became so popular that Barnes & Noble built its own called Express Lane, which caused Amazon to sue it for patent infringement. The case was settled out of court, and the terms were kept private. In the wake of the settlement, Apple licensed the software from Amazon for its iTunes store.

Besides attracting more shoppers, the invention played another less obvious but just as important role in Amazon's history: 1-Click gave the company the ability to store and collect financial data, including credit card numbers, addresses, and how much its customers spent, on what, and how often. And the e-tailer could do this over long stretches of time, because these customers had set up permanent accounts. Although the purchases were made by credit cards controlled by the big banks, Amazon now had access to financial data on a large group of well-heeled and loyal customers.

Amazon not only holds the financial information of its customers but also data on the millions of independent retailers who sell goods on its site. This presented an attractive opportunity to start a lending business. In 2011, Bezos decided to start providing loans to these small merchants so they'd have the cash they needed to grow. Christened Amazon Lending, the program became another important element in driving the company's AI flywheel. If small merchants had the capital to expand, there'd be more selection on Amazon.com, which would attract more customers, which in turn would attract more merchants.

Lending to small businesses with shaky credit histories is risky, but Amazon reduced that risk by designing algorithms that know almost in real time a merchant's sales growth and inventory turns and whether its products are getting positive or negative reviews. If those numbers started stalling or the number of negative reviews started piling up, Amazon could cut off the seller's credit line. From the borrower's perspective, Amazon Lending required no long forms to fill out or interviews with bank managers. One day a button simply appears on the seller's Amazon account page asking if they'd like to borrow some money. The button, which is controlled by an algorithm, can just as easily disappear, potentially leaving some borrowers short of cash just when they need it, as, in an earlier chapter, London-based seller John Morgan discovered the hard way.

Like most Amazon innovations, Amazon Lending started out slowly, then took off. From 2011 through 2015, Amazon was issuing on average roughly $300 million a year in small-business loans. Then Bezos started to push the business hard. By 2017, the company had boosted its annual lending rate to $1 billion. More than twenty thousand small businesses that sell on its Marketplace—not only in the U.S. but in England and Japan— have borrowed from Amazon. According to Peeyush Nahar, vice president for Amazon Marketplace, the company hopes to expand to other countries where it operates Marketplaces, such as Canada and France. Loans range from $1,000 to $750,000. Sellers say interest rates can be as high as 12 percent. "Small businesses are in our DNA," Nahar wrote in a company release. "Amazon is providing capital to small businesses to help them expand inventory and operations at a critical period of their growth. We understand that a small loan can go a long way."

It's not inconceivable that Amazon in the not-too-distant future could become a digital financial service business that offers checking accounts, personal loans, mortgages, and even insurance. It already offers its own Visa card in partnership with Chase and is expanding its Amazon Pay business, which allows shoppers to pay for products and services they buy from businesses outside the Amazon orbit. Amazon Pay works very much like PayPal, Apple Pay, and Stripe, which allow customers to easily make purchases on laptops or on mobile phones. Amazon's service has only a fraction of the customers that PayPal does, but it's growing fast as the company's Prime members discover the ease of using their account to make purchases at places other than Amazon, such as gas stations and restaurants. At the same time, more and more retailers who sell on their own sites are using Amazon Pay because of the trustworthiness that comes with the Amazon name.

The business model that Amazon is pursuing in many ways resembles that of Ant Financial, the Alibaba affiliate that operates Alipay, the largest mobile payments service in the world, with some 1 billion users. Ant Financial is expanding into credit scoring, wealth management, insurance, and lending. It even offers a money market fund called Tianhong Yu'e Bao, which as of 2018 had $211 billion in deposits. An October 2018 report by the research firm CB Insights pointed out that Ant Financial had a stock market valuation of $150 billion, higher at the time than that of Goldman Sachs, Morgan Stanley, Banco Santander, or the Royal Bank of Canada.

Amazon would be hard put to crack the mobile payment business in China because Ant Financial and Tencent, with its WeChat Pay, together control 92 percent of that market. America, however, lags China in mobile payment systems. According to the research firm eMarketer, only a quarter of smartphone users in the U.S. used mobile payment systems to buy an item in a store in 2018, compared to 79 percent in China. America is where Amazon could make inroads against mobile and online payment leaders such as PayPal, Google Pay, and Apple Pay.

The good news for Amazon is that consumers seem perfectly willing to try e-banking. A survey by Accenture found that 70 percent of global consumers would take advantage of robo-advisory services for their banking, insurance, and retirement planning. *Hello Alexa, what's my bank balance?* The Boston consultancy Bain conducted a survey that found that nearly three-quarters of Americans between the ages of eighteen and twenty-four said they'd buy a financial product from a tech company. As part of the same survey, Amazon was named the tech company they would most trust with their money—ahead of Apple and Google.

The road to becoming a financial powerhouse will be bumpy. To be a commercial bank, for instance, Amazon would have to jump through daunting regulatory hoops both in the U.S. and abroad. What's more likely is that Amazon will partner with one or more big banks to climb this steep learning curve. In March 2018, the *Wall Street Journal* reported that Amazon had been talking to JPMorgan Chase, Capital One, and others about a partnership that would allow it to offer checking accounts. In such a setup, because the big banks—and not Amazon—would hold customers' deposits, the e-commerce giant wouldn't be subject to banking regulations. Amazon would become the slick digital face of consumer banking with a traditional financial institution doing the heavy lifting behind the scenes.

In a 2018 report, "Banking's Amazon Moment," Bain sketches a scenario in which the e-tailer would not only collect fees from its banking partner for the Amazon checking accounts it creates, but also would be able to collect payments directly from those checking accounts for whatever its customers buy on Amazon.com. This means Amazon would avoid the heavy fees it currently pays credit card companies. Bain estimates that in the U.S. alone, Amazon would save more than $250 million in annual credit card fees. Once Amazon builds a basic banking service, Bain's Gerard du Toit and Aaron Cheris foresee the e-tailer moving "steadily but surely into other financial products, including lending, mortgages, property and casualty insurance, wealth management (starting with a simple money market fund to hold larger balances), and life insurance." Bain believes that Amazon could end up with 70 million banking customers—about as many as Wells Fargo—by the mid-2020s.

When a company spends more than any other company in the world on R&D, it gets to do a lot of experimentation. Amazon, as we've seen, is making major pushes into advertising, health care, and finance, but that's just the beginning. Bezos is placing a number of longer-term bets on other sectors that could morph into major businesses.

At the same time that Amazon is expanding its advertising

business, it's creating its own streaming TV service, a move that could eventually not only provide another valuable platform for selling advertising, but could also become a major stand-alone business. The company's Fire TV, a small black device that attaches to a TV and allows customers to stream their favorite shows over the Internet, competes with Apple TV, Android TV, and Roku in the race to persuade millions of cable TV customers to cut the cord. With Fire TV, a viewer can get a wide variety of programs if they subscribe to streaming services such as Netflix, HBO Go, Hulu, ESPN+, and, of course, Amazon Prime Video. As of 2019, Fire TV offered 320 channels in four markets: the U.S., the UK, Germany, and Japan. And the selection of programs is growing. Besides the deal to stream NFL Thursday Night Football, Amazon in the UK and Germany offers Eurosport, which attracted 386 million viewers for the 2018 South Korea Winter Olympics. Says Amazon's Greg Hart, who oversees Prime Video: "We want to keep giving people access to more and more types of content, and oftentimes those channels are the same ones that they can get on traditional cable."

And the list of new ventures for Amazon keeps growing. In late 2018, Amazon announced that it was manufacturing its own computer chips to help better integrate its hardware and software in its cloud computing business, saving costs in the process. It's not hard to imagine that before long Amazon could start selling its chips to other tech firms. That same year, the company said that it had formed a partnership with Korean carmaker Hyundai to sell its vehicles on Amazon.com. Shoppers can compare models, read reviews, check inventory at local dealers, and even order a test-drive with the vehicle driven to the person's home. This digital showroom is different from other auto research sites in that the car manufacturer's site is embedded in Amazon—shoppers don't have to go to a dealer's site to get purchasing information and test-drives. Hyundai gets access to Amazon's 300 million customers, and Amazon collects valuable data on car shoppers and perhaps the opportunity to sell more car wax.

As 2019 rolled in, Amazon led a $700 million investment round in electric pickup truck and SUV maker Rivian. While the e-commerce giant had been working with other companies to install Alexa in cars and to develop autonomous delivery vans, this was its first direct investment in the electric car manufacturing business. Later that year, Bezos announced that Amazon had ordered 100,000 Rivian electric vans—to date, the largest order of such vehicles ever. The vans should start hitting the road in 2021. Around the same time as the Rivian investment, GeekWire broke the news that Amazon planned to launch 3,236 satellites that are intended to provide high-speed Internet to just about anywhere in the world. Allowing millions more people to get access to the web certainly wouldn't hurt Amazon's e-commerce and cloud businesses.

Some wagers—such as Amazon's venture capital arm's investment in a prefab homebuilding company—seem not to be a good fit. When the company says it wants to provide the smart home of the future with Alexa-driven security systems, thermostats, and appliances, does that really need to include the walls and roof? But as Bezos puts it: "Even the best innovators always look a little clueless at the beginning because to get a great return you have to be doing something most people aren't. So, look in the mirror and ask if you agree with your critics. If not, water the garden and ignore the weeds."

As Amazon invades industry after industry and gains more and more power with its AI flywheel, the impact on society and the economy will be epic.

CHAPTER 14

Bezos Under Fire

As the richest man in the world, Jeff Bezos had become a favorite target of politicians and the press, but right after the Labor Day weekend of 2018, as vacationers straggled back from their holiday, he drew flak like he'd never seen. Suddenly, he came under sharp attack for the pay and working conditions at his company. Perhaps most disturbing to him was that the most vicious jabs came from the political Left—something the owner of the liberal *Washington Post* could hardly have expected. In the days and weeks that followed, Bezos responded swiftly, drawing on his competitive spirit and displaying a series of aikido-like public relations moves that not only mitigated the damage but also, in one way, at least, turned a fraught situation to his advantage—as he's done so many times in his career.

The first shot came from Senator Bernie Sanders, the Democratic socialist from Vermont, who targeted Amazon's CEO as a bad corporate actor. On September 5, 2018, Sanders introduced a bill called the Stop BEZOS Act, which stands for Stop Bad Employers by Zeroing Out Subsidies. The law would require big companies like Amazon that employ people who are on federal welfare such as Medicaid and food stamps to pay back the government for the massive costs of those programs.

Two days later, the media picked up on a story about two AI researchers who discovered a 2016 Amazon patent that proposed to house workers in cages to protect them while working in warehouses. While the cages might keep the workers safe, the researchers had written a scathing paper that concluded that Amazon's design was "an extraordinary illustration of worker alienation, a stark moment in the relationship between humans and machines." The next week, Senator Elizabeth Warren (D-Mass.) followed with a charge that Amazon had become too powerful and needed to be broken up.

Bezos surely must have been mystified by the level of hostility, because at the time of these attacks, U.S. unemployment was the lowest it had been since the 1960s, and the S&P 500 stock index was rising to historic highs. All the good economic news, however, wasn't enough to keep many Americans from feeling anxious about what the future would bring—not just for their own careers but for their children's. A 2017 survey by the American Culture and Faith Institute found that four out of ten American adults preferred socialism to capitalism. The next generation seemed even less enamored with the way things were going. A 2016 Harvard study that polled young adults between the ages of eighteen and twenty-nine found that 58 percent didn't support capitalism.

The reasons for this discontent were varied—the rise of the gig economy, wage stagnation, the lingering effects of the 2008 financial crisis, and the looming threat of automation. But perhaps the biggest issue was the growing wealth gap in America. In a statement Sanders released around the same time he introduced his Stop BEZOS bill, he said: "At a time of massive income and wealth inequality, when the three wealthiest people in America own more wealth than the bottom 50 percent and when 52 percent of all new income goes to the top one percent, the American people are tired of subsidizing multi-billionaires who own some of the largest and most profitable corporations in America." Sanders had a point. Consider that as of early 2019, Jeff Bezos, Microsoft's Bill Gates, Berkshire Hathaway's Warren Buffett, and Facebook's Mark Zuckerberg together were worth $357 billion. They could write a $1,000 check to every man, woman, and child in America and still be multibillionaires.

The kind of income inequality Sanders was talking about was starkly profiled in a 2018 article by the *New York Times*. Karleen Smith, who once worked as a clerk at Macy's in the Landmark Mall outside Washington, D.C., has now taken up residence in her former store, which has been turned into a homeless shelter. Ms. Smith, fifty-seven at the time, told the *Times*: "It's weird to be moving into this building. I used to work here. It's called survival." The defunct Macy's now holds sixty beds and offers hot meals and showers for those who can't afford to live in the city.

And the wealth gap isn't just an American problem. The world's 2,208 billionaires grow $2.5 billion richer every day, according to an Oxfam study, at a time when the poorest half of the global population is seeing its net worth dwindle. And the wealth at the very top of society is staggering. The combined fortunes of the world's twenty-six richest individuals reached $1.4 trillion in 2018—equal to the total wealth of the 3.8 billion poorest people. Signs of this imbalance are rising in Europe. France has endured the working-class "yellow vest" protests over social inequality while in Britain the wealth gap has helped drive the Brexit movement.

As Amazon, Alibaba, Alphabet, and other big tech companies grow in power, more wealth will assuredly accumulate at the top of the income pyramid. The AI-fueled automation that these companies are unleashing—whether it's warehouse picking robots, autonomous vehicles, or Alexa taking care of our shopping and health-care needs—will reduce, as this book has argued, the number of blue-collar jobs. On top of that, the small number of companies that master the AI flywheel will dominate globally, and their founders and shareholders will continue to rake in more than a fair share of global wealth.

In the 1960s and 1970s, corporations tended toward a more balanced approach by taking into consideration the needs not only of their shareholders but also their employees and communities. The 1980s saw the advent of corporate raiders such as Carl Icahn, Victor Posner, and T. Boone Pickens, who put pressure on boards and management to run their corporations solely for shareholders. Since then, running a business to maximize returns for shareholders has become the modus operandi. Commonly, CEOs today will do whatever it takes—cutting R&D, firing employees, slicing benefits—to make the latest quarterly earnings, because if they don't deliver, activist investors will find someone who will.

Unfortunately, the focus on shareholder value will only get worse as the next generation of powerful corporations, fueled by big data and AI, becomes even more dominant. Yes, shareholders' interests certainly need to be taken into account, but so must those of the employees and the communities in which corporations operate. The solution offered by many on the left is simple to state but hard to execute: corporations need to pay their employees more, and governments need to pick up the slack when a business can't economically pay a living wage or create enough jobs to meet the needs of society.

Amazon, of course, is right in the middle of this debate and serves as a good proxy for where capitalism is headed. For years, the company caught the wrath of unions and liberal politicians for the way it compensated its workforce. The argument was that Bezos, who drove his workforce hard, was so focused on costs that he was short-changing his rank-and-file employees. And to a certain extent they were right.

In the summer leading up to the announcement of the Stop BEZOS Act, Senator Sanders and his coauthor of the bill in the House, Ro Khanna, a progressive Democratic congressman from California, were turning up the political heat. They gave speeches and appeared on television to explain why big companies like Amazon and Walmart—two of the largest employers in the U.S.—should reimburse the federal government for the costs of providing welfare to its employees. Sanders estimated that food stamps, Medicaid, and other federal benefits that the federal government pays low-wage workers amounted to $153 billion a year. Senator Sanders had been pounding Bezos over Amazon's pay practices. In one tweet, he wrote: "No one working for the wealthiest person on Earth should have to rely on food stamps. No one working for a man who earns $260 million a day should be forced to sleep in their car. Yet that is what's happening at Amazon."

For all of Senator Sanders's good intentions, the Stop BEZOS Act is, in essence, a tax on employers. A single parent with two children who worked for Amazon and earned $20,000 a year received on average $2,100 in food stamps and $770 in school meal support. If the family incurred medical costs, add to that amount the federal government's share of their Medicaid benefits. Under the act, Amazon would have to pay back the federal government the total amount of those benefits.

Even some on the political right piled on Amazon, but for reasons that had less to do with the plight of workers and more to do with squandering hard-earned, taxpayer dollars. As Fox News talk-show host Tucker Carlson put it during an August 2018 broadcast: "A huge number of Amazon workers are so poorly paid, they qualify for federal welfare benefits. . . . Jeff

Bezos isn't paying his workers enough to eat, so you made up the difference with your tax dollars."

Bezos went on the attack. In an August 2018 blog post, Amazon responded by accusing Sanders of playing politics and making misleading claims about what it pays workers: "Amazon is proud to have created over 130,000 new jobs last year alone. In the U.S., the average hourly wage for a full-time associate in our fulfillment centers, including cash, stock, and incentive bonuses, is over $15/hour before overtime." That was higher than what either Walmart or Target paid its workers.

Amazon has 648,000 full-time and part-time employees and almost all receive benefits depending on the number of hours worked. Most of the workers who don't get benefits come from a pool of 100,000 seasonal workers who sign on to help with the holiday rush. One can appreciate the dilemma of a business that needs to hire an army of temporary workers for a couple of months during the holidays. Should Amazon be held responsible for what these workers do with their lives over the other ten or eleven months of the year—especially if some decide not to work and go on welfare?

The bigger problem with the Stop BEZOS Act was that it was more likely to hurt the very workers it aimed to help. Under this bill, Amazon would be less likely to hire workers on federal welfare because it would know that its wage costs would rise if one of its employees had another child or became eligible for Medicaid payments because of high medical bills. One could imagine a scenario where a single mother, whose cost of employment spiked because of this legislation, would be in danger of losing her job and becoming even more dependent on government largesse. "The long and short of it is," argues Ryan Bourne, an economist and the R. Evan Scharf Chair for the Public Understanding of Economics at the libertarian Cato

Institute, "is that Bernie's bill makes welfare recipients more expensive. In economics, if something becomes more expensive you use less of it."

Logic and politics, however, don't always mix. With the political zeitgeist shifting against Amazon, Bezos on October 2, 2018, surprised his critics by implementing an across-the-board $15 minimum wage for all 350,000 hourly employees, including seasonal workers. As he said in a statement announcing the wage hike: "We listened to our critics, thought hard about what we wanted to do, and decided we want to lead. We're excited about this change and encourage our competitors and other large employers to join us."

Even in the months before the unveiling of the Stop BEZOS Act, Amazon had already been engaged in a vigorous internal debate over a wage hike for its employees. Dave Clark, the senior vice president of worldwide operations, whose bailiwick includes Amazon's warehouses, believed that—political theater aside—raising wages would help attract and keep good workers in a tight job economy. The discussion was mostly over how to implement the hike—gradually or all at once. Clark and other members of the senior team brought a number of different scenarios to Bezos that included graduated wage increases. The most aggressive and expensive option was to implement a $15 minimum wage across the board immediately. Bezos, who likes bold action, jumped on the idea and without hesitation told the group to do it as soon as possible. Says one senior executive who was at the meeting: "Jeff appreciated the idea because it would make Amazon a leader in the wage debate and not just a fellow traveler."

Without a doubt, Bezos was concerned about the plight of his workers when he gave them a raise. More corporations need to follow his lead. But as we shall see, the wage hike was both a brilliant public relations move and—remember this is Bezos, one of the most competitive people in the world—a tactic that put his competitors at a disadvantage.

For most Amazon workers, that raise was welcome, but for some, the boost to $15 an hour came at a cost. As part of the deal, the company would cut out restricted stock units for call center and warehouse employees as well as monthly incentive-based pay bonuses for warehouse workers tied to production goals. Some workers complained in the press that the raise was at best a wash, and others complained that they'd actually lose money on the deal. When those press reports reached the desk of Dave Clark, he told his team to find those workers who were disadvantaged by the decision and make sure they were made whole.

For Amazon, however, it was a master stroke. By giving his workers a raise to a minimum of $15 an hour, Bezos defused Sanders's attack. The senator actually praised Bezos for the move and hoped other companies would follow his lead, and it also put the Stop BEZOS Act—which in any event had a slim chance of passing as long as Republicans controlled the White House and the Senate—on the back burner.

What many missed, however, was that the raise to $15 an hour was actually a brilliant strategic move not only politically but economically—another example of Bezos's win-at-all-costs ethos. Yes, the move would cost Amazon as much as $1.5 billion a year in increased labor costs, but by doing so Bezos threw his competitors off-balance. Amazon's wage increase was likely to lead to a more productive workforce because it would help attract and keep better, more motivated workers—allowing the online retailer to maintain superior customer service, its perpetual holy grail. If Amazon offers $15 an hour and a competitor offers $11, who's going to be able to hire the best workers?

Bezos wasn't done tormenting his competitors. By hiking wages, Amazon was playing the long game. While others were fighting to keep wages low, Bezos was adjusting Amazon's business model to stay ahead of a national trend of rising pay. Many cities and states throughout America had already started to boost their minimum wages. Seattle and New York City, for example, already had a $15 minimum wage and California had passed legislation to raise its minimum wage to $15 in 2022. Bezos wanted to make sure that his business model could handle the shift.

In 2018, Amazon employed ninety registered lobbyists to support its causes, which ranged from antitrust to taxes to drones to labor issues. According to the nonprofit Center for Responsive Politics, Amazon spent $14.4 million on its lobbying efforts that year. After Bezos's decision to hike wages to $15 an hour company-wide, Amazon's lobbyists began pushing hard to get a federal minimum-wage bill passed. A more than doubling of the $7.25-an-hour federal minimum wage to match Amazon's $15 an hour would make life much more difficult for the e-tailer's brick-and-mortar rivals. And with that kind of lobbying muscle, getting a federal minimum wage passed wasn't out of the question. "You could conceivably see in the next four or five years, especially if a Democrat is elected to the White House, a big hike in minimum wage," says Cato's Ryan Bourne.

Retailing is a tough, low-margin business, and so it is for Amazon. The company, however, owns a string of high-margin businesses, including the cloud, advertising, and its subscription services, and therefore it can more easily handle the hit on profits from its wage hike to $15. Many of the company's retail competitors, which *don't* have those kinds of profitable businesses in their portfolios and which lack Amazon's cash generation capacity, will find it difficult to deal with such a dramatic pay hike.

Of course, Sanders and Bezos's tussle aside, the long-term

worry for Amazon's lower-rung workers is not that their compensation will dip below that which is sufficient for a comfortable middle-class lifestyle (even at $15 an hour, which works out to $31,000 a year, that goal remains elusive), but that their jobs may be automated out of existence. On this topic, Bezos is a techno-optimist. He believes that the economy will provide jobs for those displaced by automation and AI. That said, from time to time he *has* pondered the need for a universal basic income (UBI) to make up for lost jobs. In essence, with a UBI the federal government steps in and pays every American a basic wage to make up for the disruption that technology is about to wreak on the job market.

Bezos, who has libertarian leanings, hasn't made up his mind yet on a UBI. In general, he is a social progressive who is not politically outspoken and has limited his public advocacy. That puts him at odds with his fellow tech titans, including Facebook's Mark Zuckerberg and his cofounder Chris Hughes, Tesla's Elon Musk, and venture capitalist Marc Andreessen, all of whom support some form of a universal basic income.

The UBI is simply a logical response to a socially and politically complex problem. It's designed to make sure that those holding jobs that will be disrupted by technology will have enough money to retrain for a new job or, if untrainable, survive on minimum-wage jobs. Many western European nations already have a social safety net in place—although the frequent protests by France's yellow vests in 2018 and 2019 suggest that in some corners of the continent it's not enough. In many parts of Asia and South America, safety nets, generally speaking, aren't as strong as in Europe. Governments there will be hit by the same kind of massive job disruption caused by AI and automation and will need to seek similar solutions to those being explored in America.

In the U.S., various UBI plans have been proposed, but basically the way it would work is that all citizens—no matter how much they make—would get paid an amount each month to ensure that no matter how little they earn, they'll have enough money on which to live. Different proposals bandied about at Washington, D.C., think tanks put that number between $500 and $1,000 a month. The idea is not a new one. Historically, intellectuals and politicians across the political spectrum, including Dr. Martin Luther King Jr. and Richard Nixon, have supported a variation of the idea. The appeal today is that it would eliminate poverty for 41 million Americans—the current yardstick for poverty in the U.S. being $12,000 a year for an individual—and it would make it easier for those earning minimum wage or toiling in the gig economy to get by.

What has kept the UBI from becoming a reality is that it costs a lot. Robert Reich, a former labor secretary under President Bill Clinton and a professor of public policy at Berkeley, calculates that a $1,000-a-month stipend to every American—yes, even to billionaires, to make it politically palpable—could cost taxpayers about $3.9 trillion a year, which is $1.3 trillion more than current federal welfare programs and about the same size as the entire federal budget. Another way to look at it is that the program would cost roughly 20 percent of U.S. GDP. This staggering tab would have to be paid by raising taxes on the wealthy or by imposing a carbon tax, a national sales tax, or a tax on robots—or some combination of all of those.

In this current era of political tribalism both in America and in Europe, it's hard to imagine that enough votes could be garnered for a massive tax hike and a historic redistribution of wealth. In the U.S., campaign finance laws are structured in such a way that the richer you are the more political power you amass—power that can be used to block income redistribution. The prime example: billionaire brothers David and Charles Koch, owners of the chemical and fossil fuel giant Koch Industries, who, prior to David's death in August of 2019, spent hundreds of millions of dollars in election years to roll back the reach of government.

Chris Hughes, who cofounded Facebook with Mark Zuckerberg when they were undergrads at Harvard and is the former owner of *The New Republic* magazine, published a book in 2018 called *Fair Shot: Rethinking Inequality and How We Earn*, which argues for a basic income that is more limited and thus politically more palatable. Those earning up to $50,000 a year would get a monthly $500 tax credit. Hughes told me that his plan would cost just about the same as the $1 trillion tax cut the Republicans passed in 2018 and would help people not only make ends meet but also enable them to better themselves, by pursuing training, being able to pay for a babysitter so they can attend job-training classes, or have gas money to look for a new job. "I'm not interested in money for nothing," he says. "People need to know they can get ahead by working hard, and that's just not true now. And the way to do that is by restructuring the tax code."

Yet if the labor situation becomes a crisis over the next decade or two, a full-blown UBI might be the only choice. "Eventually the cost of not doing it exceeds the cost of doing an UBI," says the futurist Martin Ford. "Socially, wealth inequality becomes so disruptive that you have to do something. And it might not be a bad thing for the economy." As Reich argues: "It seems a safe bet that increased automation will allow the economy to continue to grow, making a UBI more affordable. A UBI would itself generate more consumer spending, stimulating additional economic activity. And less poverty would mean less crime, incarceration, and other social costs associated with deprivation."

In that tumultuous period following Labor Day 2018, Bezos made one final gambit, which helped diffuse the cloud of criticism surrounding Amazon and the impact it was having on society. On September 13, fast on the heels of the attacks from Sanders, Warren, and Fox News, Bezos announced that he would donate $2 billion to help eradicate homelessness and to support early child education. It was his first significant donation, and although it represented less than 2 percent of his $163 billion net worth at the time, it was still serious money.

Up to this point in Bezos's life, philanthropy had been mostly an afterthought. The CEO had given tens of millions of dollars to the Fred Hutchinson Cancer Research Center in Seattle, but that was a paltry amount compared to his wealth. He'd spent almost all of his time and energy on Amazon, his space exploration company Blue Origin, and his family. What Bezos does he likes to do well, if not better than anyone else, so it's plausible that in the years leading up to his $2 billion donation, he didn't feel he could dedicate enough time to doing philanthropy properly.

It would be easy to be cynical about the timing of Bezos's donation and see it simply as a tool to help fend off political attacks from Sanders and his ilk. However, an argument can be made that Bezos should be given the benefit of the doubt. A year earlier—before the politicians turned up the heat—Bezos was already thinking about creating a major philanthropy. In a June 2017 tweet, he wrote: "This tweet is a request for ideas. I'm thinking about a philanthropy strategy that is the opposite of how I mostly spend my time—working on the long-term." Bezos wasn't going to stop thinking long-term, but he was making a dramatic concession by helping people in the here and now.

Another point in Bezos's favor is that his family members have a long tradition of working to meet the needs of many Americans. Jeff's parents, Jackie and Mike Bezos, run the Aspen-based Bezos Family Foundation, which focuses on childhood education. Among its many programs is the project Vroom, an app that provides suggestions for more than a thousand free activities—based on the latest in cognitive science—that parents can do with their children to increase their brain power. One example: when parents are out with their child, they can point out things in the real world that he or she has read about or seen on TV.

Following in the tradition of his family, Bezos designed his $2 billion Day 1 Fund to help people in immediate need. It would award grants to organizations and civic groups that shelter and feed young families and it would back a network of new, non-profit, Montessori-inspired preschools in low-income communities. Bezos seemed truly passionate about the project and in his relentless way seemed dedicated to making it work. In that September 2018 tweet announcing the new charity, he attached a vision statement that read, "We'll use the same set of principles that have driven Amazon. Most important among those will be genuine, intense customer obsession. 'Education is not the filling of a pail but the lighting of a fire.' And lighting that fire early is a giant leg up for any child."

As September 2018 wound to an end, Bezos's new philanthropy, Amazon's wage hike to a minimum of $15 an hour, and the company's lobbying for a higher national minimum wage temporarily diffused some of the political heat. At the time, no one expected the firestorm that would erupt five months later in the wake of Amazon's announcing it would build one of its second headquarters in New York City.

On Valentine's Day 2019, just an hour before the news broke in the national media, New York City mayor Bill de Blasio received a call from Amazon's head of Global Corporate Affairs, Jay Carney. A former *Time* magazine journalist and White House press secretary for President Obama, Carney told the stunned politician that Amazon had decided to walk away from a deal to bring a second headquarters and 25,000 jobs to Long Island City, an up-and-coming Queens neighborhood that ran along the East River and offered spectacular views of the Manhattan skyline. The call was brief, and Carney told the mayor the decision was final. Soon after talking with Carney, de Blasio, who'd worked hard to woo the company, struck out at Amazon in a tweet: "You have to be tough to make it in New York City."

Four months earlier, de Blasio and New York governor Andrew Cuomo, both Democrats, had sealed a deal with Amazon worth some $3 billion in state and local incentives to attract the e-commerce giant to New York. Their offer beat out those of 278 other cities competing to get those attractive Amazon jobs. At the same time, Amazon also announced that, besides New York, it would create another headquarters in northern Virginia.

The scuttled deal speaks volumes about Bezos's attitude toward dealing with the public, and it also sheds light on how little the public understands Amazon's willingness to walk away from a deal when it doesn't like the terms. In the months following the announcement of the New York City headquarters location, Amazon faced increasing resistance from a newly elected slate of progressive politicians, including U.S. representative and self-described democratic socialist Alexandria Ocasio-Cortez, fondly known as AOC by her followers, whose district is adjacent to Long Island City. AOC and a group of local politicians pointed to the $3 billion in tax incentives that Amazon would receive for creating 25,000 jobs. (Nevermind that Amazon would have generated billions more than that in tax revenues.) The opposition claimed that a billionaire like Bezos didn't need the money. Those opposed also wanted Amazon to not resist unionization, to subsidize local housing, and to help rebuild the decaying subway lines. It also didn't help that in the days before Amazon walked away, Andrea Stewart-Cousins, the new Democratic leader in the state senate, chose Michael Gianaris, a liberal state senator whose district includes Long Island City, to serve on a powerful state board that had veto power over the deal. Gianaris, an outspoken Amazon critic, seemed to have his mind already made up: "When they come in and take over a community like that, the community dies."

The bottom line is that Amazon simply didn't need the political hassles it faced in New York. As Carney, who helped lead Amazon's second-headquarters initiative, put it: "We pulled out not because we didn't think we would get the approvals we needed; we never doubted that. We knew we had broad public support, and we had faith that Governor Cuomo could deliver. We pulled out because it wasn't worth the grief." Spending months and even years trying to appease hostile politicians only takes time and resources away from Amazon's focus on its customers. In the company's eyes, rolling over to union demands only hurts customers by necessitating higher prices; getting involved in subway rehabilitation only takes time away from serving customers. Another contributing factor was that, historically, Amazon has shied away from public scrutiny. Dealing for decades with local politicians who'd be openly criticizing its every move isn't how the company likes to roll. To those who know how Bezos thinks, it was no surprise that he hit the ejector button so quickly on the New York deal. New York City needed Bezos more than he needed it.

That said, it's true that Amazon might've done a better job of explaining to local leaders its business philosophy and spent more time listening to their concerns. Because Amazon failed to explain itself fully, politicians such as AOC had an easy time painting it as yet another big, greedy corporation out for itself—the community be damned. The company's unexpected pullout only strengthened some politicians' resolve to pin society's ills on Amazon. Indeed, the number of antitrust experts who want to dismantle the company, virtual brick by virtual brick, is small but growing.

CHAPTER 15

The Rise
of Hipster Antitrust

President Trump in March 2018 lashed out at Amazon in a tweet, accusing it of "putting many thousands of retailers out of business." A little more than a year later, Treasury secretary Steven Mnuchin, commenting on the U.S. Department of Justice's launching an antitrust review of big tech, told CNBC: "I think if you look at Amazon, although there are certain benefits to it, they've destroyed the retail industry across the United States so there's no question they've limited competition." Of course, it may simply be that the president and his allies were miffed at the relentless negative coverage the commander in chief had been receiving in the *Washington Post*, which, as the president well knew, is owned by Bezos.

Trump wasn't alone in his dislike for the Seattle company. A growing chorus of critics believed that Amazon had gotten too big and too powerful. Former Walmart U.S. CEO Bill Simon said that Amazon should be dismantled. Senator Elizabeth Warren argued that Amazon needs its own version of the Depression-era Glass-Steagall Act, which split consumer and investment banks. In her scenario, the government would break

Amazon into two parts, separating Amazon's website from its direct retail business. The company's platform sells products not only from third-party sellers but also from Amazon itself. Warren said that Amazon had an unfair advantage by competing with merchants who use its e-commerce platform. Think of it as being both a player and a ref in an NBA basketball game. If a group of third-party sellers are doing well selling, say, green hooded sweatshirts, Amazon knows it and will make its own green sweatshirt and sell it at a lower price. "Pick one business or the other," she said. "You can't be in both."

The campaign against Bezos took on new momentum in the fall of 2019 when bipartisan members of the House Judiciary Committee asked Amazon and other big tech companies to hand over executive communications—including, supposedly, Bezos's emails—and financial statements, as well as information about competitors, market share, mergers, and key business decisions. Specifically, Congress asked Amazon to provide material on product searches on Amazon.com, the pricing of Amazon Prime, and the fees charged to sellers. Committee chairman Jerrold Nadler said the requests will aid a continuing investigation, citing "growing evidence that a handful of corporations have come to capture an outsized share of online commerce and communications."

One of the first academic arguments for the breakup of Amazon appeared in a January 2017 article in *Yale Law Journal*, titled "Amazon's Antitrust Paradox." The author, a twenty-nine-year-old Yale Law grad named Lina Khan, argued that the company practices predatory pricing in various markets, and that this behavior is squeezing the competition even if it's good for consumers. Khan, who works at the Open Markets Institute, a liberal think tank based in Washington, D.C., believes that if companies become too big and too powerful, they can take away Americans' basic freedoms by lobbying to change regulations in their favor, winning huge tax breaks from state governments that take funds away from education and welfare, and bulldozing neighborhoods. As she told *The Atlantic* in 2018, "For most people, their everyday interaction with power isn't with their representative in Congress, but with their boss. And if in your day-to-day life you're treated like a serf in your economic relationships, what does that mean for your civic capabilities—for your experience of democracy?" Normally, an academic legal paper written by a recent law grad would be bound for obscurity, but Khan's paper hit a nerve. It was downloaded 145,000 times, the legal equivalent of a blockbuster movie.

Then momentum began to build against the company in Europe, where Amazon is one of the largest online retailers. In mid-2019, the European Union launched a formal investigation of Amazon for antitrust violations. EU competition commissioner Margrethe Vestager, known for the high-profile and successful anticompetitiveness cases she brought against Google, believes that Amazon is using the massive amounts of data it collects on its customers' shopping habits to shut out competition. The commissioner's argument—similar to Elizabeth Warren's—is that there exists a possible conflict of interest within Amazon because it acts both as a direct seller of retail goods and as the provider of an e-commerce platform for itself and its third-party sellers. So not only does Amazon compete with third-party sellers for the best placement on its site—her argument goes—but it also collects valuable data on its rivals that it can use to its advantage.

A look at the evidence, however, tells another story. In the U.S., it's hard to make an argument that Amazon is in violation of antitrust law. Even in Europe, where such laws are tougher, it's difficult to make the case that Amazon is thwarting competition. Perhaps sometime in the not too distant future Amazon and other big-tech platforms will have so much clout that they can not only dictate the terms of competition, but also hold sway over governments and, in the darkest case, reduce our freedoms. But that day hasn't arrived yet.

Amazon is certainly disrupting business models in an array of industries from books, to retail, to entertainment, but it doesn't violate current antitrust laws in the U.S.—at least, so far as they're currently interpreted. Whether companies like Amazon help or hurt consumers has become the linchpin test for today's antitrust law. The origin of this thinking stretches back to the late 1970s when Richard Posner, U.S. Circuit Court of Appeals judge and a law professor at the University of Chicago Law School, wrote *Antitrust Law*, a book that turned the field upside down. Until then, U.S. antitrust law was characterized by the pursuit of two (sometimes conflicting) goals: protecting consumers from price-fixing monopolies and protecting "small dealers and worthy men" from larger competitors. Posner's book radically shifted antitrust thinking, placing the emphasis primarily on consumer welfare. In this libertarian view, the markets should be free and unregulated unless a company uses its monopoly power to raise prices in a way that harms consumers. This philosophy came to be known in antitrust circles as the sacred Chicago texts. Big was not bad in and of itself. It didn't matter if a company harmed or put its competitors out of business. That's how free market capitalism works.

Since its inception, Amazon has been all about making life better for consumers. It uses its AI flywheel to constantly drive down prices and speed up deliveries of products. It offers its Prime members free movies, TV series, and music as well as discounts at its Whole Foods markets. Consumers trust Amazon more than any other U.S. brand. To split up Amazon on the premise that it hurts the consumer is ludicrous.

Those calling for the breakup of Amazon on anticompetitive grounds also lack compelling evidence that Amazon is hurting small businesses more than it's helping them. Punishing the company for being more efficient than its competitors doesn't make sense, especially when it passes its savings along to consumers as lower prices. Jason Furman, an economist at Harvard's Kennedy School of Government and a former economic advisor to President Obama, studies the effect of corporate power on wealth inequality, price hikes, and quashing of innovation. He currently gives Amazon a pass, believing the company shouldn't be broken up. "Walmart figured out how to have better supply chain management and grew, and then Amazon did the same online so there's more concentration in that sector and that reflects that increase in efficiency. That has a benign impact on the economy."

To understand what worries politicians and regulators both in America and in Europe, take the case of Brooks Brothers. The hallowed American brand peddles its clothes not only on Brooksbrothers.com but on Amazon's site because it has no choice—the Seattle giant controls too much of online retailing to ignore. Amazon's algorithms scan sales on its own site and most likely those on Brooksbrothers.com to see what's selling. At one point, the algorithm must have noticed that men's khaki pants were a hot item because Amazon in 2017 started making and selling its own under the house brand Goodthreads.

A search for khakis on Amazon.com results in Amazon's khakis appearing at the prime spot at the top of the page, with the Brooks Brothers brand nowhere to be found. I bought a pair of Amazon's $39 khakis and modeled them for my fashion-snob son. He said they looked great, not knowing they were a cheap Amazon knockoff. So, in this case, Amazon is good for consumers but not so good for Brooks Brothers. Now, a specific search on Amazon.com for the Brooks Brothers brand pops open a page where its khakis are heavily discounted from $90 to $55 to try to compete with Amazon. "The question here is about the data," France's Vestager says. "Do you then also use this data to do your own calculations, as to what is the new big thing, what is it that people want, what kind of offers do they like to receive, what makes them buy things?"

Well, that's *exactly* what Amazon seems to do—although the company denies it, in all likelihood to avoid antitrust scrutiny. The question is: Does the data give Amazon an unfair competitive advantage over the retailers selling on its platform? There's no doubt that Amazon has sharp elbows and that it's a fierce competitor with the third-party merchants who sell on its site. The story of John Morgan, the London seller of travel bags who woke up one day and found that Amazon had become a direct competitor, anecdotally makes that case. Yet, the evidence doesn't support the argument that Amazon is an invincible retailer.

The research firm Marketplace Pulse did an in-depth study of Amazon's private label products in 2019 and concluded that they "aren't nearly as successful as many paint them to be . . . the brands and the tens of thousands of products launched aren't resonating with customers." An Amazon spokesperson told Marketplace Pulse that "Amazon's private label products are less than 1% of our total sales. This is far less than other big retailers, many of whom have private label products that represent 25% or more of their sales." With those kinds of numbers and the fact that private label sales are standard practice in the industry, it's hard to argue that Amazon's use of data gives its own products an unfair advantage over others who sell on its site.

Of course, Amazon sells a lot of stuff besides its private label brands and here it competes fiercely with the third-party sellers who use the company's e-commerce platform. Yet, if Amazon had the monopoly power that its critics say it does, it would be driving the merchants selling on its platform out of business. The exact opposite of that is happening. Mindful of the growing political momentum against his company, Bezos, as before noted, opened his 2018 letter to shareholders, which was published in April 2019, by pointing out that third-party sellers now account for 58 percent of all items sold on Amazon.com. That's up from 30 percent a decade earlier. These mostly small and medium-sized businesses sold $160 billion worth of merchandise, compared to $117 billion that Amazon sold directly—what it calls its "first-party" sales. As Bezos wrote in his letter: "To put it bluntly: Third-party sellers are kicking our first-party butt. Badly."

Jay Carney, the company's global head of policy and communications, puts it this way: "Critics like to charge that Amazon is crushing small- and medium-sized businesses. That's a serious allegation. There is just little evidence to back it up. In fact, there are millions of small- and medium-sized businesses selling their products in our store, and they're thriving. If we're trying to put third-party sellers out of business, we're not only bad at it—we're historically bad at it. That's because the opposite is true."

That doesn't mean that selling on Amazon isn't a hypercompetitive, Darwinian experience, but the more than 2 million merchants who operate not only in the U.S. but in Europe, China, Japan, and South America are expanding not dying, and that can't be used as an argument for breaking up Amazon. It is true that many small businesses both in the U.S. and abroad that *don't* sell on Amazon are struggling, but that has more to do with a shift in consumer taste toward wanting fast delivery and the choice between buying online or shopping in a store or buying online and picking up at the store. Small businesses that haven't made this transition aren't likely to survive.

Lacking a credible argument to break up Amazon under today's U.S. laws, its critics will ultimately have to turn to an argument with historic precedence. They will propose breaking up Amazon, Alibaba, Alphabet, Facebook, Twitter, and other tech platforms simply because they believe they've become too powerful and threaten the sovereignty of government. In 1602, the Dutch had established a monopoly over Asian trade with its United East India Company. By 1669, it had become the richest private company the world had ever seen. Its monopoly lasted until 1799, when attacks by other colonial powers, jealous of its power and markets, helped drive it into bankruptcy.

The last time business held the kind of power that Amazon and other tech giants are accused of possessing was during the Gilded Age. Late in the nineteenth century, titans such as J. D. Rockefeller, J. P. Morgan, and Andrew Mellon consolidated their industries into trusts where the stocks of their various companies were controlled by a single board of directors, a move that effectively protected their monopolies from federal antitrust laws. Lawyers for the trusts argued that even though the businesses that these boards controlled operated nationally, the holding companies themselves, because they were headquartered in a single state and because their directors were mainly engaged in finance not interstate commerce, were therefore protected from antitrust enforcement. The Supreme Court with misgivings agreed to the argument in *United States v. E. C. Knight Co.* (1895).

By the early twentieth century, J. D. Rockefeller had built Standard Oil into a behemoth that controlled 90 percent of all refining in the U.S. Andrew Carnegie merged his steel company with nine others and employed 1 million. J. P. Morgan, the most powerful tycoon of the Gilded Age, controlled a trust consisting of several banks, the Western Union Telegraph Company, the Pullman Car Company, Aetna Life Insurance, General Electric, Leyland Steamship Lines, and twenty-one railroads. As the magazine *Collier's Weekly* noted at the time: "You can ride from

England to China on the regular lines of steamships and railroads without once passing from the protecting hollow of Mr. Morgan's hand."

The dilemma that President Teddy Roosevelt faced at the time is similar to the one that the "break up Amazon" contingent faces today. Although the Gilded Age trusts were amassing great power, they were in many instances lowering prices for consumers. Edmund Morris, in his brilliant biography *Theodore Rex*, points out that by the early twentieth century, the U.S. economy under the trusts was running better, and the price of kerosene courtesy of Standard Oil had been declining for thirty years. As Morris writes: "America was no longer a patchwork of small self-sufficient communities. It was a great grid of monopolistic cities doing concentrated business with one another: steel cities and rubber cities, cities of salt and cloth and corn and copper." Amazon has had a similar impact on the economy by lowering prices and continuously improving customer service.

Roosevelt eventually broke up many of these trusts during his presidency by using a novel argument. He said that the trusts run by Rockefeller, Morgan, Mellon, and others had become so powerful they were threatening the very sovereignty of the federal government. As he wrote in 1901: "More and more it is evident that the State, and if necessary, the nation, has got to possess the right of supervision and control as regards the great corporations which are its creatures." Roosevelt worried that the trusts had become so big and wielded so much clout that the federal government would be hard put to regulate them in any way. By 1903, Roosevelt had persuaded Congress to pass bills that would eventually break up the trusts, but not before it was discovered that J. D. Rockefeller had ordered six senators to do their utmost to block the legislation.

Today, Amazon, Alphabet, Apple, Netflix, and Facebook

wield immense power over the American economy and our lives, but not nearly so pervasively as the trusts of the Gilded Age. Facebook and Alphabet together control nearly 60 percent of the online advertising market, but that only represents about a quarter of the overall U.S. ad market, and Amazon is moving up fast as a competitor. Netflix has penetrated 75 percent of the homes that subscribe to video streaming services, but it still faces plenty of competition from Amazon, Disney, AT&T, and others. Apple controls around 40 percent of the smartphone market in the U.S., but only about 10 percent worldwide.

While Amazon controls nearly 40 percent of all online retail in the U.S., online retail only accounts for about 10 percent of all retail in the U.S.—nine out of every ten of our shopping dollars still go to brick-and-mortar stores. It turns out that customers like to try on dresses and shoes, squeeze cantaloupes, and compare HD TV screens before buying. That means that Amazon only controls about 4 percent of U.S. retail. Globally the situation is even starker. Amazon controls only 1 percent of retail worldwide, and formidable competitors such as Walmart and China's three behemoths, Alibaba, Tencent, and JD.com, will make sure that Amazon will have to fight hard for every additional dollar of sales.

One similarity between Gilded Age trusts and today's big tech companies that *is* undeniable (albeit ironic) is they that can be good for the economy and society. Issues of privacy and election hacking aside, Facebook and Alphabet help manufacturers and retailers sell their goods more efficiently through targeted advertising. Apple makes a device that a billion people love—well, at least most of them—and Netflix brings affordable entertainment to the homes of its 100 million subscribers. Consumers love Amazon's big selection and fast delivery.

The only logical argument, then, that Amazon's critics can

make is that the company has become (or will become) so big and successful that it can put hundreds of companies out of business and that it can bully governments to get tax breaks and change laws in its favor.

The trouble with that argument is that disruption always has been and always will be at the heart of capitalism. If Amazon's enemies want a system where everyone plays nice, where less efficient companies get government protection, and the U.S. Justice Department is the referee, that's their prerogative. That anti-Amazon vision, however, carries a steep price. It will stifle innovation. In the 1930s, Austrian economist Joseph Schumpeter argued that capitalism at its heart was about creative destruction—the old had to make way for the new if there was to be progress. History has borne him out. The automobile wiped out the buggy makers, cell phones have wiped out landlines, cloud computing is taking the place of corporate data centers, organic food is hurting the business of packaged goods giants like General Mills and Kraft Heinz. Do we really want to go back to a world where we drive in horse-drawn carts, dial up friends and get a busy signal, and only eat Kraft macaroni and cheese?

For the foreseeable future, then, Amazon will remain a formidable force in global business and will have massive repercussions on business and society—and be more disruptive than many think. The AI flywheel will spin through industry after industry, forcing incumbents to adapt or die. The technologically weak will be culled from the herd. Hundreds of millions of jobs will be displaced by AI and automation, and enough new jobs will not take their place. We all have to get used to that because breaking up or hobbling Amazon or Alphabet or Alibaba won't stop the rising tide of AI and automation. If these current tech giants aren't the ones to cause the coming technological disruptions, others will.

That said, the day may arrive when what Amazon's critics fear comes true. The company's AI flywheel could become so pervasive and so impenetrable that it and other big tech companies like it would need to be regulated or broken up—on the grounds that whatever is going on out there simply *feels* scary. That day doesn't seem imminent, but it could happen. If these smart systems begin to make more and more decisions about our lives that we don't understand or that don't make sense, or if they become so powerful that no one can compete, then government will have to find solutions to these monumental challenges.

In the meantime, the world has to adjust to a radically new way of working and living called Bezonomics.

CHAPTER 16

Raptor Fighter Jets Versus Biplanes

In the opening of this book, Jeff Bezos said that Amazon might someday fail. It's hard to imagine a business as powerful, rich, and smart as Amazon faltering, never mind collapsing. Yet it would certainly be foolish to disagree with one of the savviest capitalists in history. Yes, Bezos is probably right. One day some upstart will find a better, cheaper, and faster way to sell online. Or someone could develop a new technology that shatters Amazon's cloud business, or perhaps Bezos's forays into health care and finance will draw the company into its own Vietnam, a long war that saps its energy and leaves it dying on the battlefield.

In one way, all this hardly matters because even if Amazon fails, the world's richest man has given birth to Bezonomics, a new way of doing business that is rippling throughout the globe with profound implications and will continue to do so long after Bezos and Amazon are gone. Bezonomics, a potent cocktail of customer obsession, crazy innovation, and long-term thinking driven by a relentless AI flywheel, is the business model of the twenty-first century. And it's profoundly changing the way we work and live.

269

Compared to a traditional business, Amazon is an F-22 Raptor stealth fighter jet in a dogfight with a World War I biplane. Despite all the hype surrounding AI, it's the first company to widely integrate machine learning into its DNA. Amazon started as a tech company, not a bookseller, and it's applying that savvy to industry after industry. The data-driven selling machine thinks, learns from its own mistakes and gets better, and then repeats that cycle incessantly in real time. It is the first company where computers have the potential to make more business decisions than humans. Bezos has created the smartest company in the world, and it's getting smarter.

The global business world will eventually divide into two camps—those who adopt their own version of Bezonomics, and those who don't. Alphabet, Facebook, Netflix, Alibaba, JD.com, and Tencent have built huge, powerful businesses based on their ability to collect and analyze data, and keep applying those learnings to make their businesses smarter and their offerings to customers more attractive. In their pursuit of AI-driven technologies such as voice and facial recognition, the Internet of Things, and robotics, they're creating automated business models that will crush traditional businesses that fail to adapt to this new world. And the emergence of 5G technology, which will replace our current digital networks, will only widen the gap. Experts predict that this next generation of Internet connectivity will be as much as a hundred times faster than today's web. (On a 5G network, a two-hour movie can be downloaded in seconds.)

For traditional companies, adaptation to this new world doesn't mean simply hiring a gaggle of data scientists to work on a few pet projects. A corporation wishing to put Bezonomics at its heart will have to completely redesign itself. The way Nike has used AI and big data to integrate online shopping with its gleaming experiential stores is a prime example. Even smaller businesses need to adopt the tenets of Bezonomics if they want to survive. Stitch Fix built its online women's clothing business around a smart algorithm that identifies which fashions its customers prefer.

The impact that Bezonomics is having on society is just as profound. Some of the big tech companies are sowing discord with fake news, interfering with elections, and violating personal privacy. As Apple CEO Tim Cook put it: "If you've built a chaos factory, you can't dodge responsibility for the chaos." The global wealth gap has become so out of kilter that politicians in America and Europe have singled out Amazon and other big tech companies for blame. These wealth-creation machines have become so efficient at creating riches for their top employees and shareholders that they're likely to engender more public outrage and become easy targets for regulators—perhaps in some cases even be broken up.

Whether or not Amazon violates current antitrust laws is beside the point. As history has shown, the law can be read in any way that those in power want to read it, and therefore it's not inconceivable that Amazon and other tech giants will face a day of regulatory reckoning. As a foreshadowing of this trend, India in 2018, in an effort to foster competition, passed a law that would prohibit big retailers like Amazon and Walmart from selling their own products on their sites. Might such regulation spur similar efforts in other markets?

The bigger concern is the impact that Amazon and other AI-driven tech giants will have on jobs.

Globally, the job disruption will be massive. Yes, the economy will eventually produce new jobs to replace some of those lost, but this time the change will be so massive that governments will need to intervene with job training, minimum-wage guarantees, and perhaps even universal basic incomes.

The key question facing societies around the globe is whether the convenience that Amazon and other big tech companies bring to customers in retail, search, media, and soon in other industries such as health care and finance is worth the price. So far, the answer is yes, as these giants continue to grow at a rapid pace. People, after all, like what they offer.

So, in the short run at least, get used to it. Amazon is here to stay, and the Bezonomics AI flywheel will turn faster and faster and faster.

Acknowledgments

Tackling a story as big, complex, and ever changing as Amazon takes a collective effort. My editor at Scribner, Rick Horgan, is the rare editor these days who enthusiastically took time and energy to get deeply involved in this project. As I was writing *Bezonomics*, Rick often sent me the latest news on Amazon, consistently challenged my ideas, and pointed me in new directions. I relished our long conversations about the many ways Amazon is invading all aspects of our lives. I am deeply grateful for his thoughtful guidance at every stage. Thanks also to those at Scribner, including Nan Graham, Brian Belfiglio, and Colin Harrison, who believed in this project from the beginning and provided the resources to give this book the kind of launch most authors can only dream about.

When the project was only a vague notion in my mind, my agent, Todd Shuster, pushed me hard to craft a proposal that became the core of this book. Without Todd's hard work and insights, this book would not have come to fruition. And thanks to the rest of the team at Aevitas Creative Management, including Justin Brouckaert and Erica Bauman, for their help.

The advantage of writing a book about Amazon, I found, is that everyone wants to talk about the topic, and I took full advantage of that with many of my friends and colleagues who enthusiastically listened to my opinions and provided me with valuable feedback. My thanks go to Emma Clurman, Hank Gilman, Peter Hildick-Smith, Rik Kirkland, Charlotte Mayerson, Tommy Nathan, Peter Petre, Judi Simmons, and Rodney Zemmel. Also a shout-out to my friends and colleagues at *Fortune*, Adam Lashinsky, Cliff Leaf, and Brian O'Keefe, who allowed me to explore the depths of Alexa for an article in their magazine. Their insights were invaluable when I was writing the chapter on that topic. I also want to acknowledge Brad Stone's book, *The Everything Store*, which skillfully captured Amazon's early years and served as an invaluable research tool.

My fact-checker Tom Colligan was a lifesaver, conscientiously chasing down facts in a book that spans industries and the globe.

I owe thanks most of all to my family: Caroline, Paul and Suz, Sophia and Alex, who for two years endured long dinner conversations about Amazon and had the good grace to hear me opine for hours without rolling their eyes too many times. I couldn't have made it to the last word of this book without their enthusiasm, wit, and good nature. I'm especially grateful to my wife and confidante, Caroline, whose support, insights, and sharp editorial ear for tone and language truly made this a stronger book.

Notes

Introduction

2 *At his all-hands meetings*: "Jeff Bezos on Why It's Always Day 1 at Amazon," Amazon News video, posted on YouTube, April 19, 2017, https://www.youtube.com/watch?time_continue=8&v=fTwXS2H_iJo.

2 *As Bezos put it*: Jeff Haden, "20 Years Ago, Jeff Bezos Said This 1 Thing Separates People Who Achieve Lasting Success from Those Who Don't," *Inc.*, November 6, 2017.

3 *As Bezos put it in Brad Stone's 2013 book*: Brad Stone, *The Everything Store: Jeff Bezos and the Age of Amazon* (New York: Back Bay Books, 2013), 12.

5 *For two decades, Iverson and his team*: Jim Collins, *Good to Great* (New York: HarperBusiness, 2001), 177.

6 *Consider that for the development*: Avery Hartmans, "Amazon Has 10,000 Employees Dedicated to Alexa—Here Are Some of the Areas They're Working On," *Business Insider*, January 22, 2019.

7 *The research firm CB Insights*: "The 7 Industries Amazon Could Disrupt Next," CB Insights, https://www.cbinsights.com/research/report/amazon-disruption-industries/.

7 *The company he founded*: Matt Day and Spencer Soper, "Amazon U.S. Online Market Share Estimate Cut to 38% from 47%," Bloomberg.com, June 13, 2019.

8 *Harit Talwar*: Speaking at the 2019 Fortune Brainstorm Finance conference in Montauk, New York.

8 *Just like Amazon was able*: Mike Isaac, "Which Tech Company Is Uber Most Like? Its Answer May Surprise You," *New York Times*, April 28, 2019.

10 *It offers a vast selection*: "How Many Products Does Amazon Sell Worldwide," ScrapeHero, October 2017, https://www.scrapehero.com/how-many-products-does-amazon-sell-worldwide-october-2017/.

10 *In the U.S., Amazon consistently ranks*: "Rankings per Brand: Amazon," Ranking the Brands, https://www.rankingthebrands.com/Brand-de tail.aspx?brandID=85.

10 *As of 2019, millions of independent businesses*: Jeff Bezos, 2018 Letter to Shareholders, April 11, 2019.

10 *Worldwide, Amazon says*: "Small Business Means Big Opportunity," 2019 Amazon SMB Impact Report, https://d39w7f4ix9f5s9.cloud front.net/61/3b/1f0c2cd24f37bd0e3794c284cd2f/2019-amazon-smb -impact-report.pdf.

11 *On top of all that*: Richard Rubin, "Does Amazon Really Pay No Taxes? Here's the Complicated Answer," *Wall Street Journal*, June 14, 2019.

Chapter 1: Bezonomics

14 *Around the globe, an estimated 200 million*: "150 Amazing Amazon Sta-tistics, Facts, and History (2019)," Business Statistics, DMR, https://expandedramblings.com/index.php/amazon-statistics/.

15 *During the 2017 holiday season*: Courtney Reagan, "More Than 75 Per-cent of US Online Consumers Shop on Amazon Most of the Time," CNBC, December 19, 2017.

15 *The Republicans polled*: "2018 American Institutional Confidence Poll," Baker Center for Leadership, https://bakercenter.georgetown.edu /aicpoll/.

15 *That perhaps helps explain*: Scott Galloway, *The Four: The Hidden DNA of Amazon, Apple, Facebook, and Google* (New York: Portfolio/Penguin, 2017), 14.

16 *An astounding 44 percent*: "How America's Largest Living Generation Shops Amazon," Max Borges Agency, https://www.maxborgesagency .com/how-americas-largest-living-generation-shops-amazon/#slide-2/.

16 *A ranking of the world's most valuable brands*: Martin Guo, "2019 BrandZ Top 100 Most Valuable Global Brands Report," November 6, 2019, https://cn-en.kantar.com/business/brands/2019/2019-brandz-top -100-most-valuable-global-brands-report/.

16 *Amazon has become so addictive*: Karen Webster, "How Much of The Consumer's Paycheck Goes to Amazon?," PYMNTS.com, October 15, 2018.

17 *Aronowitz saw using Amazon*: Nona Willis Aronowitz, "Hate Amazon? Try Living Without It," *New York Times*, December 8, 2018.

17 *As he told the* Wall Street Journal: Khadeeja Safdar and Laura Stevens, "Amazon Bans Customers for Too Many Returns," *Wall Street Journal*, May 23, 2018.

17 *"Whenever someone likes or comments"*: Simon Parkin, "Has Dopamine Got Us Hooked on Tech?," *The Guardian*, March 4, 2018, https://www.theguardian.com/technology/2018/mar/04/has-dopamine-got-us-hooked-on-tech-facebook-apps-addiction.

18 *"We thought we could control it"*: Nellie Bowles, "A Dark Consensus About Screens and Kids Begins to Emerge in Silicon Valley," *New York Times*, October 26, 2018.

19 *The Max Borges Agency poll*: "How America's Largest Living Generation Shops Amazon."

19 *Amazon and the millions*: "How Many Products Does Amazon Sell?," ScrapeHero, January 2018, https://www.scrapehero.com/many-products-amazon-sell-january-2018/.

20 *A deep dive into the Mariana Trench*: Jason Notte, "25 Bizarre Products Sold on Amazon You Need to Know About," *The Street*, July 19, 2017.

20 *One customer warned*: Brandt Ranj, "7 Crazily Heavy Things That Ship for Free on Amazon," *Business Insider*, March 21, 2016.

20 *In 2016, the company had*: Jason Del Rey, "Surprise! Amazon Now Sells More Than 70 of Its Own Private-Label Brands: The Biggest Push Has Come in the Clothing Category," *Vox*, April 7, 2018.

21 *By 2018, that number had grown*: Jessica Tyler, "Amazon Sells More Than 80 Private Brands," *Business Insider*, October 8, 2018.

21 *By 2022, they are expected*: Nathaniel Meyersohn, "Who Needs Brand Names? Now Amazon Makes the Stuff It Sells," CNN Business, October 8, 2018.

21 *She found that about a third*: Alina Tugend, "Too Many Choices: A Problem That Can Paralyze," *New York Times*, February 26, 2010.

22 *A Nintendo NES Classic*: Steven Musil, "Amazon Prime Customers Bought 2 Billion Items with One-Day Delivery in 2018," CNET, December 2, 2018.

23 *From the time the customer*: Ben Popper, "Amazon's Drone Delivery Launches in the UK," *The Verge*, December 14, 2016.

23 *In late 2018, the company announced*: Rebecca Ungarino, "Amazon Is Building an Air Hub in Texas—and That Means More Bad News for FedEx and UPS, Morgan Stanley Says," *Business Insider*, December 16, 2018.

23 *Morgan Stanley lowered its outlook*: Michael Larkin, "These Are the Latest Stocks to Sink on a Potential Amazon Threat," *Investor Business Daily*, December 4, 2018.

23 *One key to fast delivery*: "Amazon Global Fulfillment Center Network," MWPVL International, December 2018, http://www.mwpvl.com/html/amazon_com.html.

23 *In early 2019, it bought*: "Why Amazon Is Gobbling Up Failed Malls,"

Wall Street Journal, May 6, 2019, https://www.wsj.com/video/why-amazon-is-gobbling-up-failed-malls/FC3559FE-945E-447C-8837-151C31D69127.html.

23 *The scale of Amazon's distribution network*: "An Amazon Puzzle: How Many Parcels Does It Ship, How Much Does It Cost, and Who Delivers What Share?," *Save the Post Office*, July 29, 2018.

24 *Wall Street analysts predict*: Rani Molla, "Amazon's Cashierless Go Stores Could Be a $4 Billion Business by 2021, New Research Suggests," *Vox*, January 4, 2019.

25 *the service has created scores*: "The Marvelous Mrs. Maisel: Awards," IMDb, https://www.imdb.com/title/tt5788792/awards.

25 *In 2019, Amazon spent approximately*: Eugene Kim, "Amazon on Pace to Spend $7 Billion on Video and Music Content This Year, According to New Disclosure," CNBC, April 26, 2019.

25 *That number still trails Netflix*: Todd Spangler, "Netflix Spent $12 Billion on Content in 2018," *Variety*, January 18, 2019.

26 *As Steve Boom*: Micah Singelton, "Amazon Is Taking a More Simplistic Approach to Music Streaming. And It Isn't Alone," *The Verge*, April 25, 2017.

Chapter 2: The Richest Man in the World

29 *He runs Amazon as if every penny*: "10 Most Expensive Things Owned by Jeff Bezos," Mr. Luxury video, posted on YouTube, December 17, 2018, https://www.youtube.com/watch?v=G-IwSI1cDrM.

29 *His most recent purchase*: Vivian Marino, "Luxury Sales Spike as Buyers Rush to Avoid Higher Mansion Taxes," *New York Times*, July 5, 2019.

30 *He portrays himself online*: Jeff Bezos Instagram photo, https://www.instagram.com/p/BhkcyHpn_J1/?utm_source=ig_embed.

30 *Yet, in 2019, he divorced*: Aine Cain and Paige Leskin, "A Look Inside the Marriage of the Richest Couple in History, Jeff and MacKenzie Bezos—Who Met Before Amazon Started, Were Married for 25 Years, and Are Now Getting Divorced," *Business Insider*, July 6, 2019.

31 *"Jeff Bezos" wasn't always*: "Jeff Bezos Talks Amazon, Blue Origin, Family, and Wealth," video interview by Mathias Döpfner, the CEO of Axel Springer, with Jeff Bezos (4:51), posted on YouTube, May 5, 2018, https://www.youtube.com/watch?v=SCpgKvZB_VQ.

31 *His father, Ted*: Stone, *The Everything Store*, 140–42.

31 *Ted's unicycling job*: Ibid., 142.

32 *Bezos never saw his biological father again*: Ibid., 321–24.

32 *After Stone unearthed Jorgensen*: Laura Collins, "Amazon Founder Jeff Bezos's Ailing Biological Father Pleads to See Him," *Daily Mail*, November 17, 2018.

32 *Jorgensen died*: Kim Janssen, "Who Was Jeff Bezos' Tenuous Personal Tie to Chicago?," *Chicago Tribune*, February 20, 2018.

32 *After Jackie got divorced from Jorgensen*: Stone, *The Everything Store*, 143–46.

33 *It seems that Jeff Bezos inherited*: "Jeff Bezos Talks Amazon, Blue Origin, Family, and Wealth," video (5:00).

33 *As Bezos later recalled his first summer*: Ibid. (6:00).

34 *Bezos's grandfather was*: Chip Bayers, "The Inner Bezos," *Wired*, March 1, 1999.

34 *Gise was also a top manager*: Christian Davenport, *The Space Barons*, (New York: PublicAffairs, 2018), 59–62.

34 *Among other things, DARPA created*: Ibid., 60–61.

34 *During those summers*: Mark Liebovich, "Child Prodigy, Online Pioneer," *Washington Post*, September 3, 2000.

34 *The significance of that business*: Mimi Montgomery, "Here Are the Floor Plans for Jeff Bezos's $23 Million DC Home," *Washingtonian*, April 22, 2018.

35 *In late 2018, a group of 450 Amazon employees*: Anonymous Amazon employee, "I'm an Amazon Employee. My Company Shouldn't Sell Facial Recognition Tech to Police," Medium, October 16, 2018; Christopher Carbone, "450 Amazon Employees Protest Facial Recognition Software Being Sold to the Police," Fox News, October 18, 2018.

35 *Bezos didn't respond publicly*: "Jeff Bezos Speaks at Wired25 Summit," CBS News, posted on YouTube October 18, 2018, https://www.you tube.com/watch?v=cFyhp1kjbbQ.

35 *Bezos's positive attitude*: Mallory Locklear, "Google Pledges to Hold Off on Selling Facial Recognition Technology," *Engadget*, December 13, 2018.

35 *In a 2018 experiment using Amazon's Rekognition*: Brian Barrett, "Lawmakers Can't Ignore Facial Recognition's Bias Anymore," *Wired*, July 26, 2018.

36 *In 1974, when he was ten years old*: Jeff Bezos, "We Are What We Choose," Princeton commencement speech, May 30, 2010.

37 *On the ranch, Pop Gise*: Interview with Jeff and Mark Bezos, Summit LA17, November 14, 2017.

37 *Bezos even helped his grandfather*: David M. Rubenstein, conversation with Jeff Bezos, the Economic Club, Washington, D.C., September 13, 2018, https://www.economicclub.org/events/jeff-bezos.

37 *Part of being a resourceful person*: Summit LA17 interview, November 14, 2017.

37 *When Bezos was in Montessori school*: Rubenstein, conversation with Jeff Bezos, September 13, 2018.

37 *When he was in sixth grade*: Julie Ray, *Turning On Bright Minds: A Parent Looks at Gifted Education in Texas* (Houston: Prologues, 1977).

38 *After graduating from high school*: Alan Deutchman, "Inside the Mind of Jeff Bezos," Fast Company, August 1, 2004, https://www.fastcompany.com/50541/inside-mind-jeff-bezos-4.

38 *Not long after arriving in New York*: Summit LA17 interview, November 14, 2017.

38 *He found that woman in MacKenzie Tuttle*: Stone, *The Everything Store*, 22, 34, 39.

38 *He let them play with knives*: Summit LA17 interview, November 14, 2017.

39 *This former cohost*: Alexia Fernandez, "Who Is Lauren Sanchez? All About the Former News Anchor Dating Billionaire Jeff Bezos," *People*, January 9, 2019.

39 *In those early days in New York City*: Robin Wigglesworth, "DE Shaw: Inside Manhattan's 'Silicon Valley' Hedge Fund," *Financial Times*, March 26, 2019.

39 *One day Bezos figured out*: Stone, *The Everything Store*, 25.

39 *When he decided to start Amazon in 1994*: Summit LA17 interview, November 14, 2017.

39 *Bezos wrestled with the decision*: Ibid.

40 *In 1997, the two-year-old company was growing*: James Marcus, *Amazonia: Five Years at the Epicenter of the Dot.com Juggernaut* (New York: New Press, 2004), 100–3.

41 *During a holiday season*: Stone, *The Everything Store*, 73.

41 *When, in the late 2000s*: Ibid., 299.

42 *Bezos jumped on the strategy*: Summit LA17 interview, November 14, 2017.

42 *"The whole point of moving things forward"*: Ibid.

Chapter 3: In God We Trust, All Others Must Bring Data

43 *The company's web page*: Liebovich, "Child Prodigy, Online Pioneer."

43 *At the company, some managers*: Eugene Kim, "One Phrase That Perfectly Captures Amazon's Crazy Obsession with Numbers," *Business Insider*, October 19, 2015.

44 *In the early days of Amazon*: Gregory T. Huang, "Out of Bezos's Shadow: 7 Startup Secrets from Amazon's Andy Jassy," Xconomy, May 9, 2013,

https://xconomy.com/boston/2013/05/09/out-of-bezoss-shadow-7-startup-secrets-from-amazons-andy-jassy/.

46 *Then, one day he appeared*: Marcus, *Amazonia*, 51.

50 *The first Echos were shipped*: Joshua Brustein, "The Real Story of How Amazon Built the Echo," Bloomberg.com, April 19, 2016.

51 *"I'm very happy"*: Eugene Kim, "Jeff Bezos' New 'Shadow' Advisor at Amazon Is a Female Executive of Chinese Descent," CNBC, November 20, 2018.

51 *Early in Amazon's history*: Stone, *The Everything Store*, 216.

51 *Jassy, who shadowed Bezos*: Max Nisen, "Jeff Bezos Runs the Most Intense Mentorship Program in Tech," *Business Insider*, October 17, 2013.

53 *If someone isn't prepared*: Stone, *The Everything Store*, 177.

54 *A few years later he left Amazon*: Sarah Nassauer, "Wal-Mart to Acquire Jet.com for $3.3 Billion in Cash, Stock," *Wall Street Journal*, August 8, 2016.

55 *Apple's Steve Jobs was famous*: Ira Flatow interview with Walter Isaacson, "'Steve Jobs': Profiling an Ingenious Perfectionist," *Talk of the Nation*, NPR, November 11, 2011.

56 *In 2015, the* New York Times *ran a long piece*: Jodi Kantor and David Streitfeld, "Inside Amazon: Wrestling Big Ideas in a Bruising Workplace," *New York Times*, August 15, 2015.

56 *When Bezos started the company*: Marcus, *Amazonia*, 17.

57 *All are brilliant technologists*: Evan Osnos, "Can Mark Zuckerberg Fix Facebook Before It Breaks Democracy?," *The New Yorker*, September 10, 2018.

58 *As Bill Gates told* The New Yorker: Ibid.

Chapter 4: The 10,000-Year Man

61 *This sleepy outpost*: "Geographic Identifiers: 2010 Census Summary File 1 (G001): Van Horn town, Texas," U.S. Census Bureau, American Factfinder, 2015, https://factfinder.census.gov/faces/nav/jsf/pages/community_facts.xhtml?src=bkmk.

61 *Just to the north*: "Three-Peat for Bezos," The Land Report, June 21, 2016.

62 *In 2014, Bezos told Henry Blodget*: Henry Blodget, "I Asked Jeff Bezos the Tough Questions—No Profits, the Book Controversies, the Phone Flop—and He Showed Why Amazon Is Such a Huge Success," *Business Insider*, December 14, 2014.

62 *"If everything has to work"*: Summit LA17 interview, November 14, 2017.

63 *As Bezos puts it*: Ibid.

63 *At an off-site meeting in 2003*: Leslie Hook, "Person of the Year: Amazon Web Service's Andy Jassy," *Financial Times*, March 17, 2016.

64 *In mid-2019, the investment*: Yun Li, "Amazon Could Surge 35% with AWS Worth More Than $500 Billion, Analyst Says," CNBC, May 28, 2019.

64 *In 2014, Amazon launched the Fire Phone*: Ben Fox Rubin and Roger Cheng, "Fire Phone One Year Later: Why Amazon's Smartphone Flamed Out," CNET, July 24, 2015.

65 *The phone never caught the public's imagination*: Ibid.

65 *As painful as that litany*: Amazon 2015 Letter to Shareholders.

65 *"I've made billions of dollars"*: Blodget, "I Asked Jeff Bezos the Tough Questions."

67 *He has given money to candidates*: Sean Sullivan, "The Politics of Jeff Bezos," *Washington Post*, August 7, 2013.

67 *In 2018, he donated $10 million*: Rachel Siegel, Michelle Ye Hee Lee, and John Wagner, "Jeff Bezos Donates $10 Million to Veteran-Focused Super PAC in First Major Political Venture," *Washington Post*, September 5, 2018.

67 *As he told Charlie Rose*: Charlie Rose, "A Conversation with Amazon's Founder and Chief Executive Officer, Jeff Bezos," video, CharlieRose.com, October 27, 2016.

68 *When his friend and former*: Rubenstein, conversation with Jeff Bezos, September 13, 2018.

68 *Since the acquisition*: Ibid.

68 *To the relief of the* Post's *staff*: Dade Hayes, "Jeff Bezos Has Never Meddled with Washington Post Coverage, Editor Marty Baron Affirms," Deadline, June 6, 2019.

68 *In 2003, Amazon*: Saul Hansel, "Amazon Cuts Its Loss as Sales Increase," *New York Times*, July 23, 2003.

68 *For Bezos, it was more than a rich man's hobby*: Summit LA17 interview, November 14, 2017.

69 *He has pledged that each year*: Irene Klotz, "Bezos Is Selling $1 Billion of Amazon Stock a Year to Fund Rocket Venture," Reuters, April 5, 2017.

69 *"In space," says Bezos*: Summit LA17, interview with Jeff and Mark Bezos, November 2017.

69 *By 2018, the company had secured a contract*: Samantha Masunaga, "Blue Origin Wins $500-Million Air Force Contract for Development of New Glenn Rocket," *Los Angeles Times*, October 10, 2018.

69 *The company has also said*: Eric M. Johnson, "Exclusive: Jeff Bezos Plans

to Charge at Least $200,000 for Space Rides—Sources," Reuters, July 12, 2018,

69 *In the spring of 2019*: Kenneth Chang, "Jeff Bezos Unveils Blue Origin's Vision for Space, and a Moon Lander," *New York Times*, May 9, 2019.

70 *The clock rests*: Kevin Kelly, "Clock in the Mountain," blog, The Long Now Foundation, n.d., http://longnow.org/clock/.

70 *Near the top of the five-hundred-foot-tall tunnel*: Ibid.

Chapter 5: Cranking the AI Flywheel

74 *Then he came up with Amazon.com*: Stone, *The Everything Store*, 35.

74 *to make life a little easier*: Ibid., 50.

75 *In 2002, he instituted*: Ibid., 169.

77 *From 2000 to 2005, the stocks*: Olivia Oran, "5 Dot-Com Busts: Where They Are Today," *The Street*, March 9, 2011.

77 *A devastating article published*: Jacqueline Doherty, "Amazon.bomb: Investors Are Beginning to Realize That This Storybook Stock Has Problems," Barron's, updated May 31, 1999.

77 *It was cutting costs*: Stone, *The Everything Store*, 103–4.

80 *"I warn people that customer obsession"*: Summit LA17 interview, November 14, 2017.

81 *Bloomberg's Justin Fox unearthed*: Justin Fox, "Amazon, the Biggest R&D Spender, Does Not Believe in R&D," Bloomberg View, April 12, 2018.

82 *And he was able to persuade*: "Amazon's Quarterly Net Profit," chart, Atlas/Factset, https://www.theatlas.com/charts/BJjuqbWLz.

82 *All of Amazon's major innovations*: Rubin and Cheng, "Fire Phone One Year Later."

82 *"I know that if I am energized at work"*: Summit LA17 interview, November 14, 2017.

84 *So instead of hiring*: Stone, *The Everything Store*, 163.

86 *It comes as little surprise*: "IDC Survey Finds Artificial Intelligence to Be a Priority for Organizations, but Few Have Implemented an Enterprise-Wide Strategy," Business Wire, July 8, 2019.

87 *Today an estimated 35 percent*: Stephen Cohn and Matthew W. Granade, "Models Will Run the World," *Wall Street Journal*, August 19, 2018.

89 *This is why a computer science graduate in the U.S.*: Entry Level Data Scientist Salaries, Glassdoor, https://www.glassdoor.com/Salaries /entry-level-data-scientist-salary-SRCH_KO0,26.htm.

89 *Facebook's algorithms keep getting better*: "Number of Monthly Active Facebook Users Worldwide as of 2nd Quarter 2019 (in Millions)," Statista, 2019, https://www.statista.com/statistics/264810/number-of -monthly-active-facebook-users-worldwide/.

90 *In 2019, Britain's*: Haroon Siddique, "NHS Teams Up with Amazon to Bring Alexa to Patients," *The Guardian*, July 9, 2019.

90 *As Tony Ma*: Tony Ma, "Tencent's Founder on the Future of the Chinese Internet," *Washington Post*, November 26, 2018.

90 *In the two years from 2016 through 2017*: Vishal Kumar, "Big Data Facts," Analytics Week, March 26, 2017, https://analyticsweek.com /content/big-data-facts/.

90 *The research group IDC*: David Reinsel, John Gantz, and John Rydning, "The Digitization of the World—from Edge to Core," white paper, IDC, November 2018.

Chapter 6: Earn Your Trident Every Day

93 *As an experiment, Kashmir Hill*: Kashmir Hill, "I Tried to Block Amazon from My Life, It Was Impossible," Gizmodo, January 22, 2019.

95 *The result was Super Saver Shipping*: Stone, *The Everything Store*, 129.

96 *As he told* Vox: *"So I threw out"*: Jason Del Rey, "The Making of Amazon Prime, the Internet's Most Successful and Devastating Membership Program," *Vox*, May 3, 2019, https://vox.com /recode/2019/5/18511544/amazon-prime-oral-history-jeff-bezos -one-day-shipping.

96 *Others at the company say*: Stone, *The Everything Store*, 186.

96 *Whoever's idea it was*: Del Rey, "The Making of Amazon Prime."

96 *At the time, Amazon charged*: Ibid.

97 *Responding to the power of Prime*: Adam Levy, "Walmart's $98 Delivery Subscription Could Take on Amazon and Target," The Motley Fool, September 14, 2019.

97 *In China, Alibaba has the invite-only*: Hilary Milnes, Alibaba's Tmall Woos Luxury Brands to Sell to Its Invite-Only Loyalty Club for Big Spenders," *Digiday*, April 17, 2018.

99 *Bezos, in his 2017 shareholder letter*: Amazon 2017 Letter to Shareholders, page 1.

100 *That's exactly how it has played out*: Consumer Intelligence Research Partners (CIRP), https://www.fool.com/investing/2017/10/20 /amazon-prime-has-nearly-as-many-subscribers-as-cab.aspx.

100 *As Bezos once summed it up*: Video, Summit LA17 interview, November 14, 2017.

101 *The streaming service*: Andrew Liptak, Westworld Creators Jonathan Nolan and Lisa Joy Have Signed On with Amazon Studios," *The Verge*, April 5, 2019.

102 *In 2018, Reuters obtained*: Jeffrey Dastin, "Amazon's Internal Numbers on Prime Video, Revealed," Reuters, March 15, 2018.

102 *The papers also revealed*: Peter Kafka, "Netflix Is Finally Sharing (Some of) Its Audience Numbers for Its TV Shows and Movies," Recode, January 17, 2019.

Chapter 7: Sexy Alexa

107 *For centuries humans*: William of Malmesbury, *Chronicle of the Kings of England*, Bk. II, Ch. x, 181, c. 1125.

107 *The first breakthrough*: Melanie Pinola, "Speech Recognition Through the Decades," *PC World*, November 2, 2011.

107 *Around that time*: Andrew Myers, "Stanford's John McCarthy, Seminal Figure of Artificial Intelligence, Dies at 84," *Stanford Report*, October 25, 2011.

107 *By the 1980s*: Pinola, "Speech Recognition Through the Decades."

107 *A product called Dragon*: Ibid.

108 *By 2010, computing*: Bianca Bosker, "Siri Rising: The Inside Story of Siri's Origins—and Why She Could Overshadow the iPhone," *Huffington Post*, December 6, 2017.

109 *Alexa and the Echo were hits*: Amazon 2018 Annual Letter to Shareholders, April 11, 2019. The 100 million number included Alexa devices made by both Amazon and other manufacturers. As of August 2019, Amazon had sold 53 million smart devices for a 70 percent U.S. market share.

109 *So popular was Amazon's device*: Dieter Bohn, "Amazon Says 100 Million Alexa Devices Have Been Sold: What's Next?," *The Verge*, January 4, 2019.

110 *As of 2019, Amazon's Alexa*: Bret Kinsella, "60 Percent of Smart Speaker Owners Use Them 4 Times Per Day or More," Voicebot .AI, July 12, 2017. To derive the 500-million-questions-a-day figure, I took the weighted average of the number of questions a day (5) from the IFTTT study cited in the Voicebot.AI story and multiplied by the 100 million Alexa devices that have been sold.

110 *Alexa will play music*: Brian Dumaine, "It Might Get Loud," *Fortune*, November 2018.

110 *If there's still any doubt*: Avery Hartmans, "Amazon Has 10,000 Employees Dedicated to Alexa—Here Are Some of the Areas They're Working On," *Business Insider*, January 22, 2019.

111 *Says Nick Fox, a Google vice president*: Dumaine, "It Might Get Loud."

114 *Nearly 70 percent of Amazon Echo*: "Amazon Echo, Google Home Creating Smart Homes," Consumer Intelligence Research Partners, September 25, 2017.

116 *The research firm OC&C Strategy*: "Voice Shopping Set to Jump to $40 Billion by 2022, Rising from $2 Billion Today," OC&C Strategy Consultants, Cision PR Newswire, February 28, 2018.

117 *At the Neural Information Processing Systems conference*: Karen Hao, "Alibaba Already Has a Voice Assistant Way Better Than Google's," *MIT Review*, December 4, 2018.

119 *In May 2018, Amazon mistakenly*: Niraj Chokshi, "Is Alexa Listening? Amazon Echo Sent Out Recording of Couple's Conversation," *New York Times*, May 25, 2018.

119 *In late 2018, an Amazon customer in Germany*: Jennings Brown, "The Amazon Alexa Eavesdropping Nightmare Came True," *Gizmodo*, December 20, 2018.

120 *In 2017, a six-year-old*: Jennifer Earl, "6-Year-Old Orders $160 Dollhouse, 4 Pounds of Cookies with Amazon's Echo Dot," CBS, January 5, 2017.

120 *Linguist John McWhorter*: John McWhorter, "Txting is Killing Language, JL!!!," TED Talk 2013.

Chapter 8: Warehouses That Run in the Dark

123 *Compared to Amazon's*: J. Clement, "Number of Full-Time Facebook Employees from 2007 to 2018," Statista, August 14, 2019, https://www.statista.com/statistics/273563/number-of-facebook-employees/.

124 *By 2022, there will be*: "Growth of the Internet of Things and in the Number of Connected Devices Is Driven by Emerging Applications and Business Models, and Supported by Standardization and Falling Device Costs," Internet of Things Forecast, Ericsson.com, https://www.ericsson.com/en/mobility-report/internet-of-things-forecast.

124 *When Henry Ford proved*: "Celebrating the Moving Assembly Line in Pictures," Ford Media Center, September 12, 2013, https://media.ford.com/content/fordmedia/fna/us/en/features/celebrating-the-moving-assembly-line-in-pictures.html.

125 *In 1961, a California start-up*: David Laws, "Fairchild Semiconductor: The 60th Anniversary of a Silicon Valley Legend," Computer History Museum, September 19, 2017.

125 *Tim Berners-Lee, a computer scientist*: "World Wide Web," *Encyclopaedia Britannica*, https://www.britannica.com/topic/World-Wide-Web.

126 *The consulting firm McKinsey*: James Manyika et al., "Jobs Lost, Jobs Gained: What the Future of Work Will Mean for Jobs, Skills and Wages," McKinsey Global Institute, November 2017.

126 *McKinsey is also quick to point out*: James Manyika and Kevin Sneader, "AI, Automation, and the Future of Work: Ten Things to Solve For," McKinsey Global Institute, June 2018.

127 *Daniel Susskind of Oxford*: Geoff Colvin, "How Automation Is Cutting into Workers' Share of Economic Output," *Fortune*, July 8, 2019.

128 *After the company bought Kiva*: Evelyn M. Rusli, "Amazon.com to Acquire Manufacturer of Robotics," *New York Times*, March 19, 2012.

128 *Amazon's warehouses that use these robots*: Ananya Bhattacharya, "Amazon Is Just Beginning to Use Robots in Its Warehouses and They're Already Making a Huge Difference," Quartz, June 17, 2016.

128 *Even after installing all these robots*: Author interview with Amazon's Ashley Robinson, April 29, 2019.

132 *James Bloodworth is a British*: James Bloodworth, "I Worked in an Amazon Warehouse. Bernie Sanders Is Right to Target Them," *The Guardian*, September 17, 2018.

133 *He describes a workplace*: Ibid.

136 *It opened its Andover*: "A 360° Tour of Ocado's Andover CFC3 Automated Warehouse," Orcado Technology video, posted on YouTube May 10, 2018, https://www.youtube.com/watch?v=JMUNI4UrNpM.

136 *Under each square*: James Vincent, "Welcome to the Automated Warehouse of the Future," *The Verge*, May 8, 2018.

136 *In February 2019, a fire*: "Ocado Warehouse Fire in Andover Started by Electrical Fault," BBC News, April 29, 2019.

136 *On the day the deal beacame public*: Naomi Rovnick, "Ocado Profits Dip as Costs of Robot Warehouses Climb," *Financial Times*, July 10, 2018.

137 *One of China's largest online retailers*: Craig Smith, "65 JD Facts and Statistics," DMR Business Statistics, https://expandedramblings.com/index.php/by-the-numbers-15-amazing-jd-com-stats/.

137 *JD.com opened a warehouse in 2017*: "JD.com Fully Automated Warehouse in Shanghai," JD.com, Inc., video, posted on YouTube November 10, 2017, https://www.youtube.com/watch?v=RFV8IkY52iY.

137 *That's because this vast warehouse*: Steve LeVine, "In China, a Picture of How Warehouse Jobs Can Vanish," Axios, June 13, 2018.

138 *The winner was Cartman*: Evan Ackerman, "Aussies Win Amazon Robotics Challenge," IEEE Spectrum, August 2, 2017.

141 *In America, there are 3.6 million cashiers*: "Cashiers," *Occupational Outlook Handbook*, Bureau of Labor Statistics, U.S. Department of Labor, https://www.bls.gov/ooh/sales/cashiers.htm.

141 *That report was delivered*: Martin Ford, "How We'll Earn Money in a

Future Without Jobs," TED Talk, April 2017, https://www.ted.com /talks/martin_ford_how_we_ll_earn_money_in_a_future_without _jobs.

142 *Consider that, globally*: "Robots Double Worldwide by 2020," press release, International Federation of Robotics, May 30, 2018, https:// ifr.org/ifr-press-releases/news/robots-double-worldwide-by-2020.

142 *That doesn't bode well*: "Related to: Data Industry," American Trucking Associations, https://www.trucking.org/News_and_Information _Reports_Industry_Data.aspx.

143 *In the hotel industry*: Vibhuti Sharma and Arunima Banerjee, "Amazon's Alexa Will Now Butler at Marriott Hotels," Reuters, June 19, 2018, https://www.reuters.com/article/us-amazon-com-marriott-intnl /amazons-alexa-will-now-butler-at-marriott-hotels-idUSKBN1JF16P.

143 *Stanford University researchers*: Taylor Kubota, "Stanford Algorithm Can Diagnose Pneumonia Better than Radiologists," Stanford News, November 15, 2017, https://news.stanford.edu/2017/11/15/algorithm -outperforms-radiologists-diagnosing-pneumonia/.

143 *Deutsche Bank CEO*: Laura Noonan, Patrick Jenkins, and Olaf Storbeck, "Deutsche Bank Chief Hints at Thousands of Job Losses," *Financial Times*, November 8, 2017.

143 *In 2017, Tencent's Dreamwriter*: Tony Ma, "Tencent's Founder on the Future of the Chinese Internet," *Washington Post*, November 26, 2018.

143 *By reading through*: Bartu Kaleagasi, "A New AI Can Write Music as Well as a Human Composer: The Future of Art Hangs in the Balance," Futurism, March 9, 2017.

Chapter 9: Dancing with the Devil

148 *President Trump in March of 2018 tweeted*: Donald Trump, "I have stated my concerns with Amazon long before the Election . . . ," @realDonaldTrump, Twitter.com, March 29, 2018, https://twitter .com/realDonaldTrump/status/979326715272065024?ref_src=twsrc %5Etfw%7Ctwcamp%5Etweetembed%7Ctwterm%5E9793267 15272065024.

148 *the number of small businesses*: "2018 Small Business Profile: United States," U.S. Small Business Administration, https://www.sba.gov /sites/default/files/advocacy/2018-Small-Business-Profiles-US.pdf.

149 *Businesses not only have to compete*: "Marketplaces Year in Review 2018," Marketplace Pulse, https://www.marketplacepulse.com/marketplaces -year-in-review-2018#amazonsellersfunnel.

149 *In its defense*: "Small Business Means Big Opportunity."

150 *To say that these sellers*: Adam Levy, "Amazon's Third-Party Market-place Is Worth Twice as Much as Its Own Retail Operations," The Motley Fool, March 7, 2019.

151 *At one point, some 90 percent*: Kevin Roose, "Inside the Home of Instant Pot, the Kitchen Gadget That Spawned a Religion," *New York Times*, December 17, 2017.

152 *In late 2018, Amazon*: Eugene Kim, "Amazon Has Been Promoting Its Own Products at the Bottom of Competitors' Listings," CNBC, October 2, 2018.

153 *They also seem designed*: Julia Angwin and Surya Mattu, "Amazon Says It Puts Customers First. But Its Pricing Algorithm Doesn't," ProPublica, September 20, 2016.

154 *Complaints about Amazon's capricious closings*: Natasha Lomas, "Amazon Amends Seller Terms Worldwide After German Antitrust Action," Techcrunch, July 20, 2019.

155 *company offers them an exclusive*: Chris Pereira, "A Look at Dragon Boat: Amazon's Plan to Disrupt the Shipping Industry," SupplyChain 24/7, October 18, 2016.

156 *As of 2018, about a third of all*: Chad Rubin, "Is It Time to Copy Chinese Sellers? Eight Tips for Amazon Sellers," Web Retailer, February 19, 2018, https://www.webretailer.com/lean-commerce/chinese-sellers -amazon/.

157 *The data sold included*: Jon Emont, Laura Stevens, and Robert McMillan, "Amazon Investigates Employees Leaking Data for Bribes," *Wall Street Journal*, September 16, 2018.

158 *An FTC complaint*: *Federal Trade Commission v. Cure Encapsulations, Inc. and Naftula Jacobowitz*, United States District Court, Eastern District of New York, February 19, 2019, https://www.ftc.gov/system/files /documents/cases/quality_encapsulations_complaint_2-26-19.pdf.

158 *Amazon has sued freelancers*: Kaitlyn Tiffany, "Fake Amazon Reviews Have Been a Problem for a Long Time. Now the FTC Is Finally Cracking Down," *Vox*, February 27, 2019.

160 *And a Tennessee family*: Alana Semuels, "Amazon May Have a Counterfeit Problem," *The Atlantic*, April 20, 2018.

Chapter 10: The Game of Drones

163 *Globally, the industry*: "Total Retail Sales Worldwide from 2015 to 2020 (in Trillion U.S. Dollars)," chart, eMarketer, https://www.emar keter.com/Chart/Total-Retail-Sales-Worldwide-2015-2020-trillions -change/194243.

164 *Traditional retailing is undergoing*: "Our History," Walmart, https://corporate.walmart.com/our-story/our-history.

165 *A 2018 survey*: "Same-Day Delivery For Retailers," Dropoff, https://www.dropoff.com/same-day-delivery-matters.

166 *As of 2019, a number of prominent retailers*: Karen Bennett, "These Dying Retail Stores Will Go Bankrupt in 2019," Cheat Sheet, January 30, 2019.

167 *When the company opened in New York's*: Jon Caramancia, "The Amazon Warehouse Comes to SoHo," *New York Times*, November 28, 2018.

167 *If Bloomberg is correct*: Rani Molla, "Amazon's Cashierless Go Stores Could Be a $4 Billion Business by 2021, New Research Suggests," *Vox*, January 4, 2019.

168 *Online sales account for only*: Jennifer Smith, "Inside FreshDirect's Big Bet to Win the Home-Delivery Fight," *Wall Street Journal*, July 18, 2018.

168 *So far, Walmart is the king*: "Grocery Store Sales in the United States from 1992 to 2017 (in Billion U.S. Dollars)," Statista, August 26, 2019, https://www.statista.com/statistics/197621/annual-grocery-store-sales-in-the-us-since-1992/.

168 *At the time of the takeover*: Tracy Leigh Hazzard, "Why Did Bezos Do It? An Inside Look at Whole Foods and Amazon," *Inc.*, September 28, 2018.

169 *Consider that in 2018*: "An Amazon Puzzle."

169 *By taking control of the packages*: Greg Bensinger and Laura Stevens, "Amazon's Newest Ambition: Competing Directly with UPS and FedEx," *Wall Street Journal*, September 27, 2016.

169 *To put that in perspective*: "About FedEx: Express Fact Sheet," FedEx.com, https://about.van.fedex.com/our-story/company-structure/express-fact-sheet.

170 *In an investor call*: Ethel Jiang, "FedEx: We Aren't Afraid of Amazon," *Business Insider*, December 19, 2018.

170 *In a signal that it finally*: Paul Ziobro and Dana Mattioli, "FedEx to End Ground Deliveries for Amazon," *Wall Street Journal*, August 7, 2019.

170 *Indeed, it disclosed*: Rich Duprey, "FedEx Finally Admits Amazon Is a Rival to Be Reckoned With," The Motley Fool, August 5, 2019.

171 *Some customers complain*: Dennis Green, "Amazon's Struggles with Its Fresh Grocery Service Show a Huge Liability for Prime," *Business Insider*, July 1, 2018.

171 *In the 2018 Temkin Experience Ratings*: "Wegmans, H-E B, and Publix Earn Top Customer Experience Ratings for Supermarkets, According to Temkin Group," Cision, PR News Wire, April 5, 2018.

172 *And the work is tough*: Alana Semuels, "I Delivered Packages for Amazon and It Was a Nightmare," *The Atlantic*, June 25, 2018.

Notes

173 *In 2018*, Business Insider *reported*: Hayley Peterson, "'Someone Is Going to Die in This Truck': Amazon Drivers and Managers Describe Harrowing Deliveries Inside Trucks with 'Bald Tires,' Broken Mirrors, and Faulty Brakes," *Business Insider*, September 21, 2018.

173 *Around the same time*: Hayley Peterson, "More Than 200 Delivery Drivers Are Suing Amazon over Claims of Missing Wages," *Business Insider*, September 13, 2018.

173 *Amazon said it would*: Hayley Peterson, Leaked Email Reveals Amazon Is Changing How Delivery Drivers Are Paid Following Reports of Missing Wages," *Business Insider*, October 2, 2018.

174 *The consultancy McKinsey & Company*: Martin Joerss, Jürgen Schröder, Florian Neuhaus, Christoph Klink, and Florian Mann, "Parcel Delivery: Future of the Last Mile," McKinsey, September 2016, 15.

175 *In 2016, the company earned*: Patent No: US 9,547,986 B1, U.S. Patent Office.

175 *Toyota, Amazon is developing*: "Amazon Rides Along with Toyota's Delivery Alliance for Self-Driving Cars," Bloomberg News, January 8, 2018.

175 *Ford later that year*: Emma Newburger, "Ford Invests $500 Million in Electric Truck Maker Rivian," CNBC, April 24, 2019.

175 *Amazon is far from alone*: "46 Corporations Working on Autonomous Vehicles," CB Insights, September 4, 2018.

176 *Subsequently, Udelv*: "Announcing Our Walmart Partnership," Udelv blog, January 8, 2018.

176 *In 2019, a start-up named Nuro*: Russell Redman, "Kroger Goes Live with Self-Driving Delivery Vehicles," Supermarket News, December 18, 2018.

178 *In 2013, Bezos appeared*: "Amazon's CEO Jeff Bezos Unveils Flying Delivery Drones on '60 Minutes,'" Charlie Rose, *60 Minutes*, video posted on YouTube February 28, 2013, https://www.youtube.com /watch?v=Fbq6gQVLhWE.

178 *And that's just the start for drones*: "How e-Commerce Giant JD.com Uses Drones to Deliver to Far-Out Areas in China," CNBC, June 18, 2017, https://www.cnbc.com/video/2017/06/18/how-e-commerce -giant-jd-com-uses-drones-to-deliver-to-far-out-areas-in-china.html.

178 *In 2018, the Federal Aviation Administration*: Jessica Brown, "Why Your Pizza May Never Be Delivered by Drone," BBC News, December 14, 2018.

179 *Bob Roth, a director with Amazon Prime Air*: Day One Staff, "Another New Frontier for Prime Air," *Dayone* blog, Amazon.com, January 18, 2019.

179 *A 2017 NASA study found*: Andrew Christian and Randolph Cabell,

"Initial Investigation into the Psychoacoustic Properties of Small Unmanned Aerial System Noise," NASA Langley Research Center, March 2018.

179 *The community group*: "See This Drone Deliver Coffee and Divide an Australian Suburb," video, *Daily Telegraph*, December 26, 2018.

179 *But that wasn't enough of a reason*: Jake Kanter, "Google Just Beat Amazon to Launching One of the First Drone Delivery Services," *Business Insider*, April 9, 2019.

180 *In a pilot program*: Rachel Metz, "Apparently, People Say 'Thank You' to Self-Driving Pizza Delivery Vehicles," *MIT Review*, January 10, 2018.

Chapter 11: Godzilla Versus Mothra

183 *At the time, Jet.com had been valued*: Miriam Gottfried, "Jet.com Is No Amazon Killer for Wal-Mart," *Wall Street Journal*, August 3, 2016.

184 *With nearly 40 percent of all U.S.*: "U.S. Ecommerce 2019," eMarketer, June 27, 2019, https://www.emarketer.com/content/us-ecommerce-2019.

184 *According to Cowen analysts*: April Berthene, "My Four Takeaways from NRF 2019," Digital Commerce, January 28, 2019.

185 *Venture capital firms backed the start-up*: Stone, *The Everything Store*, 296.

185 *When Bezos learned of Walmart's*: Ibid., 299.

186 *According to a 2016* Women's Wear Daily *study*: Kathryn Hopkins, "EXCLUSIVE: Retail's Highest-Paid Executive Has Just Sold His Modest New Jersey Home," *Women's Wear Daily*, November 3, 2017.

186 *In a 2011 analyst call*: "Wal-Mart Stores Inc.—Shareholder/Analyst Call," Seeking Alpha, October 12, 2011, https://seekingalpha.com/article/300141-wal-mart-stores-inc-shareholder-analyst-call?part=single.

187 *Its sales hit $500 billion*: 2018 Global Fortune 500 list, http://fortune.com/global500/list/.

Chapter 12: Amazon-Proofing Your Business

193 *A 2019* New Yorker *cartoon*: Kim Warp cartoon, *The New Yorker*, March 11, 2019, 48.

196 *Over a five-year period*: Benjamin Rains, "Nike (NKE) Q3 Earnings Preview: North America, China, Footwear & More," Zacks.com, March 7, 2019.

196 *Not to be outdone by its rival*: "7 Case Studies That Prove Experiential Retail Is the Future," Retail Trends, *Storefront Magazine*, 2017, https://www.thestorefront.com/mag/7-case-studies-prove-experiential-retail-future/.

197 *The New York City bedding maker Casper*: Pamela Danziger, "Casper Has Figured Out How to Sell More Mattresses: Sleep Before You Buy," *Forbes*, July 12, 2018.

197 *According to the company*: Alex Wilhelm, "How Quickly Is Casper's Revenue Growing?," Crunchbase, January 19, 2018.

198 *FaceFirst's CEO*: "Facial Recognition in Retail," podcast, eMarketer, March 6, 2019.

198 *Alibaba's payment arm*: John Russell, "Alibaba Debuts 'Smile to Pay' Facial Recognition Payments at KFC in China," September 4, 2017, https://techcrunch.com/2017/09/03/alibaba-debuts-smile-to-pay/.

198 *A 2018 survey of shoppers*: "Creepy or Cool 2018: 4th Annual RichRelevance Study," RichRelevance, June 20, 2018.

199 *Credit card numbers*: "Facts + Statistics: Identity Theft and Cybercrime," Insurance Information Institute, https://www.iii.org/fact-statistic/facts-statistics-identity-theft-and-cybercrime.

201 *Bain estimates that share*: "Global Personal Luxury Goods Market Returns to Healthy Growth, Reaching a Fresh High of €262 Billion in 2017," *Business Insider*, October 25, 2017.

201 *"With this new step"*: Richemont press release, January 22, 2018.

202 *That's exactly what Williams-Sonoma does*: Arthur Zaczkiewicz, "Amazon, Wal-Mart Lead Top 25 E-commerce Retail List," *Women's Wear Daily*, March 7, 2016.

202 *Williams-Sonoma has differentiated itself*: Khadeeja Safdar, "Why Crate and Barrel's CEO Isn't Worried About Amazon," *Wall Street Journal*, March 20, 2018.

202 *Its brick-and-mortar stores*: Avi Salzman, "Retailer Williams-Sonoma Is 'Amazon Proof,' " *Barron's*, June 11, 2016.

203 *The retailer has to be competitive*: Ibid.

204 *The company's sales*: Panos Mourdoukoutas, "Best Buy Is Still in Business—and Thriving," *Forbes*, March 2, 2019.

206 *In 2018, Morgan Stanley said*: Lauren Thomas, "Amazon's 100 Million Prime Members Will Help It Become the No. 1 Apparel Retailer in the US," CNBC, April 19, 2018.

207 *As she told the* Los Angeles Times: Tracey Lien, "Stitch Fix Founder Katrina Lake Built One of the Few Successful E-Commerce Subscription Services," *Los Angeles Times*, June 9, 2017.

208 *"Fundamentally what we're offering"*: Tren Griffin, "Opinion: 7 Busi-

ness Rules from Stitch Fix's CEO That Don't All Come in a Box,"
MarketWatch, November 25, 2017.

209 *It is, however, the company's shrewd*: Samar Marwan, "Mother-Daughter
Duo Raise $120 Million for Their Fast-Fashion Brand Lulus," *Forbes*,
May 16, 2018.

210 *As Noelle Sadler*: Kimberlee Morrison, "How Instagram Is Growing Its
Social Shopping Efforts," *Adweek*, April 7, 2017, https://www.adweek
.com/digital/how-instagram-is-growing-its-social-shopping-efforts/.

Chapter 13: Amazon Unbound

216 *The conglomerates of the 1960s and 1970s*: Jeffrey Cane, "ITT, the
Ever-Shrinking Conglomerate," *New York Times*, January 12, 2011.

217 *What is particularly worrisome*: Jeff Desjardins, "The Jeff Bezos Empire
in One Giant Chart," Visual Capitalist, January 11, 2019.

217 *When Amazon thought*: Pascal-Emmanuel Gobry, "How Amazon
Makes Money from the Kindle," *Business Insider*, October 18, 2011.

217 *after years of losses and some false starts*: Mike Shatzkin, "A Changing
Book Business: It All Seems to Be Flowing Downhill to Amazon,"
The Idea Logical Company, January 22, 2018.

220 *The truth is that Amazon*: Corey McNair, "Global Ad Spending
Update," eMarketer, November 20, 2019.

220 *Amazon, however, is still a distant*: "US Digital Ad Spending Will Sur-
pass Traditional in 2019," eMarketer, February 19, 2019; Taylor Sopor,
"Report: Amazon Takes More Digital Advertising Market Share from
Google-Facebook Duopoly," GeekWire, February 20, 2019.

220 *A 2019 report*: "Digital Ad Spend to Reach $520 Billion by 2023, as
Amazon Disrupts Google & Facebook Duopoly," Juniper Research,
June 24, 2019.

220 *Morgan Stanley estimated*: Karen Weise, "Amazon Knows What You
Buy. And It's Building a Big Ad Business from It," *New York Times*,
January 20, 2019.

221 *It's no surprise, then*: Suzanne Vranica, "Amazon's Rise in Ad Searches
Dents Google's Dominance," *Wall Street Journal*, April 4, 2019.

221 *One advertiser found that 20 percent*: Weise, "Amazon Knows What You
Buy."

221 *In 2018, according to eMarketer*: "In China, Alibaba Dominates Digital
Ad Landscape," eMarketer, March 20, 2018.

222 *When asked about disruption in the health-care industry*: Doerr said
"120 million Prime Members," but Amazon now confirms 150 million.

222 *A 2018 survey of senior health-care executives*: "Healthcare Disruption: The Future of the Healthcare Market," Reaction Data, 2018.

222 *The same survey found that 29 percent*: Meg Bryant, "Healthcare Execs Worried About Business Model Disruption, Survey Shows," HealthcareDive, March 18, 2019.

223 *Besides its acquisition in 2018*: Amazon 2018 Annual Report, 52.

223 *Over the years, Amazon had acquired licenses*: Natalie Walters, "4 Ways Amazon Is Moving into Healthcare," The Motley Fool, July 19, 2018.

223 *As for the very long view, Amazon*: Eugene Kim and Christina Farr, "Inside Amazon's Grand Challenge—a Secretive Lab Working on Cancer Research and Other Ventures," CNBC, June 5, 2018.

223 *In the late 1990s, the company*: Christina Farr, "Amazon Is Hiring People to Break into the Multibillion-Dollar Pharmacy Market," CNBC, May 16, 2017.

224 *A job posting for the lab*: Kim and Farr, "Inside Amazon's Grand Challenge"; Amazon attributed the quote to Carl Sagan, and this has often been attributed to the astronomer, but apparently it was actually written by a *Newsweek* reporter in a profile of Carl Sagan in the late eighties.

225 *For example, it's using AI to clean up*: Ibid.

225 *In May 2017, Amazon put together a team*: Christina Farr, "Amazon Continues Its Push into the Pharmacy Business, and Has Appointed a 14-Year Vet to Run It," CNBC, February 27, 2019.

227 *In its complaint, Optum argued*: Reed Abelson, "Clash of Giants: UnitedHealth Takes On Amazon, Berkshire Hathaway and JPMorgan Chase," *New York Times*, February 1, 2019.

228 *The COO added*: Angelica LaVito, "New Court Documents Give Insight into Ambitions of Joint Health-Care Venture Between Amazon, JP Morgan, Berkshire Hathaway," CNBC, February 21, 2019.

228 *The combined company*: Reed Abelson, "CVS Health and Aetna $69 Billion Merger Is Approved with Conditions," *New York Times*, October 10, 2018.

228 *CVS stores, for example, now contain*: "CVS Reports First Quarter 2019 Results," CVSHealth, https://www.cvshealth.com/newsroom/press-releases/cvs-health-reports-first-quarter-results-2019.

229 *So far, six companies*: Rachel Jiang, "Introducing New Alexa Healthcare Skills," Amazon.com, https://developer.amazon.com/blogs/alexa/post/ff33dbc7-6cf5-4db8-b203-99144a251a21/introducing-new-alexa-healthcare-skills.

230 *Amazon has filed a patent for Alexa*: Amazon has filed a patent: http://patft.uspto.gov/netacgi/nph-Parser?Sect1=PTO2&Sect2=HITOFF&u=%2Fnetahtml%2FPTO%2Fsearch-adv

.htm&r=1&p=1&f=G&l=50&d=PTXT&S1=10,096,319&OS =10,096,319&RS=10,096,319.

231 *A survey by the Commonwealth Fund*: Robinson Osborn et al., "Older Americans Were Sicker and Faced More Financial Barriers to Health Care than Counterparts in Other Countries," Health Affairs, December 2017, https://www.commonwealthfund.org/sites/default/files /documents/___media_files_news_news_releases_2017_nov_embar goed_20171048_osborn_embargoed.pdf.

232 *The project took nearly six months*: AMAZON.COM, INC., *Plaintiff-Appellee, v. BARNESANDNOBLE.COM, INC., and Barnesandnoble .Com, LLC, Defendants-Appellants*, No. 00-1109, Decided: February 14, 2001, United States Court of Appeals, Federal Circuit; George Anders and Rebecca Quick "Amazon.com Files Suit over Patent on 1-Click Against Barnesandnoble.com," *Wall Street Journal*, October 25, 1999.

232 *The case was settled out of court*: "Amazon.com and Barnes & Noble .Com Settle 1-Click Patent Lawsuit," Out-law.com, March 7, 2002, https://www.out-law.com/page-2424.

234 *According to Peeyush Nahar*: "Amazon Loaned $1 Billion to Merchants to Boost Sales on Its Marketplace," Reuters, June 8, 2017.

234 *"Small businesses are in our DNA"*: "Amazon Loans More Than $3 Billion to Over 20,000 Small Businesses," *BusinessWire*, June 8, 2017.

235 *An October 2018 report by the research firm CB Insights*: "What the Largest Global Fintech Can Teach Us About What's Next in Financial Services," CB Insights, October 4, 2018.

235 *America is where Amazon could make inroads*: Rimma Kats, "The Mobile Payments Series: US," eMarketer, November 9, 2018; "About Pay-Pal: Top Competitors of PayPal in the Datanyze Universe," Datanyze .com, https://www.datanyze.com/market-share/payment-processing /paypal-market-share.

235 *A survey by Accenture*: "Seven out of 10 Consumers Globally Welcome Robo-Advice for Banking, Insurance and Retirement Services, According to Accenture," Accenture Press Release, January 11, 2017.

235 *As part of the same survey*: "Alexa, Move My Bank Account to Amazon," Bain Press Release, March 6, 2018, https://www.bain.com/about /media-center/press-releases/2018/alexa-move-my-bank-account -to-amazon/.

236 *In March 2018*: Emily Glazer, Liz Hoffman, and Laura Stevens, "Next Up for Amazon: Checking Accounts," *Wall Street Journal*, March 5, 2018.

236 *In a 2018 report, "Banking's Amazon Moment"*: Gerard du Toit and Aaron Cheris, "Banking's Amazon Moment," Bain, March 5, 2018.

237 *in the UK and Germany*: Georg Szalai, "Olympics: Discovery Reports

386M Viewers, 4.5B Videos Watched Across Europe," *The Hollywood Reporter*, February 26, 2018.

238 *As 2019 rolled in, Amazon led a $700 million investment*: Kris Holt, "Amazon Invests in Truck-Maker Rivian," *Engadget*, February 15, 2019.

238 *Around the same time as the Rivian investment*: Alan Boyle, "Amazon to Offer Broadband Access from Orbit with 3,236-Satellite 'Project Kuiper' Constellation," GeekWire, April 4, 2019.

Chapter 14: Bezos Under Fire

239 *The law would require big companies*: Abha Bhattarai, "Bernie Sanders Introduces 'Stop BEZOS Act' in the Senate," *Washington Post*, September 5, 2018.

240 *While the cages might keep the workers safe*: Matt Day and Benjamin Romano, "Amazon Has Patented a System That Would Put Workers in a Cage, on Top of a Robot," *Seattle Times*, September 7, 2018.

240 *A 2017 survey by the American Culture and Faith Institute*: Dave Namo, "Socialism's Rising Popularity Threatens America's Future," *National Review*, March 18, 2017.

240 *A 2016 Harvard study*: Harvard, Institute of Politics, "Clinton in Commanding Lead over Trump among Young Voters, Harvard Youth Poll Finds," Harvard Institute of Politics, The Kennedy School, April 25, 2016.

241 *Consider that as of early 2019*: Tami Luhby, "Jeff Bezos, Microsoft's Bill Gates, Berkshire Hathaway's Warren Buffett and Facebook's Mark Zuckerberg, Together Were Worth $357 Billion," CNN Business, January 21, 2019.

241 *The kind of income inequality Sanders was talking about*: Michael Corkery, "A Macy's Goes from Mall Mainstay to Homeless Shelter," *New York Times*, June 13, 2018.

241 *The combined fortunes*: Tami Luhby, "The Top 26 Billionaires Own $1.4 Trillion—as Much as 3.8 Billion Other People," CNN Business, January 21, 2019.

243 *"No one working for the wealthiest person on Earth"*: Tami Luhby, "Amazon Defends Itself from Bernie Sanders' Attacks," CNN Business, August 31, 2018.

243 *A single parent*: Ryan Bourne, "In Bernie Sanders vs. Amazon's Jeff Bezos, Only Workers Lose," *USA Today*, September 16, 2018.

243 *If the family incurred medical costs*: "Policy Basics: Introduction to Medicaid," Center on Budget and Policy Priorities, https://www.cbpp.org/research/health/policy-basics-introduction-to-medicaid.

244 *One could imagine a scenario*: Ryan Bourne, "In Bernie Sanders vs. Amazon's Jeff Bezos, only workers lose," Opinion contributor, USA Today, September 16, 2018.

246 *As part of the deal, the company*: Thomas Barrabi, "Bernie Sanders Reacts to Amazon Slashing Stock, Incentive Bonuses for Hourly Workers," Fox Business, October 4, 2018.

247 *Seattle and New York City, for example*: Laura Stevens, "Amazon to Raise Its Minimum U.S. Wage to $15 an Hour," *Wall Street Journal*, October 2, 2018.

248 *That said, from time to time*: Scott Galloway, "Amazon Takes Over the World," *Wall Street Journal*, September 22, 2017.

249 *Robert Reich, a former labor secretary*: Robert B. Reich, "What If the Government Gave Everyone a Paycheck?," *New York Times*, July 9, 2018.

250 *As Reich argues*: Ibid.

251 *In a June 2017 tweet*: Catherine Clifford, "Jeff Bezos Teased Plans to Give Away Some of His $140 Billion in Wealth," CNBC, June 15, 2018.

252 *In that September 2018 tweet*: "Amazon Chief Jeff Bezos Gives $2bn to Help the Homeless," BBC News, September 13, 2018.

253 *The call was brief*: Bill de Blasio, "The Path Amazon Rejected," *New York Times*, February 16, 2019.

253 *Soon after talking with Carney*: Chris Mills Rodrigo, "De Blasio Responds to Amazon Cancelation: 'Have to Be Tough to Make It in New York City,'" *The Hill*, February 14, 2019.

254 *Gianaris, an outspoken Amazon critic*: Berkely Lovelace Jr., "Amazon Ruins the Communities It Takes Over, Says NY State Senator Who Opposed NYC Deal," CNBC, February 15, 2019.

Chapter 15: The Rise of Hipster Antitrust

257 *A little more than a year later, Treasury secretary Steven Mnuchin*: Maggie Fitzgerald, "Amazon Has 'Destroyed the Retail Industry' So US Should Look into Its Practices, Mnuchin Says," CNBC, July 24, 2019.

258 *"Pick one business or the other"*: James Langford, "Amazon Needs a Glass-Steagall Act, Elizabeth Warren Suggests," *Washington Examiner*, September 13, 2018.

258 *Committee chairman Jerrold Nadler said*: Ryan Tracy, "House Committee Requests Tech Executives' Emails in Antitrust Probe," *Wall Street Journal*, September 13, 2019.

258 *Khan, who works at the Open Markets Institute*: Meyer Robinson, "How to Fight Amazon (Before You Turn 29)," *The Atlantic*, July/August 2018.

259 *As she told The Atlantic in 2018*: Ibid.

260 *The origin of this thinking stretches back*: Richard A. Posner, *Antitrust Law*, 2nd. ed. (Chicago: University of Chicago Press, 2001).

261 *"Walmart figured out how"*: "FTC Hearing #1: Competition and Consumer Protection in the 21st Century, September 13, 2018," https://www.ftc.gov/system/files/documents/videos/ftc-hearing-1-competition-consumer-protection-21st-century-welcome-session-1/ftc_hearings_21st_century_session_1_transcript_segment_1.pdf.

262 *"The question here is about the data"*: David Meyer, "Why the EU's New Amazon Antitrust Investigation Could Get the Retailer into a Heap of Trouble," *Fortune*, September 20, 2018, http://fortune.com/2018/09/20/amazon-antitrust-eu-vestager/.

262 *An Amazon spokesperson told Marketplace Pulse*: Juozas Kaziukenas, "Amazon Private Label Brands," Marketplace Pulse, 2019, https://www.marketplacepulse.com/amazon-private-label-brands.

263 *Mindful of the growing political momentum against his company*: Jeff Bezos, Amazon Annual Letter to Shareholders, April 2019.

264 *By the early twentieth century, J. D. Rockefeller*: Edmund Morris, *Theodore Rex* (New York: Random House, 2001), 28.

264 *Andrew Carnegie merged his steel company*: Ibid., 29.

264 *As the magazine* Collier's Weekly *noted*: Ibid., 65.

265 *As he wrote in 1901*: Ibid., 30.

265 *By 1903, Roosevelt had persuaded*: Ibid., 206.

266 *Facebook and Alphabet together control nearly 60 percent*: Molla Rani, "Google's and Facebook's Share of the U.S. Ad Market Could Decline for the First Time, Thanks to Amazon and Snapchat," Recode, March 19, 2018.

266 *Netflix has penetrated 75 percent of the homes*: Sarah Perez, "Netflix Reaches 75% of US Streaming Service Viewers, But Youtube Is Catching Up," TechCrunch, April 4, 2017, https://techcrunch.com/2017/04/10/netflix-reaches-75-of-u-s-streaming-service-viewers-but-youtube-is-catching-up/.

266 *Apple controls around 40 percent*: "US Smartphone Market Share: By Quarter," Counterpoint Research, August 27, 2019, https://www.counterpointresearch.com/us-market-smartphone-share/.

Chapter 16: Raptor Fighter Jets Versus Biplanes

270 *On a 5G network*: Chris Hoffman, "What Is 5G, and How Fast Will It Be?," How-To Geek, March 15, 2019.

Index

Index

Index

Index

317

Index

Index

Index